KULU

The End of the Habitable World

KULU

The End of the Habitable World

PENELOPE CHETWODE

JOHN MURRAY

*Printed in Great Britain by
The Camelot Press Ltd., London and Southampton*

0 7195 2431 8

To my husband
John Betjeman

Contents

Illustrations

Illustrations

Photographs not otherwise acknowledged are by the author

Acknowledgements

It is the fashion today, especially among the young, to denigrate the British Raj. Imperialism was a phase in the history of Mankind which is now nearly over and personally I think that in the assessment of future historians the Roman, Gupta, and the British Empires will rank high.

One of the finest legacies of the British to India was the work of her scholar administrators, both civil and military. Sir William Jones, General Sir Alexander Cunningham and Lord Curzon, the pioneer conservationist, come at once to mind. But there were hosts of others, less well remembered than these titans, whose stores of knowledge are for the most part locked up in little read Imperial Gazetteers, journals of learned societies, and in files of notes and typescripts which they have never had the opportunity to revise and publish.

To four such men I am particularly indebted for my background reading. The first is Captain (later Colonel) A. F. P. Harcourt, who was Assistant Commissioner in Kulu (then a subdivision of Kangra District) from 1869–71 and who was the only one of the four who succeeded in publishing a book, *The Himalayan Districts of Kooloo, Lahool and Spiti*, compiled from his notes while on tour. Published in London in 1871, it is a mine of information about the area. In addition to his scholarly work Harcourt, like so many British officials and their wives in India before the days of amateur photography, was an accomplished water-colour artist, and a large collection of his Kulu sketches may now be seen at the India Office Library, ably catalogued by Mildred Archer, having been presented a few years ago by Mr. Duncan Grant, whose mother was a first cousin of Mrs. Harcourt.

The second is Mr. A. C. Howell, I.C.S., Assistant Commissioner in Kulu from 1907 to 1910, who introduced trout into the Béas River, did much for the preservation of the temples, and published some excellent articles in the *Journal of the Punjab Historical Society*.

The third is Mr. H. Lee Shuttleworth, I.C.S., A.C. Kulu from 1917 to 1919 and again from 1923 to 1924, another passionate devotee of the Western Himalaya, who began his career at a time when the sketching phase was nearing its end and was being replaced by photography with those enormous plate cameras, each of which needed two porters to carry them and their appurtenances over the mountain ranges. Mr. Lee Shuttleworth always toured with his camera and now his magnificent collection of photographs of the Western Himalaya is in the possession of his widow, my friend Inez Shuttleworth, to whom I am much indebted for many things. Sir Michael O'Dwyer who, as Lieutenant-Governor of the Punjab, was responsible for appointing Shuttleworth as A.C. Kulu in 1917, once said that one of his reasons for the appointment was the fact that the maiden name of Mrs. Shuttleworth was MacGillicuddy of the Reeks—'And I thought a young lady who at home was in the habit of running up MacGillicuddy's Reeks would equally be at home at 18,000 feet in the Himalayas.' His belief proved well-founded, for Inez accompanied her husband all over the Kulu sub-division, including the remote Tibetan border provinces of Lahul and Spiti, with their high passes up to 18,000 feet. In addition to the photographs, Inez lent me a bound volume containing her husband's collected articles and published lectures for which I can never be sufficiently grateful. After his retirement from the service Lee Shuttleworth was for twenty years a part-time lecturer in Tibetan dialects at the London School of Oriental Studies.

The fourth to whom I am indebted is Sir Herbert Emerson, I.C.S., who has already gone down in history as a great administrator, played a leading part in the Irwin–Gandhi conversations which took place in Simla in 19–? when he was Lieutenant-Governor of the Punjab. During his earlier terms of office in the Punjab Hills he acquired such an extraordinary knowledge of the temples, religion and folk-lore of this vast mountain region that had he been able to devote his entire time to these studies he would certainly have become an Indologist of world renown. As it is the fruits of his scholarship are mainly preserved in official government publications, such as the 1920 edition of the *Mandi State Gazetteer*, for which he was doubtless paid the standard rate of Rs. 500 (then £35) with no royalties to follow. To his son, my old friend Gerald Emerson, I am deeply indebted for the loan of many of Sir Herbert's unpublished typescripts which contain his erudite research in out-of-the-way places.

When I come to reflect on all the other people who have helped me in so many ways I realise that it is really they who have written this book and not me at all. I have picked their brains unmercifully and it is impossible to acknowledge individually the bits of this book for which each is responsible: but they themselves will know. I thank them one and all from the bottom of my heart. But among them especially are Tom Tyson (former Government Printer at Lahore) and his wife Marcelline, whose garden at Katrain was famous and who still uses Kulu horticultural implements on her allotment in Twickenham; Barbara and Hilary Donald, Margaret and Peter Snell, John Banon, Pandit Balak Ram Gaur, Wendy and Dennis O'Flaherty, Lester Doniger, Madeline Brown, Sardar Sarcharn Singh, Liz and Malcolm McLaughlin, Vivyan Tweedy, John Burton Page, Mildred Archer, Robert Skelton, Timothy Gee, Terence Craig, Dr. Herman Goetz, Christina Noble, Dr. K. P. Nautiyal and the Director and staff of the Indian Government Tourist Office in Kulu, who gave me consistently good advice.

I am also deeply grateful to Margaret White, Kitty Connolly, to my husband John Betjeman, and to Jane Boulenger of John Murray for their work in preparing my typescript for the printer. Finally I must point out that the Indian Institute in Oxford is largely responsible for the delay in completing this book. I have spent so many fascinating hours there—first in its old home at the top of 'the Broad', and then in its present spectacular one on the roof of the New Bodleian—following up one reference after another into the most obscure periodicals, so that it has needed a super-human effort to get down to writing at all, as everyone will understand who has worked in great libraries. To the librarian and his assistants, especially Mrs. de Goris, I offer my warmest thanks for attending to my every want, and providing me with some of the happiest and most self-indulgent days of my life.

Introduction

Certain landscapes imprint themselves upon the mind's eye and for me the most persistent picture throughout the years has been that of the Upper Béas valley of Kulu in the Western Himalaya, with the great snow ridge above the Solang *nala* and the twin Gyephang peaks at its far end. Ever since I left India in 1933, the vision of this valley has repeatedly come before me during the day as well as during the night and on downland rides at home in Berkshire I have sometimes half closed my eyes and there it is again, replacing the distant view of White Horse Hill.

According to an ancient tradition the original name of the Kulu valley was Kulanthapitha, meaning 'the end of the habitable world', and anyone who has stood at the top of the Rohtang Pass, the boundary between Kulu and Lahul, will understand this name.

In September 1931 my mother and I trekked from Simla to Kulu on hill ponies, and rode in short stages some hundred and forty miles as far as the base of the Rohtang Pass. My father was then Commander-in-Chief and we set off from Snowdon, his official residence in the summer capital. The route was well supplied with rest-houses, also known as dak bungalows, where we slept at night, and we took our own cook, servants and stores. All the arrangements were made by our efficient A.D.C., Geoffrey Kellie, who accompanied us, together with Gerald Emerson whose father, Sir Herbert, was at that time Governor of the Punjab.

In 1963 I returned to India after an interval of thirty years and the following summer I was able to indulge my whim of riding once again to Kulu by the same route. But this time I had to make my own arrangements.

In Simla I was lucky enough to be invited to stay at the Convent of Jesus and Mary, which was founded in 1864 for the Roman Catholic orphans of British regiments stationed in

4

India. Since Independence it has become a popular Indian girls' school, attached to which is the Teacher Training College of St. Bede's. While there I decided, for old time's sake, to go to Sipi fair in mid-May and I hired Bulbul, a delightful thirteen-hand skewbald pony whose usual occupation was giving rides to children along 'the Ridge,' a broad level stretch of road between Jakko Hill and 'the Mall'.

Sipi is a grass clearing in the deodars about a thousand feet below the village of Mashobra, six miles from Simla. It used to be a favourite picnic place of the British, especially by moonlight, and features in several of Rudyard Kipling's stories. It was also great fun to ride out there for the day to the annual spring fair and most officials did this with members of their families at least once during their term of office.

Arriving at the fair everything seemed the same and I was filled with nostalgia for the days of my girlhood: there were the crowds of gaily-dressed *pahari* (hill) girls sitting in rows along the stepped bank; the booths selling the traditional sticky sweets such as *burfi* (a sort of fudge) and *jalebis* (sticky fritters); the primitive creaking wooden wheels with four chairs attached to each in which children revolved round and round in vertical circles; there was the little chalet-type wooden temple under the giant deodars with offerings of flowers laid beside the door; and there was the *shamayana* (marquee) under which we used to sit with the local Raja to watch the goings-on.

And yet there were differences. I was the only European present and Bulbul was the only pony; the tent no longer sheltered the Raja and his guests but instead spraying machines and sample seeds and instructional posters provided by the Himachal Pradesh Agricultural Department. Among all these aids to modern husbandry I had the great good fortune to meet Dewan B. N. Chopra, the official in charge of the exhibits. He told me he was an artist who trained in Manchester and now combined his own creative work with poster painting for the Department and the organising of special teaching exhibitions in Simla and the surrounding villages. We soon found that we shared a passion for wandering and he told me that he had once spent two years walking and sketching in the Western Himalaya all over Kangra, Kulu, Chamba, Saraj and Indian Tibet. I told him I was no walker but greatly longed to ride to Kulu and asked him to act as interpreter in order to find out from my pony-boy whether I could hire Bulbul for a month, together with a second pony to carry baggage. The boy replied that for such an expedition his master would charge twenty rupees a day per pony to include their keep and that of the *syces* (grooms). He also added that they would not do more than a single stage on any one day, which was ridiculous as some of them are only six or seven miles. These stages are based on the old system of *begar*, now obsolete. This used to entail forced labour when each village had to provide men at a low daily rate to carry a traveller's baggage on to the next rest-house or camp site. The stages varied roughly between six and twelve miles according to whether the track went steeply up and down mountainsides or kept fairly level along a ridge or a river valley. Time had to be allowed for the men to return to their own village by nightfall.

I told Dewan Chopra that forty rupees a day (then £3) for two ponies with my own keep on top of that was out of the question and asked him if mules would be cheaper and whether he knew where to hire some. He promised to approach a merchant friend of his in San Jauli, a mile to the north-east of Simla, and a week later took me to see Sri Milklu Ram in his little grocer's shop in the bazaar there. The upshot of our interview was that this nice, white-haired and honourable old gentleman agreed to let me have two mules for twenty rupees a day for a period of four weeks—exactly half the price of ponies.

I next set about preparations, which most unfortunately could not include the purchase of maps as all the large-scale editions have had to be withdrawn by the government because of the ever-present fear of another Chinese invasion.

I went to the Mall and bought a good supply of tinned food from Gainda Mal Hem Raj's excellent store, together with a packet of candles, several packets of biscuits and slabs of chocolate, and an oblong cake called 'Rich Fruit Bar'. After this I went to another shop where I bought two roomy canvas haversacks to act as saddlebags; and then I began the complicated task of trying to get permits to stay in the bungalows en route.

Apart from the good hotels in most of the chief towns and tourist centres in India, the traveller must rely on the old dak bungalows, which are liberally scattered all over the plains and the hills. Owing to the great influx of tourists and holiday-makers in the Western Himalaya in recent years the government has added to the number of dak bungalows by building a lot of special tourist bungalows, and all of them, both old and new, are listed as Class 1, 2 or 3 by the National Tourist Board, and preferably a permit should be obtained in advance if one wants to stay in one for a night. But, oh, the difficulty of finding out under whose jurisdiction a particular bungalow comes! Some belong to the Public Works Department, some to the Legal Department (when they are known as 'Circuit houses' and are very superior Class 1), some to the Forest Department, others to the Tourist Board; yet others are known as 'Civil rest-houses' and the Lord alone knows who is entitled to issue a chit for them. To add to my particular problem, all the bungalows I wanted to stay in between Simla and the river Sutlej belonged to various departments in Simla itself, whereas all those further on between the right bank of the Sutlej and Kulu, were under the jurisdiction of the Kulu Forestry Department or the Government Tourist Board. I therefore wrote to the appropriate offices to make my bookings but evidently not in time to get a reply and, due to my incurable habit of procrastination, I left the Simla bookings until the last day, thinking I would hire Bulbul and ride round from one office to another collecting the magic chits with ease. But I had not bargained for Indian bureaucracy. At one office I was told that a particular bungalow came under the Forest Department at Mahasu eight miles outside Simla. At the Public Works Department office I learnt with dismay that another bungalow had been transferred only last week to the jurisdiction of the civil authorities. So downhill I rode in search of the relevant office which was most difficult to find and when I arrived at 4 p.m. it was already shut. I thought this was odd. Mad with frustration, having spent several hours alternately riding up and down slippery tarred roads and queueing in dusty corridors, I decided to give up the unequal struggle and return home with only one chit to my credit. As I rode up the Mall from the direction of Gorton Castle there was a curious atmosphere about the town, and shopkeepers and bank officials were standing in the street looking towards a vast crowd of men on the Ridge. Suddenly a rhythmical succession of wails rose into the air and upon enquiry I learnt that the news of Pandit Nehru's death had come through half an hour before.

It was foolish, and also discourteous, I felt to attempt to ride through such a grief-stricken crowd, so I returned home a longer way by a path leading round the western slopes of Jakko. On arrival at the Convent I found the girl students at St. Bede's Teacher Training College in a deep state of emotion: 'What will happen to us now that Panditji has gone?' asked one of the lovely Sikh girls, as though referring to her own father.

CHAPTER I

The Start

Dewan Chopra had advised me to order the mules at noon. He said they might then arrive at the convent by 1 p.m. and that we should be able to start at 2 p.m. as planned. Quite contrary to expectations the mules arrived at 12.15 p.m. Sweet Sister Inez had looked after me so well during the past six weeks that I dreaded leaving her care; she helped me to carry my baggage to the back gate—a brown canvas kit-bag containing my bedding and clothes and my two new haversacks filled with stores, films, writing things and a large number of oddments. While the muleteer was fixing them on to my pack-mule, I went and had a quick luncheon up at St. Bede's, after which I mounted the younger of the two little thirteen-hand she-mules. The 'saddle' consisted of a sort of thick, quilted mattress stretching the whole length of the animal's back, over which Shri Milklu Ram had spread what was evidently one of his best bedcovers. I found to my great surprise— and relief—that some make-shift stirrups had been fixed to the saddle. I thought that I would certainly have to ride without any and that I ought not to mind, considering that Alexander had ridden stirrupless all the way from Macedon to the Punjab because stirrups had not been invented till long after his time. The muleteer had had the ingenious idea of putting a double length of white webbing over the saddle and under the cover with rusty old stirrup irons at either end. If I put my weight on one stirrup it went right down, but I got used to keeping them level and they added very greatly to my comfort on the trek. The saddle was held in place in front by a wide webbing breast strap and at the back by a similar breeching strap. When I sat on top I seemed to have no contact whatsoever with my mount: I was perched so high above her little head and neck that her withers were completely covered and the aids with which one rides a horse were impossible to apply because she had no bit and my legs had no contact with her sides since they were held out by the thick padding. But she wore a very pretty red string halter and three rows of blue and white wooden beads round her sleek brown neck.

We were seen off by Mother Peter Claver, Principal of St. Bede's, and had progressed a bare fifty yards up the track leading to the Jakko road when there was a soft thud and all my baggage lay on the ground beside the other little mule. Shri Milklu Ram's son, who had accompanied the muleteer to the convent, assured me that all would be properly secured when we got to his father's shop a mile further on, and meanwhile the bags were shoved aboard again and held in position by the two men. We proceeded along the 'Ladies' Mile' where the phantom rickshaw (in Kipling's short story) first appeared below the coloured cliffs known as the 'Giant's Paintbox', and I very soon realised that I had better abandon myself at once to being merely a passenger on my mule as the single halter rope had no effect whichever way I pulled it, neither did she pay the slightest attention to my voice, though she obeyed her driver's instantly and sometimes anticipated his commands in the manner of a rather too intelligent horse.

At the Milklu Ram Stores in San Jauli my baggage was ingeniously fixed by a network of ropes and rings: the kitbag lying along one side of the animal's back and the two haversacks along the other; the weight cleverly balanced by two little sacks of barley for the mules, the amount of grain being adjusted daily according to the rations we all consumed. I asked Shri Milklu Ram the names of his mules but he said they had not got any: they were simply called 'the young mule' and 'the old mule'. He gave me four stamped addressed postcards to send him at weekly intervals, wished me a very good journey, and said he had every confidence in Bhagavat Ram the muleteer, a good-looking man in his early thirties with as frank and honest an expression as you could wish for.

We then set off through the San Jauli tunnel, which was built in 1850 to take the road through a rocky hill at this eastern approach to Simla. One day in the early years of the present century the then Commander-in-Chief, Lord Kitchener, had a nasty fall from his horse in the middle of the tunnel. He had spent Sunday at his country house, Wildflower Hall, and was returning to Simla in the evening when his horse shied at a coolie in the, then, dimly lit tunnel, banging his leg against the wall and breaking both bones above the ankle. The coolie fled in terror. Lord Kitchener somehow or other managed to drag himself from the saddle and lay on the damp ground for several hours before an Englishman, a Mr. Jenn, found him there and immediately fetched a rickshaw which carried the Chief back to Snowdon. The tunnel was subsequently widened, whitewashed, and electrically lit.

It was a dull summer afternoon and it soon began to rain so that B.R. (as I shall call Bhagavat Ram from now on) pulled out his large umbrella, which seemed to be his only baggage, from beneath my kitbags and put it up. I disentangled my sou'wester from the brass ring to which it was tied and rode along in silence towards Fagu, our first halting place only eleven miles away.

The full significance of what I was doing revolved round and round in my mind: I was going to ride for a month at an average rate of three miles an hour with a man who would walk just behind me all the way and to whom I could make no conversation —for to my shame I had learned only a few Hindustani phrases in the imperative mood as a girl—and I had no idea whether I would get a room in any of the dak bungalows after Fagu for it was the only one for which I had a permit. I had been warned not to ride the thirty-nine miles along the Hindustan–Tibet road between Simla and Narkanda because of the public transport buses and long convoys of military lorries which were continually chugging along it and raising clouds of dust; but I chose to turn a deaf ear to what I did not want to hear. I remembered this romantic highway so well as a girl with its long trains of mules and ponies ambling along the untarred surface carrying goods to and from the inner Himalaya, when the only cars allowed to use it were the Viceroy's, our own, and that of the Lieutenant-Governor of the Punjab.

While one part of me longed to discover the new India, the other part thought nostalgically of the old days when my father was Commander-in-Chief and our expeditions were organised down to the last detail so that all we had to do was to enjoy them to the full, completely carefree. Now Geoffrey Kellie, whom my father always called 'the perfect A.D.C.', was seven thousand miles away, market-gardening in Berkshire. In 1931 he had reserved the bungalows for us all along the route, hired our hill ponies and our baggage mules, taken command of the *syces* and muleteers and servants, and interpreted my mother's daily wishes to the *khansama* (cook).

Mr. F. St. John Gore who, with his brother, had travelled the route fifty years earlier, describes the track along which his cavalcade proceeded, and along which I was now riding from Simla to Narkanda, in his superb book *Indian Hill Life,* as 'an excellent and very level path, made at the commencement to the famous Hindustan–Tibet road . . . admirably laid out years ago by English engineers and scarcely rising more than a thousand feet, keeping along the top of the winding ridge the whole way.' This 'path' had now been widened into a motor road by blasting away the rock on the inner side. It is, alas, tarred for most of its length except for a few odd sections which are unaccountably still a mixture of gravel, mud and ruts with gangs of beaming Tibetans, both men and women, working on them who shouted '*namasteji!*' (a greeting) whenever I appeared round a bend.

The unforested southern faces of the so-called Himalayan foot-hills—they are 'foot-hills' up to about ten thousand feet—are a dull drab brown until they are transformed in July by the miracle of the monsoon, but the other three faces are usually well afforested with cedars, firs, hollies, yews, rhododendrons and evergreen oaks, and as we approached the village of Kufri, where there is now a flourishing ski-club, the road wound pleasantly up through a forest of deodars. On one of the rare level patches of burnt-up grass we passed a largish military camp with a long row of lorries drawn up beside it. Further on, there were several smaller camps for the Tibetan refugee road-workers, with strings of prayer flags, looking like festive streamers, tied to tall poles to protect their tents from evil spirits.

We reached the beautifully situated Fagu rest-house (Class 1 with running water) soon after 4 p.m., but it was cloudy to the north-east so that we could not see the snows which I knew lay there. I proudly presented my precious, one and only, chit to the *chaukidar* (caretaker), a nice, clean-shaven man in a white cotton coat and jodhpurs who showed me into a bright, clean bedroom and brought me a cup of tea. After I had unpacked I went on to the veranda where I got into conversation with a charming young Hindu family, and the father and the two elder children decided to walk with me up the hill behind the bungalow to see a temple which I knew was at the top. The pine trees had all been lopped for fuel and cattle-bedding and presented an extraordinary appearance, like tall masts with tufted pine needles growing all the way up them. The landscape at Fagu reminded me a little of Tuscany but on a vast scale, as in the distance the lopped pines looked like Italian cypress. Half-way up the hill it started to pour with rain so that we all turned and ran down again as fast as we could—and that was the end of the temple expedition.

Dal and *chapatties* for supper: I have never raved over them as do some Europeans. They are made with whole wheat flour and I know they are nourishing but they are dry and dull, unless they are fried, when they are called *paratas*—and are doubtless not so good for you. *Dal,* a pulse food, boiled into a mush like thick lentil soup, supplies the protein which Hindu vegetarians do not get from the meat they may not eat. I decided to make do with this popular north Indian diet and to conserve my stores for those rest-houses which had no supplies at all.

During the night I thought of names for my mules: Bhalu (Bear) for my little brown one and Ullu (Owl) for the bay baggage-mule with grey hairs round her eyes and muzzle which made her look old and wise. The next morning B.R. brought them to the door at 7.50 a.m., ten minutes before they were ordered, giving the lie to all the bad habits of muleteers recorded in Victorian travel books. In ten minutes he had the baggage securely roped on to Ullu and I was just about to tell him their names when he instinctively forestalled me—evidently he too had done some thinking in the night—'This one is Durgi and that one is Shanti,' he announced with a beaming smile. I mounted Shanti while B.R. held the stirrup webbing (as opposed to leather) on the off-side and then proceeded down the slope leading from the rest-house to the handful of shacks which make up the hamlet of Fagu. That day I rode a double stage, totalling seventeen miles, to reach Matiana.

This stretch of the Hindustan–Tibet road is not very spectacular: the mountains are brown and bare and that morning the distant snows were still hidden and clouds of dust were raised again and again by lorries and buses and military jeeps dashing past us in both directions. Moving even more slowly than my mini-mule-train, we passed a poor spastic on his haunches with one leg crossed over the other in front of him, propelling himself along in a most remarkable manner by means of two wooden blocks surmounted by handles which he held in either hand.

We passed through Theog, a big village for these parts and capital of a *thesil*, a sub-district, with its own magistrate, police station, public library, two schools and a 'Dental Station'. Leaning against the wall of the latter I saw several giant probes—sticks with pointed iron spikes on the ends—and wondered if they were used to pick out the teeth of occasional abominable snowmen who might chance to drop in.

The road was shaded and we went through a magnificent grove of yews and saw many minute pink primulas and groups of wild delphinium, varying in colour from dirty mauve to the brilliant blue that one always associates with this flower. At one point I saw the wreck of a military jeep some two hundred feet below me, jammed against a pine tree. I learned later that it had come too fast round the corner and that both the driver and his mate had been killed. Every day I realised more forcibly that my Simla friends had been right in trying to dissuade me from riding along these first stages of the Kulu route. We were repeatedly enveloped by clouds of dust from passing motor traffic which spoilt my delight in nature. I remembered what a popular pony trek this used to be in the old days of the British Raj and I could not believe that 'progress', in the form of the beastly internal combustion engine, had so completely metamorphosed this well-trodden route. I am probably the last Englishwoman to ride from Simla to Narkanda along the Hindustan–Tibet road.

I found I could calculate travelling time almost to a minute on a mule, whereas on a horse one cannot be quite so accurate because one may trot or canter along stretches of untarred road. But on a little mule such as Shanti you can bank on a steady 3 m.p.h. which is reduced to 2 m.p.h. up or down steep hills. Thus we covered the seventeen miles from Fagu to Matiana in just under 6 hours. I had to tackle the *chaukidar*, on this occasion a dishevelled unshaven old man, and ask for a room without being able to produce a permit, but I got one without any difficulty as this rest-house is quite correctly listed as 'third-class', and consequently no holiday-makers from Simla were staying in it. I unpacked my old green flea-bag and rolled it down the bed.

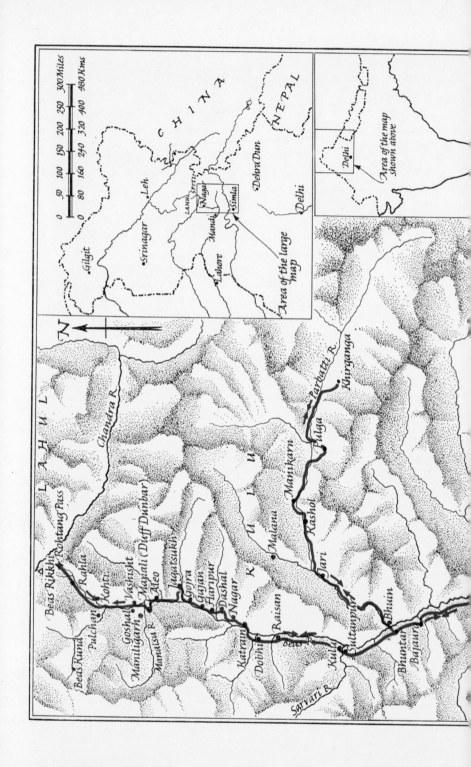

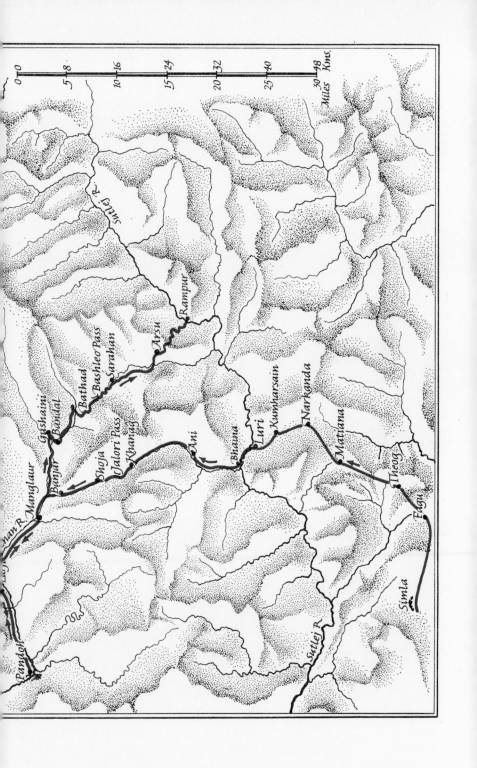

Miles Kms.

0 — 0
5 — 8
10 — 16
15 — 24
20 — 32
25 — 40
30 — 48

Sutlej R.

Rampur

Avsu

Sarahan

Bashleo Pass

Bathad

Gushaini

Bandal

Banjar

Manglaur

Larji (Tirthan) R.

Beas R.

Pandoh

Shoja

Jalori Pass

Khanag

Ani

Bhaina

Luri

Kumharsain

Narkanda

Matiana

Theog

Egu R.

Simla

Sutlej R.

The room contained a dirty dusty dressing-table without a mirror, one chair and a well-worn old blue *durree* (cotton rug) on the otherwise bare board floor. In the small adjoining room there was the usual dusty commode (still known today as 'the thunder-box') and a large bucket of cold water standing in a concrete enclosure sunk in the floor.* A hole in the outside wall lets out the dirty water which you tip out of the bucket. Beside the commode stood a dirty wooden washstand with a large enamel basin and a soap dish. This is all exactly as it was in the dak bungalows of my girlhood, except that there was sometimes a hip bath as an added luxury and the servants with whom one invariably travelled always heated water over a log fire in the compound.

The old *chaukidar* could not speak a word of English but made me understand only too clearly that he had no stores at all. However, he pointed to the bazaar along the road, so I commanded imperiously: 'Bazaar go: bring eggs, rice and *dal*!' Meanwhile I made the first hole in my private stores and ate a late lunch of good tinned tunny fish followed by a slice of 'Rich Fruit Bar' cake. It turned out to be as dry as sawdust with a very little fruit at the bottom, but eaten with plain chocolate it was filling.

After writing my diary on the veranda during the heat of the afternoon, I went and explored a glorious flower-filled gully which ran steeply down the *khud* below the village school near the rest-house. There was a little mountain stream tumbling among boulders, its banks covered with flowering shrubs: berberis, indigofera, spiraea, *rosa macrophylla*, with its erect red stems and deep pink flowers, and *rosa moschata*, the most prolific wild white rose of the western Himalaya which climbs twenty or thirty feet up a tree then flings itself over a branch in a great billowing cascade. The tall evergreen holly oaks which grew among the shrubs in the gully were all lopped, and I saw a man half-way up one chopping off the leafy branches for his goat's supper with a sort of billhook. In these parts the villagers have ancient lopping rights with which the Forest Officers are powerless to interfere and on one occasion when the government Forest Department brought an action against some loppers the latter won the case.

To my plate of rice, *dal* and hard-boiled egg at supper I added the remains of the tunny fish to form a kedgeree which proved

* Since writing the above the majority of H.P. rest-houses have 'W.C.'s installed.

the prelude to a night of alternate sleeplessness and nightmares.

The charge for occupying a bedroom in a first-class rest-house is four rupees* but for this third-class bungalow it was only two rupees with another fifty neve paise for the light—a single-wick oil-lamp which had a large piece out of its dirty glass chimney so that it smoked if you turned it above a flicker. My total bill, with tips for the *chaukidar* and the sweeper, worked out at fifty-two and a half pence in English money, which I do not think is all that cheap for a dirty room when you have provided your own bedding and part of the food. In addition to my daily board and lodging I gave B.R. (on the instructions of Milklu Ram) five rupees every day on arrival at our destination, which took care of his needs, together with hay and barley for the mules.

B.R. was, as usual, ten minutes before time in the morning so that we were again on the road by 8 a.m. for an easy eleven-mile ride rising gently to Narkanda, 9,461 feet above sea level. I counted nineteen military lorries en route, two buses and three civilian lorries, the latter racing round the hairpin bends on the wrong side of the road, the drivers paying no attention to the frequent notices bearing such slogans as 'Safety Saves', 'Make Safety a Habit', written in both English and Hindi.

The large first-class rest-house at Narkanda is on a ledge above the little village with a view looking right across the deep Sutlej valley to the eternal snows of Spiti and Rampur Busahr. The *chaukidar* announced that all the rooms were booked for the week-end but advised me to go down to the P.W.D. office to find out if any family had cancelled. There I was informed that there was some doubt about suite Number Three and that I could have it on condition that I was prepared to turn out if it were claimed. I had no alternative but to take the risk and nobody did claim Number Three.

Narkanda is a very popular week-end resort because the rest-house is good, the scenery spectacular and there is a famous four-mile walk to Hattu, a 10,000-feet peak above the village, from where you get an even more extensive view of the snows. Families come out from Simla by bus, since private cars are still not allowed along the road because of the large number of military vehicles

---

* This was before devaluation of the rupee. All rest-houses in Himachdal Pradesh now cost Rs. 10 for a 'set', i.e. a bedroom and washroom.

using it, for there is the ever-present threat of another Chinese invasion.

'Narkanda bungalow', writes St. John Gore, 'with its *khansama* and stores, its well-swept rooms and spacious veranda, not to mention its service of blue Dresden china, was to be our last sign of civilisation, for we left the main track here which leads up the Sutlej valley towards Tibet, and plunged down the narrow path that goes through the forest straight to the Sutlej, some six thousand feet below.'* I certainly do not remember eating off Dresden china back in 1931 and this time I ate off the thick, plain white type, such as one finds in English village halls: but, as standards go, the bungalow is certainly first class, the man in charge appears to combine the offices of *chaukidar* and *khansama* in a competent manner and has several sweepers working under him.

Narkanda is a tiny place with a little wooden Tibetan shrine surrounded by prayer-flags on the ridge below the rest-house, a school, a post office, a few shack shops, the P.W.D. office, and that is the beginning and end of it.

After tea I walked up the burnt-up grass slope above the village to watch the sunset lights reflected on the long range of snows on the opposite side of the valley. Here I made friends with a nice young woman wearing the traditional Punjabi dress, known as *salwar kamiz,* that is a loose tunic worn over cotton trousers with a scarf round the neck with the two ends hanging down the back. She spoke quite good English and invited me into her little wooden house on the hilltop for a cup of tea and a gossip. She had a baby of eleven months and when I asked if this was her first she announced that she had five—four daughters and a son. The two elder girls lived with their grandparents in Mandi and came to Narkanda for the school holidays, where her husband is a surveyor in the P.W.D.

'Narkanda is very dull,' she complained. 'Here there is no society.'

'What about the schoolmaster's wife?' I asked. 'Or isn't he married?'

'He is coming from another village, he doesn't live here.'

Poor girl! One cannot talk to a view, even though it may be one of the most spectacular in India.

* Op cit., p. 16.

The *khansama* produced a good egg curry for supper with really well-boiled rice. Contrary to expectations this is quite a rarity when travelling in any part of India: the majority of rest-house *chaukidars* make no attempt at separating the grains by slow drying, but cook it to a sticky mush and leave it at that. I wrote my first postcard to Sri Milklu Ram after supper, several letters and my diary till 11 p.m. and when I got up I dropped my only pair of spectacles on the floor. One side of the frame came off but I managed most ingeniously to fix it on again with a paper clip: a repair which held good until my return to England several months later. I went to bed with a hot water bottle and bed socks and kept my pink woollen combinations on under my Viyella pjyamas and put my one little blanket and my mackintosh over the top of my sleeping bag, as it was nice and cold at over 9,000 feet.

I intended to get up very early the next morning to see the sunrise over the snows but, alas, I did not wake until 6.30 a.m. I leapt out of bed and went on to the veranda in my mackintosh where I found a Sikh gentleman sitting in a cane chair in *déshabille*: a shirt over his pyjama legs and no *pagari* (turban), his long hair done up in a bun on top of his head.

'Did you see the sunrise?' I asked.

'Yes it was beautiful, really beautiful.'

I could have kicked myself: I had missed seeing the sun rise on one of the great views of the world and by now the light in the east was so blinding that I could not see the snows at all. I returned disconsolately to my room and read the Collect for the day, the second Sunday after Pentecost: 'Lord, make us at all times to fear and love thy Holy Name, for those whom thou dost firmly establish in thy love are never disappointed of thy guidance.' I sincerely hoped I loved the Lord enough for him to guide me safely through the Western Himalaya.

The maddening but understandable prohibition of maps now became exasperating, as the small tourist guide I had bought in Simla gave the next stage of the trek as twenty-six miles from Narkanda to Luri, 6,000 feet down in the Sutlej valley. It transpired that this mileage only applied to the carefully graded new motor road, whereas the much steeper old pack route was exactly half the distance. So we set off at 7.45 a.m. asking for the *chhota rasta* (little road), and were directed to a lovely shady track below the ridge. I was rejoicing at having left the highway at last when I heard the roar of an engine coming up the hill towards us and round the next bend thundered a huge green timber-lorry. Thank God it was the only one we met till we rejoined the new main road above the river several hours later. Half a mile lower down we came to the timber-yard belonging to a Simla contractor with pine trunks and sawn planks piled high in stacks, and sheds and motor-saws and several men standing idly about. Beyond this our way started to plunge down the *khud*-side in a series of steep zigzags and it seemed vaguely familiar to me, even after an interval of thirty years; it had also been used by St. John Gore some forty years before that, and by many another British trekking party. It was sad to think that it had now been superseded by the nasty modern tarmac road.

Telegraph poles and wires followed our short cut all the way and sometimes the track crossed over the new road. Creepers crept and roses rambled up many of the tall pines and deodars and poured over high branches in falls of leaves and flowers. The ground beneath was covered with a network of wild strawberry plants and as I was walking most of the time I picked the tiny scarlet fruit only to find that they tasted of nothing at all: they simply produced a drop of slightly sweet insipid water and the subtle flavour of the European *fraises des bois* was entirely absent. Other travellers in the Western Himalaya have also commented on this strange fact. Some of the pine-tree roots were above ground and formed a fine network against soil erosion and here and there there were clearings in the forest with patches of potatoes, white clover, and nurseries of baby pines.

At the end of three hours we came to the big village of Kumarsain. This was the capital of the former Simla hill State of that name and it is dominated by the Raja's palace, an architectural fantasy with a cloche-crowned tower of bright red corrugated iron at either end and a three-tiered pagoda of the same material in the middle. Apart from the palace complex the other buildings are all roofed with huge slabs of un-dressed stone—one can hardly call them tiles—characteristic of the hills.

By now it was extremely hot so I decided a rest would do us all good. A young schoolmaster who spoke English led us to a very new-looking rest-house on a knoll to the south of the village but the *chaukidar* could not be found so he led us on to a tiny Forest Department bungalow where the *chaukidar* showed me into a very clean neat little room with coarse red cotton curtains. I was hot and sticky and longed to wash my feet so I asked for some cold water. A Forest Officer then appeared and explained that there was running water in this establishment but that the tap was not working just now but would come on later. At what time, I asked.

'No time: oftenly it is coming and oftenly it is not coming.' By the time I left at 4 p.m. the tap was still dry. That day it was not coming.

Before leaving Kumarsain I photographed the fancy palace from several angles and then proceeded with my modest cavalcade to descend still further into the deep sun-parched valley. Alas, we had now got out of the forest and into the sub-tropical area so there was no more regular shade, only an occasional eucalyptus or sacred peepul. About a mile below the village there was a beautiful pagoda-type temple of dark deodar with rippling wooden fringes hanging from the eaves and panels of carving in the folk-style of the hills. These depicted the adventures of Krishna, though this *mandir* was dedicated to Shiva Mahadev, as I could tell from the stone figure of his sacred bull, Nandi, which lay outside the door. Standing beneath the sacred peepul tree (which was as dead as a doornail) in the courtyard, was a very dark soldier with a large bushy moustache. I started to speak reverently about the Lord Krishna when he announced: 'I am a Roman Catholic.' He told me that he was a native of Bangalore and that his regiment was stationed at Kasauli, the other side of Simla, but he was at present in camp near Kumarsain for a fortnight. It is a great thrill to meet someone who shares your faith in a country where the bulk of the population worships other gods, and we shook hands warmly before the soldier marched up the hill and I marched down, followed by my little mule train.

Eventually we came to the new tarred road again and had to go a mile along it before finding a track which led us to the river. We passed an army camp with several mule lines, all the animals being in splendid condition contentedly munching hay and I learnt later that the price of a good young mule had shot up to the region of

£100 owing to the emergency of the Chinese threat. We also passed an oblong cottage with plastered mud walls and a roof consisting entirely of hammered-out paraffin cans; these are sold for two rupees a dozen, which works out considerably cheaper than corrugated iron and incidentally looks much nicer, for when the 'tiles' have weathered they look like silvery slates. Two hundred yards beyond a signpost which said 'Kulu 71 miles', we came to a sprawling and very dilapidated-looking rest-house— obviously third-class—with a still more dilapidated-looking unshaven old *chaukidar* standing beside it holding a square, much-dented tin of water he had just fetched from a nearby brook. I said in halting Hindi:

'Permit no have, one room for one night want.'

He did not seem at all worried by my chitless condition and led me along the veranda into a room with an unusually high pitch-pine ceiling. It appeared he had no stores of any kind so I gave him a tin of 'spags' which he opened and tipped into an old black frying pan and proceeded to heat on a small fire of sticks in the compound. Meanwhile I tried hard to photograph the numerous large brown varanus lizards which ran up and down the bungalow walls, but as soon as they knew they were just in focus they disappeared like lightning. The 'tomato' sauce was not red but vivid pink and I shared my spags with some poor little baby thrushes which I found lying on a flower bed below the veranda, the nearby song of a cruel cuckoo revealing their sad situation.

The birds and I had just finished our supper when two young men walked up and asked for a room. They told me they were both fourth-year medical students from the Maulana Azad Hospital in New Delhi and that they were spending their summer vacation trekking, their ultimate object being to climb the Rohtang pass: Rajinder Kumar, twenty-one, plump with a bushy moustache, and Krishan Kumar Mahajan, twenty-one, tall, slim and clean-shaven. As we were all going to Kulu we decided then and there to travel together and my heart warmed towards them as heaven-sent A.D.C.'s who would supervise my arrangements at the next few rest-houses and deal with the *chaukidars*. We sealed our pact by an exchange of their dried apricots with my sticky chocolate. I lent them my torch as they wanted to cross the bridge over the Sutlej to the little village of Luri to get a meal in the bazaar but owing to a cloudburst they were back within ten minutes. By this time I was in my nightgown but I handed them a candle and a tin of sardines through my bedroom door. Then I sat and wrote my diary by the light of three slim candles stuck on to the bottom of my pink plastic plate; I resented being charged as much as one rupee by some *chaukidars,* for the use of a smoky oil lamp with a cracked chimney. It seemed odd that with the great river roaring below us neither water nor electricity was laid on at this rest-house—but then it was listed as Third Class.

In the night I suffered greatly from the heat as no electricity meant no fan and, whereas last night I had slept inside my flea-bag with a hot water bottle, now, 6,000 feet lower down the mountain, I lay, covered with insect repellent, tossing on top of it, with the ominous drone of mosquitoes in the air.

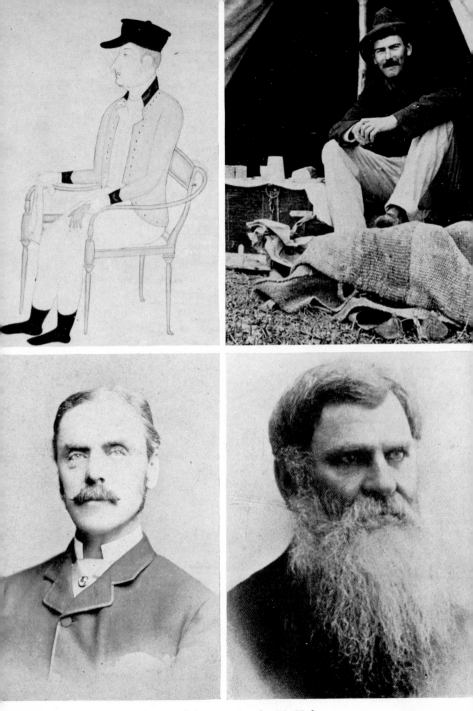

Personalities associated with Kulu:

Believed portrait (Sikh School) of
William Moorcroft

Mr. H. Lee Shuttleworth, I.C.S.

Colonel A. F. P. Harcourt

The Reverend Marcus Carleton

Members of the Ani temple band, 1931

CHAPTER II

The Ani Valley

In the morning my 'A.D.C.'s' breakfasted with me on the veranda at 6 a.m., the great heat calling for an early start. The boys had left Simla by bus only the day before which had brought them down the long tarred road from Narkanda to within a mile of the Luri bungalow, and so they had some fairly fresh bread with them for which I provided excellent tinned pineapple jam. I went to feed the little thrushes but they had completely disappeared. You never see a cat in these parts: could the monster lizards have eaten them?

The boys set off while B.R. was tying on the baggage, as they said that, being just up from the plains, they were very unfit and we would soon overtake them. On our way down to the river we watered the mules in a gurgling brook then descended to the iron suspension bridge, built in 1905 on the site of an old *sangha* (cantilever) bridge, the remains of which were used by the engineers when they constructed the new one.* On the middle of the bridge I dismounted to look up and down the dirty greeny-brown fast-moving waters of the great river Sutlej which rises some fifty miles to the north-east in the heights of Rampur Busahr. Meanwhile Durgi went off at a jog-trot with the baggage, ignoring B.R.'s loud commands to halt. When we reached the small village on the far side she had effectively disappeared, but the muleteer soon got news of her and ran down a steep stone path up which he returned cursing and kicking the disobedient animal. I had already realised that he had a grudge against her, whereas Shanti never seemed to annoy him, but my Hindi most unfortunately did not rise to reasoning with him so I was incapable of defending my elderly, erring baggage mule.

Once across the bridge we entered Kulu, actually the province of Outer Saraj which is in the Kulu sub-division of Kangra district, now both in the State of Himachal Pradesh. We proceeded along the level 'jeepable' road on the right bank of the

* This has been replaced by a modern iron bridge, wide enough for a bus.

Sutlej which was originally built as a mule track in 1912 by Mr. Willie Donald, a distinguished P.W.D. engineer who owned considerable property in the Kulu valley from the 1880's onwards. Before 1912 travellers had to ride straight up the steep hill opposite the bridge at Luri, described by St. John Gore, who reached the Jalori pass via the villages of Dalash and Kot, whereas by the newer and easier route you pass through Ani and Khanag.

The most trying thing about trekking in the Himalaya during the height of summer is the sharp contrast in temperature which one may experience from day to day. From Narkanda to Luri one descends 6,000 feet in thirteen miles and now I was riding along the Sutlej valley at a height varying between two and three thousand feet with a steep wall of baked brown *khud*-side to my right from which the heat was reflected in such intensity that I felt like an egg in a frying pan. I had discarded my jodhpurs in favour of a sleeveless brown cotton dress with an art-nouveau pattern of yellow kingcups all over it, but how I wished I had not been such a fool as to follow the current fashion of going hatless in heat! My mother and I always wore double *terais* when on trek, two thicknesses of felt superimposed one on top of the other with very broad brims, which, though they were not exactly becoming, were an effective protection against the sun; and St. John Gore's photographs show him and his brother in enormous topis.

The vegetation was still sub-tropical with masses of prickly pear cacti bursting into large yellow kingcup-like flowers—an echo of my dress—spiky aloes with their curious tall notchy blooms, the ugly *adha toda* shrub which flourishes all over the Indian plains, with its sickly green leaves and dirty white flowers which, when made into a tisane, are said to be the best possible remedy for whooping cough; an occasional eucalyptus tree, and innumerable clumps of that curious tall succulent spurge called *Tidhana* in Hindi (*Euphorbia antiquorum*) whose branches are like so many intertwined octopus tentacles.

Four and a half miles from Luri, and about 500 feet above the Sutlej, we came to the pretty little hamlet of Bhaina, where we caught up with the boys who were looking at the two-storey pagoda-type temple standing in a burnt-grass courtyard. The lower roof was square with large irregularly-shaped slices of precipice (quarzitic rock) acting as tiles, the top one round and roofed with rough wooden planks. In front there was an open pillared hall of huge square deodar pillars and a stone Nandi lying outside which indicated the dedication to Shiva. On the balcony between the *mandapa* (pillared hall) and the lower pagoda roof, each panel contained a separate beast, and further heraldic beasts in the true animal style were carved on two beams in the outer walls of the *garba griha* (*cella*). But more glorious than these was the spreading peepul in the courtyard, whose thick glossy green foliage provided us with a few minutes of blissful shade.

Leaving the hamlet the road turns sharply away from the Sutlej and up the valley of one of its many tributaries, the Ani *khud*. Here the rocks were alive with large lizards and I saw a whopper which I swear was two feet long from the tip of its nose to the tip of its tail. The road between Luri and Ani, the village we were making for, only rises a thousand feet in twelve miles and the sun was now behind us and beat mercilessly down on the back of my neck and the Bengali silk scarf I had tied round it gave very little protection. I suddenly had the bright idea of borrowing B.R.'s large umbrella to use as a sunshade, so it was pulled out from the baggage on Durgi and put up and I rested it on my right shoulder; the shade proved a marvellous relief and though I must have presented a comic spectacle from the rear, it was greatly to the credit of B.R. and my A.D.C.'s that I heard no giggling.

A little further on we came to Bhaina village school, opposite which there was a *chai khana*—an open-fronted shack tea-shop —where the boys suggested having a cup. Now I know that many young English men and women of today who hike through the East think nothing of eating and drinking at such places, but in the far-off days our English A.D.C.'s would have passed out at such a suggestion: it would have been considered dis-gracefully *infra dig* for representatives of the British Raj thus to lower themselves, besides which one would be certain to get every sort of disease from the flies crawling over the food. Little did Rajinder and Krishan realise what they were asking me to do, nor could they know the sense of liberation I felt when I sat on the hard wooden bench inside the shack and drank the weak over-sweetened brew beloved by Indians, brushing the flies off the sticky *jalebis* before eating them. I am pleased to be able to report that I suffered no ill effects whatsoever and that from then on, having jumped this fence—and a Beecher's Brook it was—I refreshed myself happily with B.R. in many a shack-shop up and down the hills.

We went on our way, the boys plodding along behind me and in spite of the fact that they were both wearing brown calico hats they complained greatly of the heat, for it was now nearing midday. Occasionally horrid little jeeps hurried by raising clouds of yellow dust, and I suggested a bathe in the river, which Krishan thought an excellent idea but Rajinder feared they might catch pneumonia if they plunged into an icy pool dripping with sweat. However, after they had dragged uphill for a further half-hour Krishan could bear it no longer and climbed down the steep boulder-strewn bank, tore off his clothes to reveal elegant trunks, and jumped into a deep brown pool under a waterfall. Rajinder then had second thoughts and soon joined him. I longed to jump in as well but thought B.R. might be shocked by mixed bathing and anyway I had not got a suit so I had to be content with paddling.

Within half a mile of Ani a jeep overtook us and stopped and out got Shri Romesh Chandra, the Conservator of Forests to whom I had written from Simla. It struck me as odd that he recognised me instantly although we had never met, but as English-women no longer regularly ride along this road I suppose it was not so odd after all. He introduced me to his companion Mr. Gordon Jones, a plump jovial Canadian forestry expert, and explained that they were touring the area with three Calcutta industrialists to see if it would be expedient to start a newsprint factory to make paper out of the sawdust and shavings of felled spruce. They were all five staying at the rest-house but would be returning to Kulu in the afternoon, and meanwhile Shri Chandra would be delighted if I would lunch with them. The food they had brought by jeep to the rest-house would not stretch to more than six, so my two A.D.C.'s said they would go to a shack restaurant and assured me there would be a good one in a biggish place like Ani, the principal village of Outer Saraj.

The rest-house lay on the far side with a good view up the Ani *khud*, where the river had been channelled into a number of little streams each working its own watermill, housed in small dry-stone buildings which proved to be a regular feature of Himalayan valleys near all the bigger villages.

We sat down to lunch just after 2 p.m. and it was a real treat to eat roast leg of lamb with beans and potatoes and gravy, after the sardines and tinned spags and the soggy rest-house rice and damned dull dal—from now on I shall refer to it as D.D.D.—to which I was accustomed. We had delicious little Lucknow melons and Kulu cherries to follow and the men drank beer cooled in the nearest ice-cold stream. How fantastic it seemed to be enjoying a big business luncheon in Ani! It made up for not having the riotous welcome we had been given in 1931, when Geoffrey thought that the blood-curdling sounds with which we were greeted signified that the villagers were about to attack us, but which turned out to come from the temple band.

After lunch my host and his friends left in two jeeps and half an hour later the boys turned up and we took possession of the rest-house. When Rajinder discussed our supper with the *chaukidar*, asking him to get us a chicken or at least some eggs from the village, he was told that there were none to be had because yesterday there had been a by-election at Ani for the Punjab Legislative Assembly and the officers conducting it, plus a lot of extra police, had fleeced the village.

Later in the afternoon we went out to explore the valley and I crossed a stream to a grassy island where Durgi and Shanti were grazing happily by one of the little mill houses. Inside, a *pahari* woman was grinding barley on a stone wheel. The barley poured out of a giant funnel and the stone wheel was kept turning by the mill-wheel itself, which lay flat in the water of the stream under the building, and revolved at a terrific rate.

My A.D.C.'s suggested calling on the Rani of Shangri, whom they had learned lived in the old mission house above the village, but on our way there we saw a new building with 'Primary Health Centre' written on it so the boys, being medicos, couldn't resist going inside. Here we met a charming young Sikh lady doctor in her tiny office who invited us all three to sit down and have coffee with her. She said she had been there a year and that her husband was the *thesildar* (district magistrate); they had two small children and lived in a dilapidated house with no mod. cons. and found it very difficult to get a *pahari* girl to mind the children and do the cleaning, for the *pahari* women much preferred taking their skinny cattle out to pasture and sitting under a tree all day gossiping to their friends. She also told us that all young doctors today, both men and women, were asked to do three years in a remote rural area as soon as they qualified. She said that she would soon forget all she had learnt as the people seldom let her or her girl health visitors into their houses and they were never called to maternity cases. Caste, she told us, is still strictly observed in the hills and she had had a Christian girl health visitor working under her who lived in a neighbouring hamlet, and who had been forbidden to get water from the well. The girl announced she would get what she wanted whereupon the village elders had threatened to kill her so she reported the matter to the police at Ani who made the hell of a row after which the girl was able to use the water freely. (Later on the boys heard another version of this story which was that the health visitor had washed her hair in the well which had understandably annoyed the elders as it was their only drinking supply!)

I asked the doctor about polyandry which used to be regularly practised in Saraj. She said that she knew of no cases where a girl officially married several brothers (which anyway is against the law in modern India) but her health visitors often reported several 'moves' among the local ladies: they would visit the house of a married woman if one of the children had fever and a month later they would find the same woman living in another house with another 'husband'.

We left the Health Centre and were directed up a long steep drive to the old wooden, Simla-style mission house, with a red corrugated-iron roof and a turret at each end. As we approached it we met a clean-shaven, middle-aged man who spoke excellent English and who turned out to be the late Rai's manager, Sri Rup Chand Johanna, a Christian whose father had worked as a catechist for the Reverend Marcus Carleton, the American missionary who had founded this settlement nearly eighty years ago. He told us that the Rai, who had died a year ago, had bought the mission house and other buildings and some land from the Church Missionary Society. Sri Rup Chand Johanna said he would be delighted to take me to call on the junior Rani but that she did not receive men visitors, so I left my A.D.C.'s talking to a young Christian boy, Fateh Chand, and followed the manager up to the house where I was presented to the pleasant-looking junior Rani of Shangri, aged about thirty-five, her lady companion and a little girl of six, who was the Rani's adopted daughter. The senior Rani was in Kulu and as neither she nor the junior Rani had any children the family was, sadly, in the process of dying out. The ladies lived in semi-purdah—as is still the custom among high caste families in the hills—in the old mission house, with no electric light, and we sat on the wide veranda and made stilted conversation about health and the weather through the interpretation of the manager, while we nibbled walnuts and a kind of pop-corn. I later reflected that if only the late Rai had kept his now celebrated illustrated manuscript, known as the *Shangri Ramayana*,* his two relicts might be spending the rest of their days not merely in comfort, but in luxury.

As Sri Rup Chand and I walked back along the path past the orchards to rejoin the boys the manager said that when I had come to Ani this morning, riding on a mule with an umbrella up, the rumour quickly got round the Christian community that a missionary had arrived. Was this indeed the case? Because if so he hoped so much that I would speak at a special memorial service to be held for the late Prime Minister tomorrow morning. I said that although I was actually only a tourist I should, nevertheless, have been delighted to oblige had I been able to speak fluent Hindi, which, alas, I could not. He then took me to see Marcus Carleton's tomb. It was marvellously situated on a grassy spur high above the valley with a few tall, lank, pale mauve Himalayan crocus growing round it. There was a simple humpback stone over the grave with the following inscription:

Reverend Marcus Carleton
Born 13th August, 1825
Died 6th May, 1898
I Cor. XV 58

The reference only was given, not the text.

* The *Shangri Ramayana* consists of illustrations of the *Ramayana* epic in the Basholi style of *pahari* painting but was executed in Mandi. A mere twenty-three leaves of it were sold at Sotheby's in July 1970, for a total of £7,080.

Kulu: the End of the Habitable World

Sri Rup Chand told me that Mr. and Mrs. Carleton had come up from the plains during a terrible famine with several convert Punjabi boys who had married local *pahari* girls and settled down to farm on land bought for them by the missionary. The chapel had originally been one of the outbuildings attached to the house but since selling it to the Rai of Shangri the Christians had built themselves a stone chapel up a side valley. They were upset because some of the Seventh Day Adventists from Simla had recently established their own mission at Ani and had built a little stone church nearer the village. Oh, that we all might be one!

I discovered later* that the Reverend Marcus Carleton was borne in Marshfield, Vermont, graduated at East Windsor Presbyterian College in 1854 and sailed to India with his wife in October of the same year. From then on he worked unceasingly in the mission field for forty-four years, never once returning to America on furlough. 'He was characterised,' says his obituary, 'by great kindness, an earnest missionary spirit and a rare child-like simplicity of character.' One has only to look at his eyes in the photograph here reproduced to see the fire and the faith that is in them.

Mr. Carleton's work in India seems to have been one long fight against the making of what used to be called 'compound Christians', that is Indians who were given work and homes on mission property as soon as they were baptised or even when they were still under instruction. As his obituary says, 'His whole life was a sort of protest against plans and methods which he felt to be detrimental to the true interests of a self-supporting and self-propagating church.'

The last eleven years of his life were spent here at Ani, in Outer Saraj, with his second wife Eliza Calhoun, the first Mrs. Carleton having died in 1881. At that time the village was far more difficult of access than it is today as Mr. Donald had not then built the present road along the river and it could only be reached by steep mule tracks via a village to the south-east named Dalash. From there you could either go north over the Jalori Pass, or south via Luri and Kumarsain to the old-

* From files in the library of the United Presbyterian Church in the U.S.A., Interchurch House, 475 Riverside Drive, New York.

established mission station at Kotgarh, some twenty miles away, from which Mr. Carleton or one of his boys had to fetch and post their letters which came and went by mail runner to and from Simla and thence to the plains.

As soon as the settlers' crops started to bring in a return they repaid the missionary on easy terms for their land and for the materials out of which they had built their timber houses, and thus became independent proprietors. On the whole the system seems to have worked well, but like every leader of men, Mr. Carleton had his failures. 'I shall also be obliged if you will kindly tell old Bind Dass', runs one letter from Ani, 'that his nephew Ram is well and works very hard and all the Christians like him. And for your information I write of the four new boys I took up, two are doing fine but the other two from Loodiana have left me. They were most abandoned characters and I am glad they are gone though I advanced them Rs 22 for food and clothing, etc.'

But Marcus Carleton's methods were not always approved of by the mission board and his letters are full of—usually un-successful—efforts to get money. In April 1887 he writes: 'I therefore fulfil my promise to tell you of my Koolloo work. I have bought a good deal of property in several places for a rural mission. The Loodiana mission made an honest attempt to take up Koolloo (at least I thought so) and lent me Rs 300 to buy confiscated property, old buildings, etc. I did so, but the Board ordered all such sums to be paid back to the mission and the Rs 300 were cut from my allowance at once and I was two whole months without the first red cent to buy my food. I had to depend two months upon my Hindoo neighbours for food I then took up Koolloo vigorously and got help from America.' (Mr. Carleton is sparing of punctuation.)

Apart from the frustration of money worries, he had, like so many saintly people, continually to fight the demon of bad health, having at the outset of his career gone to India with serious defects in his respiratory system. He was often called 'the jungle missionary', because he preferred to live constantly in the open air and to eat only the simplest food. Had Mr. Carleton chosen the text for his tomb himself I wondered? Certainly none more appropriate could have been found: for if you look up I Corinthians xv, verse 58 reads: 'Therefore, my beloved brethren, be ye steadfast, unmoveable, always abounding in the work of the Lord, forasmuch as ye know that your labour is not in vain in the Lord.'

The second Mrs. Carleton remained for a little over a year in charge of this remote Christian settlement after her husband's death in 1898. She returned to America in 1900 and died in 1929. Evidently no Presbyterian was subsequently found to supervise the work at Ani, but in 1907 the Salvation Army took it over, by which time the orange groves and orchards planted by Mr. Carleton twenty years earlier were bearing fruit. The new missionaries started a flourishing local industry making jam and marmalade which found a popular market among the British families in Simla.

I well remember the Salvation Army couple who were living in Ani in September 1931 and whom my mother invited to dinner in the rest-house. They arrived an hour before they were asked because their only watch had stopped the previous year and since then they had calculated the time by the sun, but were just a little out. They informed us that they were about to leave the settlement which was afterwards taken over by the Church Missionary Society in whose hands it still remains.

Christian mission work is not looked on with favour in the India of today, nor indeed by some Europeans who find Eastern religions superior to those of their own country. But no Gospel command is clearer than that to go out and teach all nations, and personally I cannot but admire the many men and women down the centuries who have obeyed it. On the Indian side, a considerable number of their *swamis* and *bhikkhus*, starting with the world-famous Vivekananda at the beginning of the present century, have gone to Europe and America and taught the *vedanta* and other Hindu and Buddhist religious systems and made many converts, and I am not aware that Christians have actively objected.

In the rapidly gathering dusk we rejoined my A.D.C.'s, who, together with young Fateh Chand, were looking round the orchards and gardens planted by the Carletons and their Punjabi boys in the 1880's, and which are now owned by the Ranis of Shangri. As well as terraces of orange and lemon trees, red and yellow plum, apricot, apple and pear, there were also ornamental trees such as magnolias and Italian cypress, which the missionary introduced into the valley.

I arranged to return early in the morning with Fateh Chand to photograph the tomb, then I went back to the rest-house with Krishan and Rajinder where we had a very starchy supper of D.D.D. and *chapatties* and boiled potatoes, gingered up by the boys' excellent sweet mango chutney. The next morning, after an early breakfast, Fateh Chand turned up at the appointed time and led me back to the missionary's tomb where I took photographs by the light of the rising sun. Deeply moved by the grave of this good man, I knelt down beside it and Fateh Chand did likewise and I said some prayers for the reunion of Christendom, ending up with the Lord's Prayer in the middle of which I burst into tears and was unable to finish.

The mules were ready and waiting when we reached the bungalow and as I rode along the little untarred road towards the Jalori Pass I looked back down the smiling Ani valley with its network of streams, its cornfields and orchards and thought of the Reverend Marcus Carleton looking happily from Heaven at these little farms he had bought and cultivated, and on the descendants of the young Indians he had settled on them.

CHAPTER III

The Jalori Pass and Inner Saraj

The road soon began to ascend fairly steeply and we eventually got into the shade of the forests where there were still a few vivid red flowers among the dark foliage of the tall rhododendrons. The grassy banks were bright red with the tiny tasteless wood strawberries; but at one point I found some delicious wild raspberries, with yellow fruit, which were just as good as cultivated ones at home.

At about ten o'clock I heard a shout from the river bank two hundred yards to the left and saw Rajinder and Krishan, who had walked on ahead. They were bathing again and washing in the river so I dismounted and joined them. Borrowing Krishan's Lifebuoy soap and armed with a small saucepan to pour water over my head I decided to wash my hair, and knelt down on a flat stone beside the mountain torrent. Then I sat on a rock like the Lorelei combing my, alas, not golden but silver tresses which dried very quickly in the sun and wind.

We continued up the pleasantly shaded road which later hairpinned round to the left over a white wooden bridge, leaving the Ani river altogether. Then we started climbing pretty steeply and came out into the open and saw another deep valley to the left with another torrent roaring along it towards the Sutlej. The boys sat down to rest, but I rode on followed by Durgi and B.R. and soon we entered another forest of cedar, holly, yew and white oak, many of which were covered with lichen, looped in great swags from branch to branch. Eventually we reached the rest-house at Khanag which is at 8,300 feet. A more wonderful situation could hardly be imagined. In the foreground lay a little ledge of white clover lawn with sweet-scented, carmine cabbage roses growing close to the bungalow veranda—doubtless planted by some British official many years ago—and beyond the lawn the *khud* fell steeply down to the valley where you could see the torrent a long way below dashing in and out among the

34

spurs of the mountain, while to the north-west there was a great amphitheatre of deodars going round to the Jalori Pass, which was hidden by a fold in the hills.

On the lawn sat five men who, I discovered, had been engaged in the Ani election campaign: two schoolmasters from neighbouring villages, two government officials up from the plains, and a policeman in uniform. They assured me that there would be plenty of room for us in the dak bungalow as they were about to disperse and return to their homes.

By now I was so hungry that as soon as I was shown into my bedroom by the *chaukidar* I flung everything out of my bags on to the bed, seized my last tin of food—tunny fish—opened it and ate two-thirds straight off. When the poor boys turned up an hour later, tired and thirsty after the last lap of the unshaded steep climb to Khanag with the mid-day sun beating down on their backs, I felt deeply ashamed that owing to my gluttony I only had a third of a tin of tunny fish left to offer them, but they ate it eagerly with their three-day-old Simla sliced loaf. I left them and had a nice sleep and when I awoke the jeep load of electioneers had gone. Meanwhile, Rajinder had discovered a ram-breeding station on the downs above the bungalow so we went up with him to see it. There were three modern huts—with the inevitable red corrugated-iron roofs—on the edge of the forest, outside one of which sat a nice young man who was plainly dedicated to his job. He proudly showed us four shorn rams which he used to cover the local *pahari* ewes. He said the latter only gave one pound of wool a year, but since the government had introduced these Bikaniri cross Merino rams the resulting progeny gave up to four pounds a year when they reached maturity.

From there we walked into a sacred grove of deodars in the middle of which was a tiny shrine in a walled enclosure; Rajinder put his two hands to his forehead and saluted the *devata* (the local god) within, and then we descended a few hundred feet to the hamlet of Khanag where there was a general stores at which the boys bought rice and D.D.D. and I tried on several pairs of *pulis*, the string shoes which are excellent for climbing and are much worn by the hill people. But they were all too small, and I felt like one of the ugly sisters in Cinderella trying to cram my great broad feet into them.

Kulu: the End of the Habitable World

On the unshaded path which leads for about a quarter of a mile from the village to the rest-house, I noticed a lot of juniper bushes and *cotoneaster horizontalis*—so familiar in English gardens —sprawling over banks and rocks, and the indigofera and berberis were everywhere flowering prolifically. We met some ragged schoolchildren and Rajinder got them to pose for a photograph against a brilliant background of blossom. They were carrying school boards—not slates—with a handle at one end and they told us they used them for writing practice. Back in England the following year I showed the photograph to Robert Skelton of the Victoria and Albert Museum who showed me a third-century A.D. panel of Gandhara sculpture of Prince Siddhartha, before he became the Buddha, driving to school in a little ram cart accompanied by several bigger boys who carried boards identical with those used by modern Indian schoolchildren.

The following day we had an easy climb to the top of the pass in the cool of the early morning and in addition to the usual flowers and shrubs I saw large numbers of sinister cobra plants (*arasaema Wallachiana*), their purple striped sheaths curving over like cobras about to strike. The whole of this area used to be a haunt of the two most beautiful species of Himalayan pheasant: the green and purple monal and the red crested tragopan, but although we kept our eyes open for them we were disappointed as we saw none.

The old Jalori Pass (10,720 feet) crosses the ridge about a mile and a half to the east of the present one (10,280 feet) which was constructed by Willie Donald in the years immediately preceding the First World War as a continuation of his road up the Ani valley. I was very confused by the modern guidebooks which all give the height of the pass as five hundred feet lower than the guide and travel books of before the First War until I realised that they were, in fact, describing two different passes both called by the same name.

We reached the top of what, for the sake of clarity, I will call the 'new Jalori', at about 9 a.m. and I was astonished to see two little stone huts, roughly roofed with huge irregular stone slabs, one on either side of the road. Thirty years ago the top of this pass had seemed wild and remote from civilisation: not so today for the larger of the buildings turned out to be a restaurant!

Greatly excited at the prospect of a meat meal we ordered mutton curry and rice and I told B.R. to unload Durgi and let the two little mules graze, but the grass was so closely cropped by mountain sheep that I followed the local custom—of which I so much disapproved—and stripped some small branches off the *kharsu* oaks and let my animals munch the leaves. While the mules were enjoying themselves a jeep drove up and out got three tall Sikhs, who ordered tea, put a transistor radio on the bonnet of the jeep, and turned it on at full blast to popular Indian film tunes. A few minutes later the Ani-Banjar minibus, painted red and cream, arrived. 'Really,' I thought, 'there will soon be a traffic jam', and I could not help indulging in a little silent nostalgia for the quieter days, wishing desperately that 'progress' had not come to this once lonely mountain pass. From the bus stepped our good friend Sri Rup Chand Johanna. He was on his way to inspect an orchard in Kulu belonging to the senior Rani of Shangri and to sell the apples on the trees to a contractor. The little mountain bus, he told me, now runs from Ani, in Outer Saraj, to Banjar in Inner Saraj, and from there another little bus runs to Aut on the main Mandi–Manali road where there are twelve big buses a day in either direction. He told me that the service of condolence for Pandit Nehru had lasted for one and a half hours and was attended by all the Christians of Ani.

On the roof of the shepherd's hut opposite our smart restaurant sat a young boy with two woolly black sheep dogs wearing spiked metal collars to protect them from having their throats torn out by bears and panthers. They are always worked in pairs as two dogs can usually kill a panther whereas one on its own is likely to get killed. The surrounding forests of spruce fir and brown oak still abound in panther and also red bear, which live between here and the eternal snow-line some 5,000 feet higher up. The black bear prefers life at a slightly lower altitude where he can get a good supply of maize in due season.

I walked over to the Jalori 'Boulestin' and sat down on a dirty bench in the open-fronted kitchen and watched our 'brunch' being cooked. There were two stone-lined holes in the mud floor and in one of them some pine wood was burning brightly while the other contained hot ash for simmering. The rice and roughly cut up mutton—obviously scrag end of neck—were boiling together in a large brass pan on the flaming hole and after a bit the chef-proprietor covered it with a dirty enamel plate and transferred it to the simmering hole; then he put another pan on the first burner in which he fried chopped onions and chillies in *dalda*, the popular Indian tinned cooking fat, *ghi* (clarified butter) being too expensive for everyday use. After a bit he stirred in some curry powder and poured the contents of this pan into the other one and left them all to simmer together until the meat was cooked.

At eleven o'clock our meal was ready and we took it down the *khud* on enamel plates and ate it on a bank away from the wind and close to small rhododendron shrubs (*campanulatum*) whose large creamy-mauve flowers were in full bloom. Anything is good when you are hungry, though the rice was a sloppy mess and the meat full of the little bone splinters inevitable in scrag end. Added to these inconveniences the too liberal supply of chillies nearly took the roof off my mouth but the boys loved them.

The top of the pass marks the boundary between Outer and Inner Saraj and I decided to walk the three miles down the far side to Shoja which proved to be very steep. The road was pleasantly shaded by silver fir and spruce and occasional wild cherry trees in blossom. There were quantities of iris growing on the *khud* above and below the road, thick bracken and quite a few of the tall, evil-looking cobra plants. We passed several groups of men felling spruce firs and huge piles of planks destined for a bumpy journey down mountain torrents into the Béas river and along it to the Punjab plains.

On arrival at the Shoja bungalow, which was beautifully situated in a grassy glade thick with iris, we found that the *chaukidar* was asleep and after B.R. had succeeded in waking him he came out of his go-down and pointed to his throat from which I gathered that it was sore. However, he showed me into a clean room with a single bed and I started to unpack. The boys took the only other bedroom which fortunately had two beds in it. They were only just in time, for no sooner had they settled in than a jeep drove up, bulging with baggage, and out of it got two dark, bearded giants. They turned out to be medical students,

The Ani Valley. Rajinder Kumar and Krishan Kumat Mahajan with my muleteer, Bhagavat Ram

The Jalori Pass (10,280 feet), 1964, with the Jalori 'Boulestin' in the background

too, studying in Simla where their parents run the Seventh Day
Adventist Mission Hospital next to the Cecil Hotel. The extraordinary thing was that I had recently sat between their mother
and father at a tea-party celebrating the centenary of the Jesus
and Mary Convent! The boys had walked a double stage from
Ani but were given a lift in the jeep for the last few miles over the
pass and down to Shoja. They had not had anything to eat since
breakfast that morning (fancy not stopping for a meal at the
Jalori Boulestin) and were now ravenous, but the prospects
were none too bright: the *chaukidar* declared he had no stores at
all and there was no shack-shop in the tiny hamlet below the
rest-house. The poor giants did a tour of the few chalets trying
to persuade someone to kill a sheep (I believe they could have
eaten one apiece) or at least a skinny hen—but no luck. In the
end they had to be content with our rations: the boys produced
the rice they had bought at Khanag, I unearthed a packet of
dehydrated peas, and to my surprise and delight found I had also
one tin of sausages left at the bottom of a kitbag. I longed
to make a risotto of all these goodies myself as the *chaukidar* was
too sick to cook, but the only stove was in his go-down and he
would not have liked a Memsahib intruding. As it was B.R.
most nobly volunteered to act as *khansama* and by 9 p.m. had
produced a sloppy, badly-burnt mess, God bless him.

As there were only two bedrooms in the Shoja bungalow the
Seventh Day Adventist giants had to make do with their sleeping-
bags on the dining-room floor, the *chaukidar* having produced
extra mattresses. I wrote my diary by candlelight then went to
bed in my pink silk and wool combinations, nightdress and
jersey, with a tepid hot water bottle and my heavy hunting mac
over the blanket which covered my sleeping-bag. Even then I
was cold and had to keep moving about to keep warm so that I
slept very little.

Those poor giants! Why didn't they carry a supply of stores
with them suited to their frames? All they could produce for
breakfast was a packet of digestive biscuits which they shared
with us and to which I was able to add some nasty tinned cheese
and the last remains of my chocolate which, having melted in
the intense heat of Luri, had now resolidified in the cold of the
mountain heights.

In spite of the *chaukidar*'s indisposition he turned up all right before we left in order to present the bill, get his tip, and to see that we filled in the beastly record book.

The next stage was the most beautiful part of the trek from Simla to Kulu and I walked, as the road continued steeply downhill, through glades of iris with the Jalori torrent tumbling down the *khud* and rushing northwards through the valley far below. Deodars provided shade and the brown oaks were replaced by the green holly oaks and lower still by the white oaks, and at this level, too, there were huge walnut trees, and horse-chestnuts still in flower. We passed several gangs of Tibetan road workers, both men and women, and also the large camp where they lived, consisting of rows of tents (many with blackened tops from the fires they light inside) pitched on terraces with hundreds of tiny prayer flags strung up for protective purposes. Near here a poor Tibetan woman came up to us with a septic cheek, but the boys could not help her as they carried no drugs. All they could do was to advise her to go to the dispensary at Banjar further down the valley. They both resolved on all future treks to carry tubes of penicillin ointment.

The road grew gradually less steep and as we strode easily downhill in the fresh morning air the boys started to discuss their favourite national hero, the Bengali revolutionary, Subhas Chandra Bose (Netaji or Leader, as he was known to his followers). I said I had always had the greatest possible admiration for Gandhi, but that as a Briton how could I be expected to admire Netaji who had sided with the Germans and the Japanese in the war? Krishan said that most young Indians today were far more inspired reading about the exploits of Netaji than by those of Gandhiji: the young admired action, and Gandhi's methods had been too passive. I said the Mahatma had aroused the admiration of the world by using a new weapon to fight my countrymen—*satyagraha*—non-violent non-co-operation, and that in the long run this had been far more effective in hastening our long promised exit than the tragic battles of the Indian Nationalist Army of which Netaji was the supreme commander. Then we got into a deep discussion on the subject of loyalty and I agreed that Subhas Chandra Bose had put love of his country before everything, which was wholly admirable. I promised to read more about him when I got the chance and said no doubt in a few years' time I might be able to appreciate his violently anti-British career more objectively.

At round about 5,000 feet I mounted Shanti and rode out of the pleasant shade of the great trees into a sort of shrubbery of pale pink oleanders, feathery spiraea, and flowering pomegranates all growing along the river banks. Then we got down to the level of the prickly pear and ugly *adha toda* and by the time we reached Banjar, the principal village of Inner Saraj, it was midday, and very hot indeed. I told B.R. to water the mules.

'He tells us they don't need it,' said Krishan.

I flew into a rage and said: 'You none of you have any feeling for animals: that is one of the great quarrels we British have always had with you. My mules have come a long way and the temperature must now be at least 90 degrees, please tell B.R. that I insist on his watering them as soon as we come to a good place!'

I rode on in silence down the long village street with open-fronted shops on either side, a post office, a dispensary, school, police station and the usual various government offices. At one point we came to a spring channelled into a stone basin and I stopped Shanti for a drink but before she could get her muzzle near the water some angry villagers came up and waved us on and the boys explained that this spring was reserved for people to drink from. About a mile below the village the Jalori torrent joins the larger Tirthan river which flows into the valley from the east, and here I insisted that B.R. took the mules down to water, though the going between the road and the bank was extremely stony and rough. I dismounted and stood and watched the operation to make certain he did as I wished: by now I had reassumed the authority of the British Raj and was not prepared to stand any nonsense. When at last the animals reached the sandy bank they had only to lower their heads and drink their fill. Neither of them condescended so much as to sniff at the water.

Two miles from Banjar we passed below the village of Plach, where the Reverend Marcus Carleton had once owned property, and two miles further on the road crossed to the other side of the Tirthan by a suspension bridge and then continued beside the left bank of the river through the big village of

Manglaur, where the Bah torrent tumbles down a *nala* (water-course) from the south and still further swells the Tirthan. We proceeded along the hot austere valley and passed an isolated wooden house on which the statements 'God is Great. God is everywhere. Welcome Guru', were chalked up in English.

According to M. C. Forbes, who wrote an excellent guidebook to these parts published in 1911,* the great Dharamsala earth-quake of 1905—whose activities extended far beyond Kangra—completely remodelled this valley through which we were now travelling: 'Whole hillsides carrying with them the roadway slid down into the Tirthan, blocking up and completely changing the level of its bed. Some of the avalanches of loose soil and stones went on sliding and crumbling for two years before they came to rest. In one place, where the path now makes a great curve inwards and away from the stream, it used to go straight across at the present level of the river, and so greatly has the con-figuration of this valley been altered that a cutting actually in the water is pointed out as part of the old road which used to be fifty feet above the river bed.'

Re-making this road was yet another problem for Mr. Willie Donald to whom, says Forbes, 'Kulu owes a great debt in the matter of its roads.'

We now passed the hundredth milestone from Simla, for although India has officially gone over to the metric system it will be a long time before the people use it and both measure-ments are marked up. A little further down the river another suspension bridge led back to the right bank where oleanders grew prolifically all along the water's edge.

We reached Larji in the early evening to find the little two-bedroomed dak bungalow bursting at the seams with an American family, father (agricultural adviser on drainage to the Punjab government), mother, three young flaxen-haired children and a further three boys (friends of the family) and two servants, on a fishing week-end from Chandigarh. I pleaded with the *chaukidar* saying that I was too tired to go on and asked if I could sleep on the veranda, to which he agreed, with the river as my wash-house.

Alas, here at Larji I had to say farewell to my A.D.C.'s because

* *To Kulu and Back* (Thacker and Spink, now out of print).

there was no room at all for them in the rest-house. Dead beat as they were, having so recently come up from the plains, the poor boys decided to walk the three miles on to Aut where there was a Forest Department bungalow and from where they could get the early morning bus to Manali at the far end of the Kulu valley. I thanked them profoundly for all their help and for their stimulating company and we arranged to meet in Delhi before I returned to England.

Larji is a small hamlet but the dak bungalow is in a really stunning position in the angle between two foaming torrents, for the Sainj river joins the Tirthan at this point, and together they tear down the valley into the Béas a few hundred yards below. While waiting for my supper I sat and watched two men returning home from the other side of the Tirthan by the *jhula* (rope bridge) just above the rest-house. A thick rope was attached to a post on either bank and whoever wanted to cross had to sit on a wooden seat above the torrent and propel himself along by means of another rope above his head. The surrounding hills are said to be full of game, chiefly *ghoral* and *kakur* (barking deer) and the Rungal mountain which overshadows the little village is known to contain *verde antique* but nobody has attempted to quarry it.

As Larji provides excellent trout fishing the bungalow is very popular and has a superior type of *chaukidar* who is a good cook and I had an excellent supper of rice and D.D.D., two hard-boiled eggs in a runny curry sauce, and sliced tomatoes and cucumber. I was, therefore, not as envious as I might have been of the grilled trout caught and eaten by the Americans, the delicious odours of which floated out to my veranda. I slept comfortably in my sleeping bag stretched out on a string *charpoy* (Indian-type bed consisting of a wooden frame on four short legs, with string or webbing stretched cross-wise over the frame) and was thrilled to wake up at dawn and see a black scorpion—the first I had ever seen outside a zoo—lying motionless on the concrete floor beside, but not thank God inside, my slippers. I pushed the little creature from behind with a book and it scuttled obediently off. I suppose that in the interest of my fellow-guests I should have put on a walking shoe and killed it but I could not face the crunch.

CHAPTER IV

A *Devata* Procession

Leaving Larji punctually at 6.30 a.m. on our ninth morning out from Simla we continued down the valley which got narrower and more austere as the great bare hills closed in on us, while rock pigeons wheeled overhead and the waters roared below. We overtook, and were overtaken in our turn, by the symbols of yesterday and today on Himalayan roads—a string of at least fifty pack animals—ponies, mules and donkeys and the Banjar to Aut mini-bus, closely followed by a couple of jeeps.

We crossed the torrential Sainj river first, then the Béas by a suspension bridge which led directly into the little village of Aut, which has become quite important since the opening of the 24-mile-long Mandi gorge road in the early twenties, for here the one-way traffic begins and there are several shack-restaurants where drivers and passengers can sit and pass away the time until it is their turn to use the road. When we arrived a line of lorries, buses, jeeps and private cars was drawn up behind the barrier facing south and I assumed they must all be going to Kulu and thought that B.R. knew the way (though I later learnt that this was his first journey to these parts) so, sitting on Shanti, I took my place in the queue. The milestones originally set up by the British all along the old Himalayan pack-routes are now inscribed in three scripts, the Latin, the Devanagari and the Gurumukhi (Punjabi); but not all three on one stone, each will be in a different script. This one at Aut happened to be in Gurumukhi, the only one of the three which I could not read—and B.R. could not read at all.

After a twenty-minute wait the barrier went up, the oncoming traffic thundered past us after which we followed our line of vehicles in a cloud of dust until the motors got well away and the dust settled and on we plodded into the deep dark gorge. At a point some three miles south-west of Aut, just as we were approaching the little riverside hamlet of Thalot, the most exciting

thing happened: I heard the enthralling never-to-be-forgotten
strains of a Himalayan temple band coming from somewhere
above in the rocky hills to my right. This was the first such music
I had heard on this trek and it carried me back to 1931 when my
mother, as wife of the Commander-in-Chief, was greeted in all the
bigger villages to which we rode by the temple band and the local
devata.

I leapt from my mule and rushed up the *khud* just in time to
see the first men appear over the brow of a bare brown hill,
carrying an enormous red and white standard. Next came the
musicians: a few flautists, a few drummers, two men blowing
curved 'serpents'—resembling those used in English churches in
the eighteenth century—and another two carrying six-foot silver
trumpets over their shoulders. These are so heavy that the musicians have to stand still to blow them and can only do so for about
thirty seconds at a time. The flutes play runny tunes, the serpents
arpeggios, the drums thrilling rhythms and the great trumpets
blare out octaves with such compelling force that I am tempted to
apostatise on the spot and throw myself down before the
devata: it is real primeval *Sacre du Printemps* stuff which would
surely have intoxicated Stravinsky.

Meanwhile I was leaping from rock to rock like a mountain
goat with two cameras hanging round my neck clicking first one
then the other so that I got some black and white photographs for
this book and a colour sequence of the whole procession which I
can never hope to equal. At the end of the band the *devata* himself
appeared attached to a *rath*, a wooden palanquin slung on long
poles resting on the shoulders of two young men. As he approached I signalled to the bearers to halt, which they were
delighted to do, while I photographed the group and enquired the
name of their god, which I learnt was Markanda, the Hindi form
of Markandeya, a deified Vedic sage. Like all the village gods of
these hill regions the processional image consists not of a single
figure but of several metal masks which are fixed on to the *rath*
on ceremonial occasions but otherwise kept in the *bhandar*, the
temple treasury. Brightly coloured stuffs are hung below the
masks and a gilded wooden *chhatri* (umbrella) is stuck above them
—at least on the palanquins of the Saraj and Mandi *devatas*, whereas
in Kulu they are decorated with several miniature metal *chhatris*.

The *devata* was followed by a crowd of devotees and when the untidy procession crossed over the tarred road I suddenly realised that the god was being carried down to the Béas to bathe. There was a fifty-foot drop over enormous boulders to the foaming water's edge and I shall never understand how I avoided breaking at least one of my legs attempting to follow him. The ritual ablutions consisted of tipping the *rath* right over three times so that the tip of the *chhatri* touched the water, and whenever it did so the whole band struck up with a triumphant blare. Markanda was then taken back to the road where he started to 'dance', the two young men carrying him lurching the *rath* over first to one side then to the other, jogging it up and down on their shoulders as they did so. But evidently they did not come up to scratch as an old man signalled to them to stop and then gave a demonstration of how it should be done, a tender look of devotion on his face. The women of the village took no part in the ritual but stood together in a crowd on the road. When the 'dancing' was over the *devata* was set down to rest under a precipice and some of the women went up to a cave in another precipice and fetched stacks of *chapatties*, which were being cooked on a large flat stone heated by a wood fire. These they distributed among the men who were now seated on the ground near their god. On the rock face above them, a slogan was chalked up in English: 'Work is Worship'.

Remounting Shanti I led my modest mule train on its way. Sometimes the road was cut right out of the rock and the precipice above curved menacingly over us so that it was like riding through a tunnel open on one side, but these cuttings were welcome for their shade. When the road came out of them the heat—at least 100° F.—radiated off the rocks and but for B.R.'s splendid umbrella I would have had a stroke. I rested it on my right shoulder so that it shaded my neck and back and I was able to see the view in front through dark glasses. Some of the hills rose almost sheer for about a thousand feet above the green and foaming Béas; others receded a little and brown burnt-up grass grew on their steep slopes; I even saw a small chalet-type temple perched high above on one such patch, though how any worshippers ever got near it I cannot imagine. A few isolated *chil* pines grew far up on these forbidding hills and lower down cascades of creepers with feathery white flowers tumbled on to

Devata Markanda being taken down to the Béas for a ritual bath. Mandi-Larji gorge below Thalot

Bajaura, southern face of the temple of Visvesvara Mahadeva

Panel of sculpture on the northern niche of the Bajaura temple: Durga slaying the demons, Sumbha, Nishumba and Mahisha

Looking eastward up the Parbatti Valley to the eternal snows of Spiti; B.R. with Durgi and Shanti

the road from invisible clefts in the rock face. Quite a few lorries rumbled by enveloping us in dust and I couldn't think how the wooden bridges over the innumerable *nalas* supported them: the loose boards all rattled like mad as the heavy vehicles lumbered over them.

The eleventh milestone from Aut was in English and I read 'Mandi 13 miles'. The dreadful truth struck me: we were going in bang the opposite direction from Kulu. There were no rest-houses on this road, not even so much as a *chai khana*. There was nothing for it but to turn round and ride the eleven miles back, and eleven miles out of your way is quite something on a mule as it adds up to twenty-two by the time you have retraced your steps. B.R. was—not unnaturally—in a very bad temper, which as usual he vented on poor Durgi, but two miles back we found a gurgling spring beside the road and all four of us had a drink which improved relationships all round. While we were refreshing ourselves a lorry stopped—by now all the traffic was going towards Kulu—the young driver got out, had a drink and asked me in passable English if I would like a lift. I gladly accepted, thus leaving Shanti free for B.R. to ride, and I left, telling him to meet me at the Forest Department rest-house at Aut. Half an hour later, for progress is slow even in vehicles propelled by the internal combustion engine on this twisty road with so many bridges, the kind lorry-driver, who refused flatly to take a tip, deposited me at Aut, which was only three miles from Larji where I had spent the previous night. That day we had travelled twenty-five miles to progress three! Still the *devata* procession had made this otherwise frustrating march well worth while.

I approached the rest-house through its well-kept little garden —typical of bungalows run by the Forest Department—and shouted loud and long for the *chaukidar* and banged on the go-down door without success. A few minutes later a young Forest Officer came out of the house and explained that the *chaukidar* was on leave, but that he would open up the spare bedroom for me and, as he had his servant with him, he would be delighted if I would dine with him. I thanked him profusely and accepted with pleasure.

Meanwhile—it was after 2 p.m. and I had not had anything to eat for eight hours—I went along to the bazaar for a cup of tea with which I ate a stale bun-like object without any currants in it, then I returned to the bungalow and had a good sleep till the worst of the heat was over. At 4.30 p.m. B.R. arrived, dripping with sweat, to deliver my baggage and after unpacking, I walked down to the river to see all the pack animals, mules, donkeys and ponies, which were tethered in long lines on a wide stretch of burnt-up grass. Some were being led down to water by their drivers, other were munching hay. There must have been two hundred of them altogether and I reflected that their days are numbered now that the western Himalaya is being so extensively opened up to motor traffic. On the whole, the animals were in good condition and the percentage of sore backs was small, though tell-tale patches of white hair showed that most of the animals had suffered at one time or another.

By now I was absolutely ravenous but there was no sign of the promised dinner until the Forest Officer appeared at 8 p.m. and asked when I would like to eat. I replied as soon as possible, but it was another hour before the meal was ready and I have seldom tucked in more greedily. We had a good lamb curry with rice and *dal* and excellent fresh mint and fresh pomegranate chutney, the latter made from the tiny fruits of the wild variety which grows so freely in the sub-Himalaya. To follow we had a crème caramel—one of the finest legacies of British rule—stewed apricots, and finally large ripe raw apricots from cultivated trees, the fruit being about three times the size of the wild ones.

The Forest Officer told me that the object of the Forest Department was to plant a tree for every one felled. They put barbed wire fencing round the young plantations to protect them from goats but this was extremely difficult on the steep hillsides—I had already noticed they were badly maintained—and a lot of damage was done by stray animals. I picked the young man's brains about local botany but he kept bringing the conversation round to sex by which he appeared to be obsessed. He told me that he was thirty-one and his father had been pressing him to marry for years and had even produced some girls whose parents were willing for a match but he had turned them down as so many of his friends appeared to be unhappily married. Did I think that marriage was essential to happiness? Did women like sex? He was so afraid of getting 'what I think you English call "spliced"' in case his wife didn't like it. How could she know until she had tried? How could either of them know? No, he was sure it was best to remain single.

I asked him what he thought of the goddess Durga and he said 'She is a very powerful goddess.'

'Well,' I said, 'she is married under her various forms to Lord Shiva under his various forms so I suppose you too as a good Hindu should follow the example of your gods and get married.'

'That is a point,' said the Forest Officer.

'One of the things which first attracted me to Hinduism was your doctrine of the *ashramas*, we have no single word for it in English, we say the four stages of life.'

'I have a great-uncle who is a *sannyasin*.'

'That is very good, but you are not old enough yet to follow his example. Don't you think you ought to embark on the second stage and become a *grihastha* (householder) and get married and bring up a lovely family of children?'

'That is just what I fear doing.'

'President Radhakrishnan made a very wise remark: "He who runs back from marriage is in the same boat with one who runs away from battle." I memorised it when I read *The Hindu View of Life* over thirty years ago. He says a lot of inspiring things about the married state. I strongly advise you to read the book, then perhaps you will think differently.'

Having delivered this moral lecture to the young man I thanked him very much for the excellent dinner and went to bed. After the longest and hottest march of my trek I was exhausted but was not destined to have a restful night. I tossed about for a couple of muggy hours then heard a jeep drive up to the bungalow and a minute later two men walked into my room. They were very embarrassed when they found it was occupied and quickly retreated on to the veranda. At last I dozed off only to wake again with the feeling that there was somebody in the room. It was still pitch dark but I knew instinctively that it was my host of the evening:

Forest Officer: 'I must sleep with you, I must!'

ME. 'Don't be so absurd, I am old enough to be your mother!'

F.O. 'Please, I *must* sleep with you.'

ME. 'Go away at once and don't make yourself ridiculous.'

F.O. 'But I have great desire! You *must* let me sleep with you.'

ME. 'Sorry, but I have no desire. You had better do as your father tells you and get married as soon as possible.'

F.O. 'Just this one night let me sleep with you!'

ME. 'If you don't go back to your room at once I will scream at the top of my voice and your servant will hear me.'

F.O. 'No, No! You mustn't scream. Please do not scream, please!'

ME. 'Go back to your room then.'

He tip-toed out and I got up and barricaded the door (there was no key) behind him as best I could with two chairs and the old wooden dressing table.

It was an unpleasant experience at the time, but on reflection I was flattered. It was, however, too complicated to explain to the poor young man that being called Penelope I simply had to live up to my name and remain faithful to my dear old Ulysses, John Betjeman.

CHAPTER V

We Reach the Kulu Valley

After such a disturbed night I was glad to be on the road again and the early morning air freshened me. We made no mistake about the direction this time and went northwards up the gorge where the steep bare hills hemmed us in oppressively and it was a great relief when the dark defile at last widened out and gave way to a gently undulating plain of fertile farm land framed in mountains. We passed a tract of marshy land lying between the road and the river with recently dug deep ditches criss-crossing over it, and there was a notice to tell us that the work was being carried out by the Indo-German Agricultural Project.

Though technically still in Mandi territory we had now at last reached the Kulu valley which runs some fifty miles northwards to the base of the Rohtang Pass into Indian Tibet. It is less famous in the outside world than the vale of Kashmir, but was so passionately loved by former British administrators that some of them turned down promotion in order to stay in it, and likewise by discriminating European settlers who, for some sixty odd years, formed a distinct community. In exactly three hours we had covered the nine miles from Aut to Bajaura, for true to form, on even ground, my little mules kept up their three miles an hour like clockwork.

In the old days Bajaura was a fortified border town lying on the Mandi–Kulu boundary line, and was additionally important before the opening of the Mandi–Larji gorge road to motor traffic in 1926 because the principal trade route from the plains entered the valley here after crossing the 6,760 feet Dulchi Pass, the lowest of the passes leading into Kulu and the only one which is not snowbound in winter.

It was by this route that the first Englishmen, William Moorcroft and George Trebeck, set foot in the Kulu valley at the beginning of August 1820. And it was here that they were held up for two days for lack of porters, as all business was suspended owing to the recent death and cremation of the Rani. 'We were told', Trebeck wrote, 'that eleven of her female attendants had burnt themselves with her corpse and no reason was assigned for this but that they did not wish to survive their protectress.'

Moorcroft was a native of Lancashire and qualified for the profession of surgeon in Liverpool. Upon completing his studies he was sent to investigate a local epidemic of cattle plague. (Could it have been foot-and-mouth?) This resulted in his decision to become a vet, but as there were no veterinary colleges in England at that time, he went to study in France. On his return to England he settled in London and ran a very lucrative business in partnership with a Mr. Field which continued for some years until he lost a lot of money in a project for the manufacture of cast iron horseshoes. He was, therefore, pleased to accept an offer from the Directors of the East India Company to go out to Bengal as superintendent of their military stud and accordingly sailed to India in the year 1808. He did much good work in improving the health of the horses, notably by introducing the cultivation of oats into the country. Convinced that outside blood was needed to increase the stamina of the Indian cavalry horse he suggested the importation of either English thoroughbred stallions or of Turkoman sires from central Asia. The authorities at first favoured his return to England to select suitable animals, but at the eleventh hour they changed their minds so that Moorcroft turned his attention to the trans-Himalayan countries, especially the neighbourhood of Balkh and Bokhara, famous for the strength and endurance of its horses. Accordingly he planned an expedition to Turkestan, primarily to buy good stallions for the Bengal cavalry and secondarily to try to establish trade relations which he thought would be useful to Great Britain. Russia was already importing British and continental fabrics into central Asia—an early move in the Great Game*—and Moorcroft planned to secure a part, if not the whole, of this commerce. Curiously enough the East India Company gave him only reluctant permission to go and then only on condition that he went at his own risk and expense. But he

---

* The best account of the 'Great Game' as played between England and Russia throughout the nineteenth century is to be found in *A Person From England* by Fitzroy Maclean (London, 1958).

was so fired with enthusiasm that nothing deterred him. He was accompanied by George Trebeck, a young man who went in the capacity of draughtsman and surveyor; Mr. Guthrie, a Eurasian doctor, and Mir Izzet Ullah who was already familiar with the proposed route and who acted as interpreter. In addition to these companions Moorcroft had a large caravan carrying about £3,000 worth of goods entrusted to him by two mercantile firms of Calcutta.

After setbacks, the expedition got to Bajaura in August 1820 and proceeded up the Kulu valley, over the Rohtang Pass and into Lahul. By the end of September Moorcroft reached Leh, the capital of Ladakh, where he was forced for various reasons to remain for two years. The expedition did not reach Bokhara until 1825, where Moorcroft and his companions stayed for five months, trading, and then decided to return to India. After crossing the Oxus on their way back Moorcroft, accompanied only by a few servants, made a detour to Maimana. 'Before I quit Turkestan,' runs one of his letters from Bokhara, 'I mean to penetrate into that tract which contains probably the best horses in Asia, but with which all intercourse has been suspended during the last five years. The experiment is full of hazard but *le jeu vaut bien la chandelle.*'

As it turned out the game cost him his life, for at a town called Andhko (now in north-west Afghanistan), where he spent a few days examining and buying stallions, he caught a fever and died. His servants carried his body to Balkh where he was buried. How I should like to make a pilgrimage to the tomb of this passionate horse-lover and intrepid traveller!

Meanwhile, Mr. Guthrie, the doctor, also died and was buried beside Moorcroft; and only a few days later poor young George Trebeck died in a village called Mazar where he lies buried under a mulberry tree.

Although William Moorcroft failed in the two principal objects of his mission—to bring Turkoman stallions back to Bengal and to establish British trade relations in central Asia—nevertheless he contributed greatly to the annals of geographical research in that he and Trebeck were the first Europeans to reach central Asia via Kangra, Kulu and Lahul and their journals are full of information about the hitherto unknown sources of the Béas, the Chenab and other rivers, and of great lakes which they were the first Englishmen to describe.

The account of this adventurous but ill-fated journey was compiled some fifteen years later from letters and journals written by Moorcroft and Trebeck which eventually found their way to John Murray's publishing house in Albemarle Street.

I had planned to spend a couple of hours at Bajaura looking at the famous temple, so I first rode up to the clean and well-appointed rest-house and had a refreshing wash in cold water, followed by two cups of tea. Then I walked to the temple of Basheshar Mahadev (Sanskrit Vishvesvara Mahadeva) which stands about 200 yards from the village in a fertile plain between the main road and the river, and the earliest description of which is found in Moorcroft's *Travels*.[*]

In the sub-Himalayan provinces such as Mandi and Suket, stone temples in the style of the northern Indian plains are common, but in the inner hills they are nearly all of wood or alternate courses of wood and stone. In the Kulu valley itself there are under twenty recorded temples built exclusively of stone, and these date mostly from the seventeenth century when the Rajas tried to popularise the gentle worship of Vishnu, demanding no animal sacrifice, in place of the autochtonous bloody cult of the Mother Goddess and the local *devatas*.[†]

The temple of the great God Shiva as Lord of the Universe, Basheshar Mahadev, is the largest stone monument in Kulu. It has been described in detail by the famous archaeologist Dr. Vogel[‡] but in the absence of ancient inscriptions he will not commit himself to any date, simply stating the 'The excellent workmanship of the large bas-reliefs and, in fact, all the sculptural decoration on the Bajoura temple, points to an early date'. A more recent writer on Indian art, however, Mademoiselle Odette Viennot of the Musée Guimet, writes '*Les Divinités fluviales du temple à Bajaura qui tiennent le vase et le lotus et dont les animaux véhicules accusent une grande stylisation pourraient se placer un peu plus tard.*'[§]

[*] P. 169.
[†] For a fuller description of Kulu temple architecture see Chapter XII.
[‡] J. Ph. Vogel; *Archaeological Survey of India Report*, 1909–10, pp. 18–24.
[§] Odette Viennot, *Les Divinités Fluviales Ganga et Yamuna Aux Portes des Sanctuaires de l'Inde,* Presses Universitaires de France, 1964, p. 147.

Later, that is, than the sun temple at Martand in Kashmir. As this was erected in the early eighth century during the reign of King Lalitaditya, Mlle. Viennot presumably surmises that the temple at Bajaura dates from the late eighth or early ninth century. The Indian art historian Mandanjeet Singh thinks the panels were probably carved by Pala sculptors in the eleventh century when many people took refuge in the hills after the conquest of Kanauj by Mahmud of Ghazni in 1018.* Yet another learned opinion, that of Dr. Goetz,† is that these sculptures are probably eleventh-century copies of seventh-century originals. So we are all at liberty to go on guessing.‡

The temple consists of a squat bulging tower (an unusually fat *shikhara*) the outer surface of which is covered with carvings or architectural motives above and decorative motives below, the familiar pot and foliage pattern being frequently repeated. There is no pillared hall (*mandapa*) attached to this or to any other of the ancient temples of Kulu, whereas their counterparts in Mandi mostly have them. The *garbha griha* (sanctuary) is entered directly by an open doorway on the east side of the tower and contains the *linga* of the great god set in the *yoni* of his female power (*shakti*), Devi, the goddess of a hundred names, the daughter of Himalaya. The inside of the wide door jambs are decorated with carvings of flowing flowers and foliage which frame female figures of Ganga and Jamuna—personifying the Ganges and the Jumna rivers—the customary guardians of northern Indian shrines.

On the remaining three sides of the temple there are niches containing magnificent carvings of gods in high relief, to the west a standing figure of Vishnu; to the south the most beautiful Ganesh I have ever seen anywhere (which I photographed at great personal risk, there being a colony of wild bees living in his stone stomach); and to the north, facing the eternal snows of Lahul, Devi Durga engaged in her victorious battle over the powers of Darkness. There is something noble about this figure of Good triumphing over Evil so that when contemplating it, I feel none of my usual difficulties about that extraordinary Hindu

* Mandanjeet Singh, *Himalayan Art*, Unesco, 1968, p. 136.

† Hermann Goetz, *The Early Wooden Temples of Chamba*. Memoirs of the Kern Institute No. 1, p. 64.

‡ Since writing this I have learnt from Dr. Krishna Deva of the A.S.I. that the temple can definitely be assigned to the ninth century.

phenomenon, the worship of the Terrible—difficulties which I know I share with most Christians—whereas most Hindus seem to take it in their stride. Here at Bajaura, Durga wears the triple-pointed crown edged with beading, characteristic of hill deities, and a large aureole, symbol of her sanctity, surrounds her head. With her eight arms she wields a variety of weapons, and yet she remains majestically aloof from the acts of destruction she is performing. To make my meaning clear I cannot do better than quote the late Professor Heinrich Zimmer's description of a Durga Mahishamardini at Ellora which applies equally well to the goddess of Bajaura: 'She is not in haste, for she is beyond Time. The fierce struggle is for her like some ritual act to be completed solemnly. . . . There is a majestic mocking leisureliness in her procedure. She makes herself manifest to the eyes of her devotees in an attitude of almost complete repose, expressing, as it were, her timeless superiority to the demonic self-centred forces that for a brief spell of some millenniums have been disturbing the harmony of the cosmic order.'*

Soon after 11 a.m. we continued along the hot and dusty road to Kulu, which is the modern name for the capital of the valley, though it used to be known as Sultanpur. Overcrowded buses roared by us at intervals which did not exactly add to the pleasure of the ride. Occasionally a grand car would sweep by and the smartly-dressed Indians it contained would look round in aston-ishment at the sight of an English Memsahib riding a mule and holding up a large black umbrella. Though I realised very forcibly that I was a complete anachronism in this sophisticated holiday resort, I had eyes only for the snows of the Solang ridge at the far end of the valley, which filled me with memories. This was the particular snowline which had stayed so vividly in my mind ever since my girlhood, calling me to return, and now at last here I was, thirty-three years later, obeying that persistent call. Then exas-peratingly, the great ridge of snows would do a disappearing act, blotted out by the bulk of a nearby hill, and often remained invisible for several miles at a stretch.

There were giant aloes growing along each side of the road and we passed several Forestry Department plots of young willows,

* H. Zimmer, *The Art of Indian Asia*, N.Y., 1955, p. 92.

bauhinias and poplars with their barbed-wire fences broken down in several places so that they afforded little protection against the thousands and thousands of sheep and goats which pass up and down this road every summer and autumn to and from the upland pastures in the charge of their nomadic shepherds from Chamba, known as *gaddis*.

We ambled through the big village of Bhuntar, the kicking-off place for the Parbatti valley, which I was soon to explore, and passed the neat little estate of the Bhutti hand-weaving project where each small house is roofed with pleasant stone tiles. Just outside Kulu town, we passed a *harijan* (untouchable) settlement of wooden houses on the left of the main road and a large military camp a little further on to the right. This was on a part of the wide *maidan* known as Dhalpur, round which all the modern government buildings, the hospital and the private and official bungalows stand. I rode straight uphill to the Forest Colony, but the rest-house seemed ominously full with tents in the compound taking the overspill, and I was directed by the *chaukidar* to the head office of the Forestry Department, where to my dismay I learnt that Mr. Romesh Chandra, whom I thought would be able to help me get accommodation, was in Chandigarh on business and not expected back for four days. I was advised to go to the Tourist Office. There I learnt that there was not a room to be had in any brand of rest-house or guest-house in the valley until the end of June—and it was now only the 6th. I felt like bursting into tears when I remembered what plain-sailing Himalayan travel was thirty years ago with tourists few and far between, and all our arrangements made by our efficient A.D.C. Geoffrey Kellie; when I set out I never realised that such things as accommodation problems existed. In the interval this valley of my dreams had turned into one of the major tourist centres in the hills, and the hotel-building programme had not begun to catch up with the flocks of Indians and of diplomats from the Delhi Embassies who come up here in ever greater numbers in search of relaxation and sport in each hot weather season. In fact, there are still no hotels at all, only a few privately-owned guest-houses up in Manali and some aluminium tourist huts to supplement the existing dak bungalows of various grades.* The tricky situation in

* Since writing this, hotels have opened in both Kulu and Manali.

Kashmir is largely to blame for this great influx into Kulu, but now that the valley has been 'discovered' in a big way, I feel it will hold its own as a tourist resort against the more famous vale, even if the seemingly insoluble problems of Kashmir are ever solved.

Instead of bursting into tears, however, I asked the tourist officer if I could use his telephone, for I suddenly remembered that Veena Mehra, a student at St. Bede's College in Simla, was coming to Kulu for her half-term holiday and had invited me to call. Within a quarter of an hour this slim, pretty girl and her cousin, another student at St. Bede's, had come to fetch me in a large and ancient bright blue Chevrolet with an even more ancient well-whiskered driver. We drove back up to the Forest Colony to get my baggage and I told B.R. he could have the next day off and paid him ten rupees for two days' board and lodging for himself and the mules. We then drove down to Mehra Lodge, at the southern end of the *maidan*, a large modern bungalow with a corrugated iron roof painted bright green instead of the usual red. The girls lived here on the Hindu joint family system, their fathers being brothers, in addition to which they were partners in a timber firm which floated logs down the Béas to the Punjab plains where they were sold.

My bedroom had a private washroom with a lovely cold shower and a basin; I spent the afternoon revelling in this luxury, washing my clothes and my hair. A servant brought in a tray of tea and biscuits at 4.30 p.m. after which I went next door and called on the Sikh Assistant Commissioner and his wife, Captain and Mrs. Gushardan Singh, whose daughter was another student of St. Bede's Teacher Training College. They most kindly invited me to dinner so I returned to Mehra Lodge and changed into a brown and yellow uncrushable dress which I had brought along for tidy occasions. I had also saved what little remained of my powder compact for smart life in Kulu, but my nose was peeling from sunburn so that when I had finished making up I looked like a powdered crocodile.

The Gushardan Singhs lived in a large bungalow between the Mehra's and the Forest Colony, while the A.C.'s office and court-house (he was also the chief magistrate of Kulu) were above the river on the other side of the *maidan*. Besides his attractive daughter, who I knew already, I met his grown-up son, a young man of such overwhelming charm and humour that I should have fallen head over heels in love with him had I been a girl.

Soon after 9 p.m. the other guests arrived, friends of my hosts who were on holiday in Manali: two principals of Indian colleges with their wives, and the manager of the Indian Horlick's factory and his wife. We did not eat till 10 p.m. and as I had had breakfast at 5.15 a.m. and a tin of sardines for lunch at 11 a.m., I was longing for my dinner and enjoyed it more than I can say. It consisted of excellent vegetable soup followed by a variety of egg and vegetable dishes and delicious *puris*, and ended with quantities of sweet Kulu cherries. We did not sit down for the meal but helped ourselves from the dining-room table and stood around eating and talking. In this bungalow I saw the only *monal* pheasants of my tour—stuffed in a glass case. These large, magnificent birds used to be plentiful in the temperate zone of the Western Himalaya but unfortunately they have been shot in such large numbers during the past fifty years that, together with the red-crested *tragopan* pheasant, they are now rare. The two specimens in my host's sitting-room were both cocks with the brilliant purply-green plumage which they only get in their third year, for the young male birds are the same brown colour as the hens.

As soon as we had finished eating we all dispersed, as in the manner of Indian dinner parties in Delhi: you do all your talking before and during the meal after which you go home to bed.

The next morning I spent a pleasant hour or so gossiping with the Gushardan Singhs on their wide veranda, the A.C. wearing a dressing-gown, his long black hair done up in a topknot in the usual Sikh manner when turbanless. His beard was tied up in a blue handkerchief and his moustache in a white one and I was lost in admiration at his being able to talk at all. Beside him sat his father, a distinguished-looking old gentleman with a spreading white beard, and I could not stop thinking what a wonderful Father Christmas he would make at a children's party. We talked of East and West, of the old times and the new, and both the Sikhs deprecated the decline in European morals and said how essential they considered pre-marital chastity for their daughters.

Next I repaired to the tourist office where the poor superintendent was still in despair about the lack of accommodation up and down the valley and the number of visitors in desperate straits.

'Thank God for the Mehra family!' I said.

'Yes, you can indeed consider yourself fortunate: many people I have had to send back to Mandi or Kangra where accommodation is also very limited so that they may have to proceed up to Simla or down to Pathankote.'

'I am sorry that Kulu has been "discovered" in such a big way, but since the fact is inescapable, wouldn't it be a good idea to build some hotels?'

'The government has had a project to do this for some years past: to build tourist hotels in Kulu, Nagar and Manali, but so far these plans have not materialised and we get the same confusion every hot weather.'

He then gave me some excellent advice for my own tour: he suggested riding up the Parbatti valley which I had never seen. Although, the superintendent told me, there were always many pilgrims going to and coming from Manikarn, they did not require rest-house accommodation and as so few tourists went up this valley he could easily give me chits for all the bungalows. If I returned to Kulu on June 19th, then I could have a room in Nagar Castle for two nights as he had just had a cancellation. He also suggested that I should return to Simla via the un-jeepable Bashleo Pass to Rampur Basahr. I took all his advice with excellent results.

That afternoon I went to the bazaar to buy some provisions for my Parbatti trek: a loaf of bread, a tin of ham (what a prize!), two of sardines and one of peach jam. I also bought four eggs for one rupee each which is cheap for these parts, and when I got back to the Mehra's house I asked Veena to get their *khansama* to boil them for me.

'Oh, he wouldn't know how to!'

'But he is such a very good cook and it is so simple to hard-boil a few eggs.'

'This fellow is a stupid *pahari* and does not understand these things.'

'Well, would he mind if I went into the kitchen and boiled them myself?'

'I am afraid my mother wouldn't like it: you see she is a strict vegetarian and for her it is sinful to cook eggs. Do you mind taking them up to the Commissioner's house?'

I did so, inwardly reproving myself for having been so slow in the uptake.

CHAPTER VI

The Parbatti Valley

On this, the twelfth day of my tour, everyone at Mehra Lodge was awake at 5.30 a.m. as the girls were being motored to Mandi from where they would get the express de luxe bus to Simla and so back to St. Bede's College.

Meanwhile B.R. and I and our distinguished little mule train of Durgi and Shanti set off at 7 a.m. to explore the sacred Parbatti valley in which the goddess lost her earrings. We went back along the main road as far as Bhuntar where we crossed the Béas by the Duff Dunbar bridge.

In the early nineties St. John Gore and his party also went by this route and he wrote:

'We paused to admire this marvellous structure, an iron suspension bridge made with wire ropes and rods brought all the way out from England, every bit of which must have been carried on men's or mules' backs one hundred miles at least through the mountains. Surely a magnificent example of the way not to do it, especially when the materials for the excellent native-made *sangha* bridge lie all around on the spot. It is commonly known as Duff's bridge, and the legend runs that a Mr. Duff, for many years Forest Officer in the district, on entering into his family inheritance in Scotland, wished to leave behind him some grateful token of his happy life amongst these people, and started this bridge to enable the yearly pilgrims to cross the troubled waters in peace and safety. Needless to say, the bridge had not made much progress when Mr. Duff's grant was exhausted, and after a long delay the government was forced to take up the work and finish it at a sum fabulously beyond the original estimate.'*

In point of fact the original materials cost this devotee of Kulu, Mr. Duff Dunbar of Caithness, over half a lakh of rupees, but they have since been replaced on at least two occasions: after

* *Indian Hill Life*, p. 60.

the great earthquake of 1905, and the great floods of 1947. It is doubtful whether any of the present-day pilgrims and tourists have heard the name of this devoted Forest Officer, but in the Forest Colony at Kulu his memorial is still known as the Duff Dunbar Bridge. About half a mile above this bridge, where the Béas is at its widest, its largest tributary the Parbatti foams into it from the east after a long and spectacular journey from the snows of Upper Basahr.

The village on the left bank of the Béas, opposite Bhuntar, is known as Bhuin and the rest-house is about a mile above it and very difficult to find. After riding up several wrong tracks we eventually got there a little before 10 a.m. to find the American fishing family from Larji already installed. Mrs.—I never found out her name—invited me to have tea and biscuits with them and her husband held forth about the inability of Indians to maintain anything; they would start a new 'project' with great enthusiasm but repairs and maintenance were just not in their make-up. I protested that there were exceptions, as I had been delighted to find how beautifully the gardens of the President's and the Prime Minister's houses were kept up in Delhi, and the Old Viceregal Lodge gardens in Simla.

I ate two of my sacrilegious hard-boiled eggs with my cup of tea, together with the two bread and butter sandwiches I had prepared at breakfast-time, so that I would not need to bother with lunch on the twelve-mile trek up to Jari, our destination for the night. During the course of the morning I discovered the largest earth closet I have ever seen, in a corner at the far end of the lawn, the closet itself being precariously balanced on two planks laid across a deep pit. Beside the wooden shack which enclosed this contraption there was another deeper and wider pit which one might well fall into if forced to answer a call in the middle of the night.

It was still very hot when we set off in the early afternoon up the narrow gorge through which the Parbatti pours to join the Béas. The road is wide enough to take light motor traffic and hardly had we entered the gorge when a small lorry charged into poor Durgi's quarters which made her leap forward and deposit all my baggage on the ground. Instead of apologising profusely and getting out to help B.R. put everything aboard again, the

driver shouted imprecations at us while I screamed '*Pagal, pagal!
Ullu, ullu!*' (fool, fool! owl, owl!) repeatedly back at him until
he eventually drove off.

At this end of the Parbatti valley the bare brown hills are
forbidding and the scenery would be drab were it not for the
wild pomegranate trees and shrubs which grow all along the
steep river banks. In June they are covered with little waxy
flame-coloured flowers brilliantly set off by prolific glossy dark
green leaves. As we gradually went higher I saw a few indigofera
and berberis shrubs still flowering, but the wild white roses
were over. There were occasional clumps of alder trees down by
the water and, when the hills graciously stepped back and left a
bit of room, there were a few strips of cultivated land bearing
apricot, pear and apple trees.

At one point I got off to photograph a beautiful *sangha* bridge
constructed on the old cantilever principle traditional in the
Western Himalaya and in other countries possessing a similar
climate and an abundance of timber such as Norway. The
method consists of laying successive tiers of whole trunks of
pine or cedar trees slanting upwards, each one projecting a little
beyond the one below it and held firm in great stone embank-
ments on either side of the river. Long planks are laid across the
water from one top tier to the other and sometimes a balustrade
runs along each side. These bridges, being narrow, have for
centuries provided shepherds with an efficient means of counting
their vast flocks.

On the twelve-mile trek from Bhuin to Jari we were passed by
three little lorries—in addition to the one which had run into
poor Durgi—two jeeps and a mini-bus stuffed with passengers.
This road did not exist in St. John Gore's time but the mule track
he used cuts across a steep hill to the village of Chong and if I
ever have the good fortune to go that way again I shall make use
of the old route to avoid the motor traffic.

At a tiny hamlet called Shat we had cups of tea at a shack-
shop where there was a row of elderly *pahari* ladies perched on a
narrow bench like birds on a branch. They were on their return
journey from the sacred springs at Manikarn. Just beyond Shat
a silvery modern metal bridge crossed a foaming ice-blue torrent
which roared on down into the Parbatti below. Precipices of

shrimp-pink rock rose steeply from the road until we rounded a bend where the hills receded and a series of terraces appeared on which grew some of the tallest thistles I have ever seen outside of Wales. A large notice announced 'Intensive Horticulture Programme. Parbatti Valley Camp'. The notice was perhaps a little premature.

As we neared Jari a more sinister notice, planted beside two shining aluminium huts, announced 'Project of Atomic Energy'. It seemed a far cry from the Harwell Atomic Energy Research Establishment near where I live in England and I wondered whether they were in touch with each other.

There is a small two-bedroomed rest-house at Jari to the left of the road as you approach the village. From the rest-house lawn you also get the first full view of the Baranagh range in Spiti looking like a towering Gaudi Cathedral, with its row of brilliant white spires standing out against the deep blue of the sky. The village of Jari certainly sits in a spectacular position. The river thunders through a deep gorge half a mile below and on the opposite bank a black mountain rises precipitously to a total height of 12,000 feet, Jari itself being 5,000 feet above sea level. I knew that behind this mountain lay the curious isolated village of Malana which for years I have longed to visit.

For supper I was given a trout from the Parbatti, but unfortunately the *chaukidar* succeeded in disguising the delicate flavour the fish must once have had by cutting it into thick chunks and rubbing them in curry paste. Later that evening a young man called at the rest-house, obviously to see whether there were any visitors with whom he could gossip. He told me he was the newly-appointed doctor in charge of the local dispensary, the only one in the valley, that this was his first job, that he had only arrived the week before and found it extremely lonely. However, his young brother was coming up next day and would spend a month at Jari on vacation from Agra University. While we were talking another young man suddenly appeared from nowhere, as is the habit of Indians, and I asked about Malana. He told me that it was only a six-mile walk from the village and that you could easily go there and back in a day. Recently an Englishman of sixty had done it and after an early morning start had been back at the rest-house by 4 p.m. The doctor suggested his young brother might go with me but I said it would have to be on my return trek down the valley as I had already planned to explore the upper end and had my rooms booked in the bungalows.

The *chaukidar* informed me that an oil lamp in my room would cost one rupee for the evening. What a rascal! Everywhere else they were half that price: so I made it quite clear that I would use my candles and accordingly stuck three of them on to my inverted pink plastic plate. The next morning a single cup, not a pot, of 'Indian style' tea was produced, very weak with milk and sugar in it and I hate sweet tea. For this he charged 25 *n.p.* nearly twice as much as at the shack-shops. In spite of its beautiful situation, this was the nastiest rest-house I had so far stayed in, with a terrible stink in the wash-room and a most unpleasant on-the-make *chaukidar*.

Just as we were about to set off next morning three young Sikhs appeared who spoke good English and said they had heard I wanted to go to Malana and they were going just the route I longed to try; from Jari to Malana then on to Nagar via the Chanderkhani pass, and would be pleased if I accompanied them. This would, however, have entailed sending B.R. and the mules back the way we had come as the route is too narrow for pack animals. I have seldom felt so torn between two exciting prospects, but were I to cut across to the middle of the Kulu valley now I should reach Nagar long before my bookings at the Castle rest-house; moreover, I might never have another chance of seeing the upper Parbatti valley, whereas I might be able to arrange to go to Malana with the doctor's brother on my way down. So I declined their very kind offer—perhaps fortunately for them, as I would certainly have retarded their progress up the precipitous mountain paths.

The march of seven and a half miles to Manikarn, rising only 400 feet, was very easy and beyond Jari the road goes downhill to the river past several Forest Department enclosures. We crossed a bridge over a torrent—one of the innumerable tributaries of the Parbatti—thundering down the great wooded ravine of the Kashol *nala* from the south. Just as we got to the other side, a young man caught us up and announced that he was the doctor's younger brother and would like to accompany me to

Malana on my return down the valley; meanwhile he would walk up to Manikarn with us as he had not yet been there. Our conversation was spasmodic as he spoke English with difficulty, yet he said he was studying statistics through it. Fancy if I had to study a subject through the Hindi medium! I really do sympathise with these Indian students who speak no English at home but are compelled to use it for their university studies.

We passed the village rest-house which is even more marvellously situated than the one at Jari, for it overlooks a large grassy glade with groups of cedars here and there and patches of iris and huge smooth boulders along the nearby rushing grey-green river. The snows at the head of the valley had hidden themselves on our trek down, but now they reappeared in full force, with the needle-like spires of Baranagh scintillating in the sun.

Jari is the mini-bus terminal but the road is jeepable as far as Kashol and soon will be right up to Manikarn, two miles further on.* To me the opening up of these once remote valleys in the name of Progress seems tragic: but perhaps I would think differently if I lived here. Anyway it was with a feeling of infinite relief that we crossed the border-line into unjeepable territory and I knew that for the next few days at least we should be out of the orbit of the internal combustion engine.

After passing through a tiny hamlet called Goje we crossed to the right bank of the river by a *sangha* bridge which will, sadly, all too soon be replaced by a modern metal one when the beastly buses get up here. The Parbatti here became torrential, being forced in a series of falls through a gorge of gigantic boulders two of which almost touched across the foaming waters. In St. John Gore's *Indian Hill Life* there is a spectacular photograph of a delicate little *sangha* bridge at this very point; but it had disappeared by the time Forbes published his guidebook in 1911, for he refers only to 'traces of an old bridge' on these boulders.

Approaching Manikarn we saw clouds of steam rising from the boiling springs there and the village itself appeared as through a transparent white curtain. At the bottom end, through

---

* Several buses (full-sized) a day now run regularly from Bhuin to Manikarn and during 'the season' a luxury bus takes tourists direct from Kulu town to Manikarn.

which we entered, there is an ugly modern temple built only a few years ago, enclosing in its courtyard the most sacred spring of all. But I rode on past it to the middle of the village where, opposite a tiny *maidan*, stood the little two-roomed rest-house close to the river bank. One room was already occupied but my magic reservation chit, when handed to the *chaukidar*, procured me the other. As I was standing on the veranda feeling rather claustrophobic because of the narrow sunless situation of Mani-karn closed in by steep rock hills concealing Baranagh, to my surprise a tall fair young Englishman walked across the rest-house lawn followed by a string of Indian boys. He held out his hand to me saying, 'I'm Ken Smith,' and proceeded to tell me that he was a graduate of Brasenose College, Oxford, now doing two years with Voluntary Service Overseas in one of the thirteen 'Sainik' military schools where he taught maths and physics. He went on to explain that he was in the process of giving ten Sikh and Hindu boys, aged from thirteen to seventeen, a toughening-up course in this area before their graduating to more serious mountain climbing in Lahul. They had started their present trek at Nagar, spent the first night in a shepherd's hut on the beautiful Chanderkhani downs just below the 12,000 feet pass, had been lost in the snows on the other side for two days and were just coming to the end of their rations when they struck the steep and narrow path leading down to Malana. Here they lodged with a gentleman called Panch Saghat Ram, the only man in this mystery village who will allow strangers into his house, and who gave them a good supply of *chapatties* to eat and a floor to sleep on. By this time they were pretty tired and looking forward to a good rest with a roof over their heads, but in the middle of the night their host's house caught fire so they had to form a chain of buckets from the nearest well and put it out. Yesterday they had crossed the Rashol Pass and entered the Parbatti valley just below Manikarn and had slept long and soundly in rows on the rest-house bedroom floor. Travelling in this way works out nice and cheap as a bedroom costs the same whether one or ten people choose to sleep in it.

I was filled with the deepest admiration for my countryman Ken Smith: St. John Gore calculated in the nineties that it was impossible for an Englishman to trek in the Himalaya without a

minimum of ten coolies. In the thirties I think we made do with
three or four apiece, and now in the sixties I was down to one.
Yet here was Ken, coolieless in Kulu, carrying his own pack on
his back, tackling these really tough passes without map or
guide or gun. His previous climbing experience had been confined to the Welsh mountains, an excellent school, but not
inhabited by bears and leopards, and I thought it extremely
courageous of him to undertake the responsibility of leading such
young boys through the Western Himalaya, in which neither he
nor they had ever set foot before. However, neither Ken nor the
boys thought their exploits at all out of the ordinary. They said
they had been dog tired for the first three days of their trek
after which they started to get fit and were greatly looking forward to yet tougher climbs in Lahul.

Ken announced that they were going down to the temple for
a free lunch and suggested that I went with them, and together
we walked back to the lower end of the village to the ugly
modern temple I had ridden past earlier that morning. On
arrival we descended a steep flight of steps, took off our shoes,
and entered the little courtyard where the heat of the paving
stones was such that we literally had to dance about until the
soles of our feet became used to it. There was a fairly large
concrete tank in the courtyard with a bridge over the middle,
the water being supplied by both hot and cold springs for the
convenience of pilgrims. Ken said he had spent an hour in it
earlier on and that the water was pleasantly warm, and now there
were six children happily splashing about, including two small
Sikh boys with topknots on their heads.

On the opposite side of the courtyard were several open-
fronted cells, one containing a *linga* for devotees of Shiva and
another larger one acting as a *sadhu* shelter with three occupants
sitting cross-legged on the floor, their long matted hair piled
in coils on top of their heads. In front, at the foot of the modern
temple tower, was the sacred boiling spring itself, the goal of
the many thousands of pilgrims who have trekked up this once
remote valley every summer for hundreds, perhaps thousands, of
years. Will they gain the same merit when they can come all the
way by bus?

The reason for the great sanctity of the Manikarn springs is because when the goddess Parbatti was one day bathing with her husband, Mahadeo (the great god Shiva), she left her earrings—*manikarna*—on the bank and when she emerged from the water she found they had been stolen. Shiva was very angry and commanded the lesser gods to search for them. They were eventually traced to Patala, the mysterious underground Kingdom of Sesha, the serpent. When questioned about them, however, Sesha snorted with rage and the earrings, which he had hidden in his nostrils, flew out and returned to the goddess. Ever since this event boiling water has bubbled up from Patala through the little tunnels which the earrings made in their passage from the bowels of the earth.

There are, in fact, far more than two hot springs in Manikarn, but this one, now enclosed within the temple courtyard beside the river bank, is the principal object of devotion. St. John Gore took a photograph of it some fifty years before the present temple was put up which shows it surrounded on three sides by a low stone wall. He describes how his Brahmin bearer Ram Jas 'sat by the side of the bubbling water in the centre of an admiring crowd. His raiment consisted of his black elf-locks hanging down his bare back and a small pocket-handkerchief where most needed. In his hands he held a book—upside down for he could not read—in which he was so absorbed that the bystanders no doubt imagined him half-way to heaven.'*

One of the highlights of a pilgrimage to Manikarn is to eat food which has been cooked in the sacred spring. The four-foot, square, shallow tank which encloses it, forms a perfect *bain-marie* with perpetually boiling water into which brass and earthenware pots are lowered, each with a stone on top to stop them floating. These contain rice, D.D.D. and other vegetables which are offered free to anyone of any nationality or creed who asks for them.

When we first entered the temple courtyard we met two young American nurses from a down-country mission hospital, but they refused to stay to lunch for fear of the diseases they might catch. In point of fact I have never had a meal more hygienically presented. We sat in a row, Ken and I and the ten Indian boys, on the parapet round the tank and were each given a spotless brass tray bearing a large plate of rice, a little shiny brass bowl

* Op. cit., p. 68.

of D.D.D., two of different vegetables and several *chapatties*. Unfortunately there were too many chillies in all the dishes for my taste and I could not shout my usual war cry of '*Mat mirch!*' (No chillies) when enjoying religious hospitality, so I had to have the roof lifted off my mouth and let tears stream down my cheeks. You can stay a night and get free meals at any Sikh *gurdhwara* in India and many European bummers take unfair advantage of this and outstay their welcome.

At Manikarn our trays were handed to us by the chief priest, a magnificent-looking Sikh with a radiant smile, flowing black beard, brilliant blue robes and deep blue *pagari* showing he was a *nihag*—a soldier of the guru—the sect who wear this *pagari*. I found it confusing to find Sikhs in charge of what I had always understood to be a Hindu place of pilgrimage: but it is simply another of those bewildering paradoxes of India to which everyone to whom you appeal for an explanation ('Why a *linga* when Sikhs denounce idolatry?') will give you a different answer.

Soon after luncheon Ken and the boys set off down the valley to Jari. I was depressed to see them go and consoled myself with a cup of sickly syrupy tea at a shack-shop and a few custard cream biscuits out of a packet I had bought. Then I returned to the rest-house to fetch my bath towel and a shirt as I was determined to bathe in the ladies' tank at the lower end of the temple courtyard. Slipping off my kingcup print dress I stepped down into the tank and bathed in my shirt and beige Celanese bloomers. The water was very hot and took some getting used to but I stayed in for half an hour, swimming five strokes up and five strokes down the triangular-shaped concrete tank, of which I was the only occupant. The water definitely does not smell of sulphur as some travellers maintain, but is said to be radio-active and very good for rheumatic diseases. As I am fortunate enough not to suffer from these I could not test the water's healing properties. Drying presented quite a problem as people were passing up and down the path above the tank, which overlooked the boundary wall, and I tried to dress as delicately as possible, tearing my dress in the process.

Leaving the temple precincts I went off to explore the village. I decided that the little *maidan* opposite the rest-house must have been the terrain on which St. John Gore watched the game of cricket that so delighted him: 'A few square yards of level ground had been squeezed in between two chalets, and there the game proceeded with much vigour, one of the fielders spending most of his time on the shingle roofs that always afforded a safe run from a well-placed hit. The game had, no doubt, been taught by some A.C. to the school-master, and he in coming up here to this out-of-the-way village, had brought it with him to the great delight of the boys.'* There is no sign of cricket there today, but national necessity has put the ground to more serious use, for it is where the local young men are drilled by the police to provide a defence force against a possible Chinese invasion.

To the right of the 'cricket pitch' there were several temples, none of which appeared to be of great antiquity or interest as they lacked carvings in either the classical or the folk style. This may be due to the fact that a great fire ravaged the village some years ago. The doors of one such building were open so I looked in and decided that it must be a temple treasury as it contained the *devata* masks, two undecorated *raths* (palanquins) used to carry the gods about in, and stacks of musical instruments for the use of the temple band which invariably accompanies the *devata* on an outing. I subsequently learnt that the priests of Manikarn own an ancient Sanskrit manuscript called the *Kulanthapitha Mahatmya*, believed to be a part of the *Brahamanda Purana*. It describes the geography of Kulu and the adventures of the classical, as opposed to the folk, gods. The widest part of the Kulu valley in the neighbourhood of Nagar is still sometimes called Kulanthapitha, which can be translated as 'The End of the Habitable World' or 'The End of Society.'

In the middle of the village I found the pack animal lines, mostly tenanted by mules and ponies, with an odd donkey or two, and was pleased to reflect that they provided the only means of transport in this unjeepable area. But such transport is expensive in these barren places, for hay is scarce, grazing nil and barley at a premium, so that B.R. had already asked me to increase his daily ration of five rupees to six.

Undoubtedly the most fascinating thing about Manikarn is the number of hot springs to be seen bubbling up all over the village. These provide a free round-the-clock service of boiling water to

* Op. cit., p. 81.

several of the larger private houses and they are also channelled into three or four public stone troughs for the convenience of washing clothes. In addition I found a large covered bathing pool for use in wet weather, those in the temple courtyard being exposed to the elements. This must be one of the very few small villages in India which is amply supplied with hot public, private, and sacred baths.

I returned to the rest-house for supper and before retiring to bed had a nice hot tub in water that the *chaukidar* carried in jugs from the nearest hot spring. The tiny wash-room was lit by my faithful three candles stuck on to the pink plastic plate and it was fascinating to reflect that I was washing in water which came direct from the underground kingdom of Sesha the serpent.

CHAPTER VII

Waziri Rupi—The Upper Parbatti Valley

The track to Pulga, our farthest port of call in the valley, was said to be very rough. As I wanted to get the worst of it over before the sun grew really hot, I had planned to start at 5.30 a.m. The *chaukidar*, however, did not appear until 5.20 so I decided to cut breakfast and eat something on arrival at the next rest-house only nine and a half miles away. But for the first time on the trek B.R. let me down and failed to appear on time. I had all my bags ready on the tiny veranda and when I walked along to the pack animal lines I found them empty except for my two mules with B.R. only just starting to tack up. He said he thought we were going to start at 6 a.m., though I knew I had repeated orders to start early, '*Sari panch baji*,' several times on the previous evening. The steam of the sacred springs must have gone to his head and confused his normally clear brain, as punctuality was one of his outstanding virtues.

I indicated that I would walk on ahead and that he was to pick up my baggage at the bungalow and follow on. As I passed the 'cricket pitch' I stopped for a minute to watch the local lads being drilled by two policemen and sincerely hoped they would never have to confront the Chinese pouring over the Pin-Parbatti Pass from Spiti. Then I went on, leaving the group of temples on my left, and soon reached the steep rock path which zigzags up the hill at the top of the village with steps cut here and there. There was a sharp drop to the river below so that I was pleased to be walking rather than riding. Then the path crossed a ridge from which there was a marvellous view of the Upper Parbatti valley: on either side of the river there were hamlets perched above vast golden staircases of terraced barley; and higher still, pine forests stretching up to the snow-line; and at the head of the valley the by now familiar outline of Baranagh, all the more glorious for having been hidden from view for the past twenty-four hours.

B.R. always caught me up within half an hour of starting on these mornings when I walked on ahead, thus proving that on hilly paths I walked at under three miles an hour. When we reached level ground I rode for a bit and we crossed a bridge over a *nala* littered with little water mills, after which the path again consisted of steps cut in the rock, so I dismounted and decided to walk the remaining seven miles to Pulga, bearing in mind how important it was to get into training for Malana.

During the morning we had to thread our way through a flock of sheep and goats at least a thousand strong tended by local shepherds, not *gaddis*, who are distinguished by the yards and yards of brown rope which they wind round their stomachs. Then we caught up with the train of mules and ponies I had seen in the lines at Manikarn, all the animals wearing string muzzles to deter them from slowing down the train by wayside grazing.

But as usual I found that I could not comfortably keep up for long with B.R. so I lagged behind and enjoyed the flowers. I was now above the level of the pomegranates and back with the indigofera and berberis in bloom, and the great waterfalls of wild white roses billowing down the *khud*. Then I smelt the strong scent of jasmin, and looking up I saw it growing in a crack of the precipice above my head. From now on there was a lot of it and the mixture of rose and jasmin and pine smells was a delight throughout the walk. Soon I passed through the hamlet of Ucheih, once famous for its silver mines, hidden in the hills on the opposite bank of the river—all now closed. This upper end of the Parbatti valley has always been known as Waziri Rupi, the Silver Province, and the present descendant of the Kulu kings is known as the Rai of Rupi because the only land he still owns lies in this area. The mines originally belonged to his ancestors but were abandoned during the reign of the last ruling Raja, Ajit Singh (1816–41). He is said to have sent one day for the keepers of his state archives, Hukmu and Gehru, and for some unexplained reason to have flown into a rage and had them beheaded there and then. But due to a curious premonition the two court officials had warned their wives that if any misfortune befell them the state papers were immediately to be burnt. And so it came about that the treatise was destroyed which described the methods of extracting silver from ore. Subsequent efforts by the British to work the mines in the 1870's proved a failure because of the heavy costs of refining and transport.

I finally crossed to the left bank of the river and began to climb up the beautiful forest path, shaded by horse-chestnuts giving way higher up to deodars, so that I knew we must be in the region of 7,000 feet, for you can roughly estimate the height in the Himalaya by the trees. The blue pine *kyle* (*pinus excelsa*) flourishes between 5,000 feet and 8,000 feet; the deodar (*cedrus deodara*) between 6,000 feet and 8,000 feet, as does the white oak (*quercus incana*) which is associated with it; the spruce fir (*picea Morinda*) and the green holly oak, *moru* (*quercus dilatata*), grow between 7,000 feet and 10,000 feet; and the silver fir (*Abies Pindrow*) and the brown oak, *Kharsu* (*quercus semicarpifolia*), between 8,500 feet and 12,000 feet.

Then the path led down and across some terraced clearings on which patches of fine wheat were ripening and mixed crops of potatoes and French beans. A notice informed me that these were experimental plots belonging to the Agricultural Department.

I found the rest-house at the entrance to the village in a grassy glade nearly a thousand feet above the river. It was surrounded on three sides by deodars and on the fourth by a little cornfield. Durgi and Shanti were having a good roll when I arrived, after which they got up, shook themselves, and started to make up for lost time by grazing the surprisingly green grass, having been restricted to hay and barley at our last two barren halting places. I, too, was delighted with the place—but from an aesthetic rather than a gastronomic point of view—for it was the first rest-house I have yet come across built in the *pahari* style of architecture adapted to western use. It had chimneys and fireplaces which the villagers' houses do not, and there were no cattle in the lower storey: in fact, there was only one storey because it was a bunga-low, but the walls consisted of alternate courses of dry stone and wooden beams and the roofing was of deodar planks. How beautiful Simla and other former British hill stations could have been if only we had had the sense to imitate the local styles of the Indian, instead of the Surrey, hills.

The *chaukidar* was young and clean-shaven and of a pre-possessing appearance and put himself out to be agreeable. I made him understand that I had my own lunch but would like two hard-boiled eggs with rice and D.D.D. for supper. He told me that eggs cost half a rupee apiece here in Pulga and being completely at his mercy I gave him three rupees with which to set in a little store of half a dozen. I opened a tin of sardines, for what was 'brunch', as I had gone without breakfast, and ate them with slices of wood—my by now four-day-old loaf from Kulu.

In the afternoon I explored the village which is so dramatically situated below the 1,800 feet Papidarm peaks. The houses were ramshackle in the extreme, some made entirely of timber, others with alternate courses of stone and timber, and some were covered with a coating of mud plaster, having patterns of red and yellow dots painted round the ground floor doors leading into the cattle byres. The roofs were covered with rough uneven cedar or pinewood planks lying higgledy-piggledy down the rafters—one could hardly call them shingles—evidently the custom of cutting large slices off the local precipice for roofing is not the practice up here, possibly because timber is so plentiful and lighter to handle.

In the middle of the village there was a tall tower-like building in what is almost certainly the most ancient style of Himalayan architecture: the alternate courses of dry stone wall and deodar beams with a carved wooden balcony running round the four sides of the upper storey, just below the overhanging eaves of the roof. I peeped through the keyhole and decided it must be the *bhandar* (temple treasury) for I could see the masks of the village *devata*, his furled-up banners, and the fantastic instruments of his private band stacked against the walls.

Not far away I came to a wooden chalet-type temple where twelve men of the Punjab police force were living. The gods certainly seem very obliging in these parts and often allow travellers to share their quarters. But these Punjabis were no mere travellers: they invited me in and told me that they were stationed in Pulga for two years. Their job was to drill forty-four young men from 7 to 9 a.m. each morning, after which they have nothing to do but play cards and draughts, and they told me that they got very bored. I suggested that they should take up botany or bird-watching, but their English vocabulary did not run to such terms and my Punjabi was non-existent so I failed to get these ideas across. They offered me the usual cup of syrupy tea and we sat together and drank on the floor of the closed-in veranda, just above ground level, which they had made very comfortable with rugs. I was interested to note that they were all wearing gym shoes with smart bright yellow soles and heels. There were several clean shirts hanging on a clothes line and a row of white *pagaris* sitting along a wide deodar beam.

The villagers of Pulga presented a dirty and ragged appearance and there were several idiots who made extraordinary noises whenever they saw me, but were probably happier living with their families than they would be in institutions. I later learnt from Dr. Snell of Manali that lack of iodine in the water is responsible for the high rate of mental deficiency in this area.

At the upper ends of these Himalayan valleys there is plenty of grass for the livestock, plenty of terraced cultivation growing corn and fruit and vegetables, a climate something like that of Switzerland and no over-population problem, I am always disappointed that the people are not more prosperous. I suppose the eternal cow problem is one of the reasons: with no selective breeding, no killing off of old and unproductive animals, the little black scrub cattle of the hills eat precious grass and give no meat and very little milk in return, in addition to which they take up a lot of the women's time minding them at their daily pasture, time which could well be spent in more productive ways.

When I returned to the bungalow a lovely pine-log fire was burning in the grate of the little sitting-room and I was just settling down to some ancient copies of *Blackwood's Magazine*, which I found on a dusty bookshelf, when the Forest Range Officer appeared. I asked him if there was anywhere where I could post a letter; he said there was no post office at Pulga but there was one just across the valley at a village called Barshaini, a six-mile walk there and back, as you have to go a good bit out of the way in order to cross the river by the nearest bridge. He promised to show me the way the next day. This bungalow, put up by his own distinguished Forest Department, was so superior to the others in the valley, the *chaukidar* so nice and obliging and the situation so wild and beautiful that I told the F.R.O. I would like to stay at least three nights and to spend one day walking up to the hot springs at Khirganga and back. He replied that I could go by mule and that a highly-educated hermit lived up there who had a B.A. in English. I was thrilled at this news and envisaged taking part in a great Hindu–Christian dialogue with a genuine holy man of the Himalaya.

For breakfast the following morning the *chaukidar* produced an omelette full of chopped onion and chillies so that my mouth became a fiery furnace. There was also an ominous note on the tray which read 'Please note that dearness of supplies in this area is 50% higher than at Manikarn and take this into account when the *chaukidar* is presenting his bill.' The Forest Officer appeared at 10 a.m. as promised and we walked two miles up the valley together to the bridge leading over to the right bank of the Béas. The path led gradually down to the river across gullies foaming and flaming with profusely flowering roses and purply-pink indigofera. In several places the track was nearly washed away and we had to cling precariously to the *khud*-side and I there and then decided that it would be extremely dangerous, if not impassable, for mules. Then we had great fun picking our way on stepping stones across a *nala*, with a little waterfall coming down to our right sprinkling us with spray. We crossed three small wooden bridges over torrents rushing down to the river below, then the path led steeply up into a deodar forest, and afterwards steeply down to the big metal bridge built in 1960 across the Parbatti, which here rushes a hundred feet below through a narrow rock gorge.

On the far side the kind F.R.O. and I parted, he going up-stream to his work and I downstream to the post office in the next village. The path was easy to follow leading over little hills covered with freely flowering spiraea shrubs and heavily scented jasmin, which sometimes pushed its way up through indigofera bushes. Scrubby little black and brown hill cows grazed among the shrubs and I was thrilled when a mail-runner jogged past me towards the bridge, wearing a tattered khaki uniform and carrying the insignia of his office—a spear with a circlet of bells round the base of the blade. The bells are designed to frighten away leopards and the spear is used in self-defence if the runner is attacked. There used to be a joke about the leopard waiting for his dinner bell but these creatures seldom attack a man though they are very fond of dogs for supper and will often follow a shooting party for miles in the hope of carrying off a spaniel or a nice fat Labrador. Nowadays these mail-runners only operate in remote districts where, thank God, the roads remain unjeepable, but in my young days they still carried the mail in six-mile stages from Kulu to Simla, running by daylight, and they only took forty-eight hours to do the journey. In this way I used to receive regular love letters and boxes of chocolates from my young man in the summer capital and the sight of the mail-runner produced a twinge of nostalgia deep down within me.

Barshaini is the village where Jamlu, the god of Malana, comes once a year to meet his brother Gyephang, the god of a high peak in Lahul, and they are both carried down to a place two miles distant to bathe together. When I came to the village I found that it was divided into two separate parts with a stone-paved path leading from one to the other. Right at the bottom end I found the post office which was firmly locked—I had hoped to buy some inland letter forms—so I popped two aerograms for England into the little red box stuck on to the outside wall under the veranda and wondered if they would stay there for ever. Later I learnt that both reached their destinations safely.

I returned to Pulga in heavy rain and was met by my friends the idiots whom I always seem to attract whenever I travel in out-of-the-way places. One in particular was a poor young man who made noises like a gorilla and then subsided into peals of hyena-like laughter as I passed by.

I spent the afternoon alternately patching my kingcup-patterned dress and reading stories in the tattered copies of *Blackwood's Magazine* and went to bed soon after supper in preparation for the long walk to Khirganga on the following day.

CHAPTER VIII

The Sacred Springs of Khirganga

The rain continued until dawn and after tossing ceaselessly about throughout the night discussing the relative merits of Hinduism and Christianity with an imaginary *sadhu* I was relieved to get up at 6 a.m. and walk out on to the veranda and watch the sun rise behind the snows of Papidarm.

My guide turned out to be a charming old shepherd with a white moustache, called Mesha, wearing a proper old-style Kulu suit of an off-white tweed tunic and jodhpurs with string sandals on his feet. He made it quite clear that we must walk, as I had already decided to do having seen the large sections of mountain path which had slipped down the *khud*. I set a fairly brisk pace through the village and downhill to the bridge, and slid about a great deal as the mud path was extremely slippery after the heavy rain. We crossed the bridge in the company of a vast flock of sheep and goats and I had a practical lesson in how invaluable these bridges are to the shepherds counting their flocks, in this case about two thousand strong. We worked our way to the head of the flock and continued up the right bank of the foaming river for about a mile where it turned sharply round to the right—southwards—in the direction of Rampur Busahr, where it rises. The Parbatti is joined at this point by the Tos torrent rushing down from the snows at the head of the main valley, and just above the confluence of the two we crossed another bridge and then followed a footpath which led gradually upwards over little terraced wheatfields well above the right bank of the river. The corn had been badly battered by the rain but this would not worry the farmers unduly, for with their neat little hand-sickles they get underneath it when the time comes for harvesting, unlike great combine harvesters which are quite unable to deal efficiently with flattened corn.

Bright orange Siberian wallflowers were growing all along the path, and ascending from one terrace to the next we had to scramble up steep stone-faced walls. We went through a village where a lot of men were sitting cross-legged on a roof passing the time of day, and then the path led along the side of a rocky hill with frequent waterfalls and water mills and *nalas* with flowering shrubs growing up and down the banks of the roaring torrents. One tends to think how wonderful it all is but on reflection you realise that in this temperate Himalayan zone, between 6,000 feet and 10,000 feet, you get the same flora as in England: conifers of all sorts, holly, yew, oak and ash, alder, rhododendron, horse-chestnut, wild cherry, berberis, indigofera, potentilla, cotoneaster, iris, primula, wallflowers, anemone, columbine, delphinium, spiraea, jasmin, and masses of climbing roses. Really one might be in suburban Surrey, but the background is on a far grander scale.

Eventually the path led down to a narrow wooden bridge without handrails. The Parbatti was joined at this point by another cascading torrent and united they forced their way through a deep ravine some fifty feet below the bridge. I knelt in the middle for quite five minutes mesmerised by the sound and the sight of the meeting of the waters. On the far side of the bridge there was a faded notice-board with Khirganga in *devanagari* script and I was very proud of being able to read it. From here the path led up a steep and slippery mud bank into a virgin forest. Sometimes there were convenient roots to act as banisters, sometimes we had to crawl under or over the great trunk of a huge spruce or silver fir which a mule could not possibly have done, so I realised that the F.R.O. of Pulga could not have been up this way recently or he would not have told me that I could ride to Khirganga.

Now that we were in the region of the tall spruce and silver fir trees I knew that we were somewhere around 9,000 feet up: the chil pine (*pinus longifolia*) flourishes naturally between 2,000–7,000 feet in the hills, though it can also be persuaded to grow in gardens in the plains.

The path led almost continually uphill and I sat and rested on tree trunks or boulders every few hundred yards and Mesha seemed very pleased to do likewise. I reflected on how fortunate I was to have an old man for my guide as *pahari* youths skip up and down the hills like mountain goats and would have been impatient at my slowness. When the path was extra steep I forced myself up remembering that I was in training for Malana which, by all accounts, was far steeper than this, and without shade, whereas we were now in a great forest. But to remind me that this was a well-trodden pilgrim route there were occasional empty match boxes and cigarette cartons lying on the pine needles. This upper Parbatti valley is a favourite haunt of bears and I would like to have seen one—at a safe distance—but none obliged by making an appearance, which was disappointing as I felt particularly safe in the care of Mesha, though neither of us carried a gun. The path eventually emerged from the forest to the edge of a large field sloping upwards to our destination: the hot springs of Khirganga with the snow line directly above them. Disappointingly this was not the beautiful Alpine meadow, bright with narcissi and anemones, I had imagined, but consisted of some twenty acres of docks. I searched hopefully among them for some plant a little less familiar but could only find shepherd's purse, chickweed and stitchwort. Fancy having to scale 9,000 feet in the Western Himalaya to find these common garden weeds!

A path led through the tall flowering docks for about a quarter of a mile up to the springs, and as we approached I saw a spout of water coming out of a square, concrete tank and forming a narrow stream which trickled down the field past us. Evidently alterations to the sacred water-works were in progress as I counted twenty-nine bags of cement lying around. I walked up to the stream and dipped my fingers in to find that the water was hot but nowhere near boiling, as it is at Manikarn. The tank was the size of a small swimming bath but I was disappointed to find it almost empty and the bottom covered with nasty sticky grey mud, with only a trickle of water running across it from a concrete panther's head in the wall of an upper tank.

Pearched on a boulder about fifty feet above the tanks to the west was the *sadhu*'s ramshackle hut, very home-made looking, its walls consisting of sacks and odd bits of rough wood and tin with an apricot-coloured cloth pennant flying from a pole close by. I sat down to rest while Mesha scrambled up the side of the boulder to extract the hermit. After about ten minutes he re-appeared accompanied by the holy man who had evidently not yet mastered the yoga of the psychic heat for he wore a long brown woollen tunic under an overcoat of brown homespun Kulu tweed below which his apricot *sannyasin* robe showed reaching to his ankles. He was evidently a Sikh, like the priest at Manikarn, for he had a vast flowing black beard, unrestricted by a hairnet, and wore a large royal blue *pagari* on his head.

'I am honoured to meet you: I hear from the F.R.O. of Pulga that you have a B.A. degree in English?' I said.

'No, no!' He protested, 'that is mistake, I speak not much at all.' He then invited me up to his hut for tea and indicated that while he was preparing it I might like to bathe in the sacred tank. Alas! I had brought neither a towel nor a change of clothes along with me and thought it would be injudicious to get into hot water fully dressed without any means of drying afterwards. I went up to examine the upper tank and saw that it was fed directly from the hillside through a spout. The water smelt slightly of sulphur and the smooth rocks on which it fell were covered with a slimy white deposit which made them as slippery as a bunch of eels. I sat down with a bump on my behind and got wet up to the waist and decided I might as well get wetter still so I stood with my back under the spout and let the water run over my kingcup print dress and down my legs. Then I turned round carefully so as not to fall flat again and put my head under the jet, but the water was too hot to keep it there for long. Then I scrambled out and found a highly polished *linga* and *yoni* close beside the tank with Shiva's trident cemented into the path beside it. Fancy the Indian mania for concrete reaching this remote place! Apricot-coloured prayer-flags were strung to thin poles all along the far side of the upper tank as is the custom in most Himalayan sacred places.

I then climbed up to the *sadhu*'s hut. Inside I sat on the baked mud floor beside the little open wood fire. There was no chimney but there were plenty of cracks in the walls and roof for the smoke to escape. I thought how odd I must look in my dripping print dress with streaming wet hair hanging in rats' tails round my glistening face, but my host was far too polite to comment. He was sitting cross-legged attending to a little *lota*, a brass pot of water on the fire. He broke a piece of *gur* (solid brown lump of unrefined cane sugar) into it saying as he did so: 'No white sugar.' '*Gur* much better,' I replied. Then he sprinkled in some powdered milk. I pointed out of the window (no glass or shutters) which commanded a marvellous view of the meadow with some scrubby brown cows trying to scratch a living among the docks, down to the forest and away to the wild hills on the far bank of the Parbatti where you could trace the many waterfalls coming down from the melting snows.

'Do not cow people give you milk?' I enquired.

'They do not give anything.'

'Docks don't produce milk,' I stated—but this remark was lost on him.

Then a very dark-skinned thick-set little man appeared, also dressed in local tweed but wearing an unbleached woollen cap instead of a *pagari*, and shook some tea out of a packet into the now simmering water. After two or three minutes the *sadhu* ingeniously removed it with a long pair of black tongs—pans never have handles in India—without spilling a drop, and poured the curious concoction into two enamel mugs, one of which he handed to me. It was boiling hot so he gave me a large saucer and I adopted the technique with which I was now familiar through my patronage of *chai khanas* en route: you pour some tea into the saucer which cools it and drink it out of that. I often remember how annoyed my nannie used to get when I was small and sometimes tried to drink out of my saucer for fun which she said was very bad manners indeed: and here I was indulging in this sensible practice in a country where it is regarded as perfectly normal.

It was now about noon so I ate a hard-boiled egg and one of the two *paratas* saved from breakfast and offered my host the other one, together with my last two custard creams, which he finally accepted under pressure. Mesha, who was sitting in the doorway, half in and half out of the hut, refused all food and drink but seized a peculiar pipe-like iron object from the floor which he filled with glowing embers from the fire and sprinkled brown powder—presumably *bhang* (cannabis)—on to them and started to smoke through a hole at the top end of the pipe. Whatever the magic powder was it made him very contented.

There was no furniture in the hut except a sort of ladder-like rack against one wall on one rung of which hung an apricot-coloured bath towel, on another a clean shirt, and on another an apricot *sannyasin*'s outfit. Beneath this stood a pair of worn green gym shoes and a pair of good canvas and rubber lacrosse boots, at least they looked exactly like the ones we wore at school. A natural ledge of rock about a foot from the ground formed a tiny table to the right of the doorway and on this Mesha had put ten *neue paise* as a devout offering to the holy man. The other furnishings of the hut were a few rugs, a few brass cooking pots, a few empty milk-powder tins and a huge book on yoga. On one wall near the entrance there was a drawing of Shiva as the great ascetic, which the *sadhu* informed me he had done himself. It was obviously inspired by the cheap oleographs of Hindu gods which are so common in India today. I commented again on the wonderful situation of the hut. The *sadhu* pointed to his window: 'It is like view from aeroplane!'

He then told me in halting but just comprehensible English that he had lived up here for the past eleven years and at Hardwar for some years before that. He had never been married: he knew no Sanskrit, only Punjabi and Hindi, and the enormous book *Yoga Vashist* was written in the latter language and he read it daily and meditated every morning and evening, usually on the flat boulder outside the hut. During the day he occupied himself with the rebuilding of the tanks so as to improve the bathing facilities for pilgrims. He had also modelled the concrete *linga* and *yoni*: all the cement, he said, had to be carried up by coolies because the forest path (as I well knew) was impassable for mules. He said that many *sadhus* came to Khirganga and stayed the night in his hut. He, himself, had decided to remain there permanently—I presume he is the self-appointed guardian of the sacred springs—though he sometimes walks down to Manikarn to consult his *guru*, the chief priest in the temple there who had received me so hospitably. I asked who his dark companion was.

'He is wandering *sadhu* from south India, very good tailor, he makes my clothes.'

I now introduced the subject of God to start our theological discussion.

'Love is God,' said the *sadhu*.

'Yes, God is love.'

Ken Smith with four of his pupils at Manikarn in the Parbatti Valley

The Sadhu of Khirganga

'Love is God,' he repeated.

'Your God is Shiva?'

'Yes, Shiva.'

'The great ascetic.'

'Yes, GREAT.' And his eyes gleamed.

I longed to find out why he was got up like a Sikh if he worshipped a Hindu god instead of venerating the Sikh *gurus* and renouncing all idolatry: but this was too involved.

'This is my God,' I said, pulling out a small wooden crucifix which I had in my satchel.

'What is its name?'

'Jesus.'

'Jesus?'

'Yes, Jesus is God.'

That was the beginning and end of the Hindu–Christian dialogue to which I had so much looked forward.

I felt very sleepy and when I told my kind host he said, 'You go to sleep,' which I did. Propped up against a rolled-up rug in a corner, I dozed delightfully for over an hour and when I woke up found that the little fire had more or less dried me out. I emerged from the hut and saw the *sadhu* and his *chela* (disciple) sitting cross-legged on the boulder above it, talking. My host beamed when he saw me and came down to say goodbye. I insisted on his accepting two rupees with which to buy more tinned milk at Manikarn, but he was not expecting anything and I know that he was a genuine holy man, unlike some of the three million *sadhus* who wander up and down India extracting food from villagers and money from tourists who are unwary enough to photograph them.

Mesha and I walked back down the dock-field, through the wonderful virgin forest, across the bridge, and proceeded westward along the valley of waterfalls some of which you could trace with your eye up to the snows. We arrived back at Pulga at 6 p.m. and I gave Mesha six rupees in place of the agreed five because he had looked after me so well, also a packet of Manikarn cigarettes. He was delighted and sat on the veranda and had a good gossip with B.R. before going home.

CHAPTER IX

Rejected by Jamlu

The next day I was up before 6 a.m., packing for our return journey down the valley. My breakfast of spam and *chapatties* washed down with weak tea was followed by the bombshell of the bill. After the sinister notice on my tray the morning after our arrival at Pulga I knew that the charges would be high, but as I had already paid 50 *n.p.* apiece for six very small eggs and had provided lunch from my own stores every day, I had indulged in wishful thinking and had decided that my bill could not possibly be exorbitant. It was thirty-three rupees. Enraged, I made the *chaukidar* break it down and he calculated as follows:

Room	Rs. 8
Food	Rs.15
Fire	Rs. 3
Lamp	Rs. 3

Now I am very bad at arithmetic but I added up this sum twice and each time it came to twenty-nine rupees, but it was only after much trouble I got the *chaukidar* to agree to this figure. I tried to explain that I had already paid for my eggs and provided a lot of the other food I had eaten but failed to get a further reduction. Nowhere have I been so shamelessly robbed. And when we set off down the Parbatti valley soon after 7 a.m. the rascal came with us saying that he was going to Kulu to fetch his wife. No wonder he could afford to bring her up to Pulga!

Having been so struck by the beauty of Kashol on my way up, I decided to spend a night there on my way down. I had no chit for the rest-house and the *chaukidar* was extremely off-hand being preoccupied with going through the inventory of the Forest Department's china with some sort of minor official. However, I was eventually given a dusty bedroom and, having unpacked my bags, I went to the neighbouring hamlet to buy eggs but could get none.

Rejected by Jamlu

There is a lovely *thach* (grazing ground) below the rest-house at Kashol bordered by deodars and with a band of silver sand dividing it from the river. You look across this to the pinnacles of Baranagh at the end of the valley and I spent a pleasant evening alternately paddling and contemplating the snows. Two men, probably poachers, were trying very hard to net trout and, stolen goods or not, I hoped to buy some for my supper. But they caught none and I had to be content with my last tin of spags warmed up.

Being in no hurry the next morning I decided not to ride the five miles on to Jari until the afternoon. After a breakfast of tea, *chapatties* and pineapple jam, I crossed the river by a long narrow footbridge and went for a walk downstream. It was Sunday so I took my Missal along and at one point I sat in the shade of a deodar and read the Collect, Epistle and Gospel for the day but I did not meditate on the Gospel as I should; I found my thoughts wandering around the *devatas* instead. I had read in the district gazetteers that owing to the former inaccessibility of these regions—now, alas, being rapidly opened up and defiled by jeeps —the *devatas* have mostly preserved their strange personalities instead of being absorbed into the *Shaiva* or *Vaishnava* cults of the plains. Very few of the *pujaris*, village priests, are Brahmins and even where they have penetrated and gained some influence and have given a *devata* a name from the classical Hindu pantheon, they seldom succeed in completely submerging the local god's personality.

I suddenly realised that one of the paths leading to the mysterious Malana valley over the Rashol Pass could not be very far from where I was now sitting and remembered the story I had been told as a girl about the indigenous, long pre-Aryan Himalayan god, Jamlu, a younger brother of Gyephang La, the *devata* who inhabits one of the twin Gyephang peaks in Lahul. One day a Brahmin found his way into the dark Malana glen and told the people that he knew all about the pedigree of their god and had written it on a parchment to show them. But the villagers were— and still are—illiterate, so one of the elders proposed that the Brahmin should take the document into the *devata's* treasury (curiously enough there is no image of Jamlu and the only temple is dedicated not to him but to his wife Naroi) and await

89

results. This he did, accompanied by the *pujari*, but he received worse treatment than Zacharias, for when he finally emerged, dragged out by Jamlu's servant, he was not only dumb, but paralysed into the bargain.

I looked longingly northwards to the precipitous limestone hills, partly covered with scrub jungle, which form the lower reaches of the mountain wall which separated me from Malana. Then I wandered along a path which led downstream along the right bank of the Parbatti past tiny fields of ripening barley and through pine and cedar groves until, after about an hour's walk, I came to the little village of Chhalal, where, by a stroke of good fortune, I met a young Forest Guard who spoke a bit of English. I asked him to take me to see the village temple but he said there wasn't one. He led me instead up to a sacred grove of *shisham* trees (*Dalbergia Sissoo*) with an earth platform, the middle of which, he said, was regarded as very holy by the villagers because it was where Jamdaggan Rishi used to sit and meditate. This deified hermit has now become identified with Jamlu, who has thus, in spite of the efforts of the Malana people, become involved in classical Hindu mythology, for the name Jamdaggan is but a hill corruption of Jamad-Agni, who is described in the *Vishnu Purana* as a *rishi* who retired to the Himalaya in search of peace.

My guide pointed to a path which led up the mountainside beyond the sacred grove. He said it led to the village of Rashol which I knew to be the kicking-off point for Malana. I was strongly tempted to suggest that we set off there and then, but realised that I could not possibly desert poor B.R. for two days without warning: he might well think I had fallen over a precipice or been spirited away by a *devata*. I also called to mind St. John Gore's description of the steep ascent from Chhalal over the Rashol Pass and gravely doubted my ability to cope with it. All three approaches to Malana are impassable to mules. Instead, I accepted an invitation to visit the young man's tiny cottage which consisted of one room up and one room down, the two being connected by a rickety ladder. The rooms were newly white-washed and the walls were adorned with the familiar brightly-coloured oleographs of Shiva, Durga, Parvati and other leading members of the Hindu pantheon. Upstairs the furniture consisted only of a *charpoy* and a small table with files on it. It was much cleaner than a rest-house bedroom. Downstairs we sat on the baked mud floor and conversed.

'Sir,' said the young man, 'I am sick of life: here there is no company, all the peoples are illiterate and ignorant.'

'Isn't there a schoolmaster living in the village?'

'No, he lives in Manikarn, he walks daily five miles to this village and five miles back same evening.'

'Are you married?'

'Yes, but my wife lives in Nagar. We have a small piece of land. She must cultivate it. I hope very much she is coming with small baby son for winter when harvest is over and new seed planted.'

When I suggested his walking back to Kashol with me he was delighted for the sake of the company. On the way he told me he had put down a deposit of five rupees with the shoemaker there who kept three hens: so no wonder I had been unable to buy eggs as my friend the Forest Guard had the monopoly of all local supplies! When we reached the hamlet he managed to get me two with which I returned in triumph to the rest-house and ordered them to be hard-boiled for my late luncheon.

Just as B.R. and I were setting off down to Jari that afternoon it started to rain and it did not stop for nearly twenty-four hours. Being allergic to the Jari *chaukidar* I decided, on approaching the village, to ask the doctor to put me up for the night. He and his young brother were both dressed in striped pyjamas when we arrived at 5 p.m., which appears to be the casual dress of many Indian men when at home. The doctor said he had no spare bedroom in his bungalow but that if I liked I could sleep in a small room attached to the dispensary, for which I was very grateful. It was dingy and dirty and the furniture consisted of two *charpoys* with dust lying thick on the webbing, two galvanised 'po-palaces', and a large low wooden armchair with such a big hole in the wicker seat that the behind of anyone sitting down would have touched the floor. My heart sank at the prospect of sleeping here but it sank further at the thought of the rest-house and its surly *chaukidar*. I offered to cook supper later in the evening for the two young men, and the doctor said he would be very pleased as he had no cook.

In the meantime the rain let up a little, so I went for an evening walk along the mysterious path under the deodars which led steeply down to the Parbatti which here flows through a gorge some 800 feet below Jari. I looked across it to a series of almost perpendicular black precipices. A wooden bridge spanned the river just below where I stood, and by following the footpath with my eyes on the far side I could clearly trace it ascending steeply along a ledge cut out of one of the forbidding cliffs. This I realised was the route I must follow tomorrow if I went to Malana.

By the time I reached the dispensary it was pouring really hard again. The doctor's kitchen was in a little go-down beside his bungalow. There was a small mud stove in one corner with no flue so that all the smoke from the damp wood which was smouldering in it filled the room. The only light came from a tiny window in the west wall and that was very little because the black rain-clouds had darkened the evening sky. I felt it was a real challenge to cook the risotto I had planned for our dinner menu. I knelt on the dirty mud floor close to a puddle and cut up two onions and put them to fry in *dalda* in an open brass pot. I had previously asked the young men to have some boiling water ready for me but the doctor's brother came in and said I must wash the rice, whereupon he proceeded to tip it into the precious hot water, shake it a bit and then drain the water off in the courtyard. I rather angrily seized the handleless pot with my handkerchief, threw the rice into the onions and *dalda*, half-filled the pot again with cold water from a bucket standing out in the rain and put it to warm up over the smoke hole at the back of the kitchen 'stove'. The few little bits of wood—all the available fuel—were so damp that I had repeatedly to bend right over and blow with all my might to produce a flicker, so that cooking was a slow process. At long last I produced a rather sloppy risotto with which I mixed a packet of dehydrated peas and my *pièce de résistance*, the tin of ham bought in the Kulu market. I thought this was a suitably grand occasion on which to devour such a treasure.

We ate our meal in the living-room: the boys said it was very good and we all three had second helpings. It was, in fact, the first properly-cooked meal I had had during my whole week in the Parbatti valley. The doctor complained that the *paharis* didn't understand cooking (and my word he is right!) and could only boil rice and *dal*, whereas in the Punjab plains where he came from they had a large variety of highly-spiced dishes, complicated to prepare, and which he greatly missed. He said his so-called cook-boy had walked out on him last week and that a new one was coming in from the village soon, but he knew quite well that his repertoire would begin and end with rice and *dal*. I managed to turn the conversation to Malana and said how much I wanted to go there. The doctor told me it would be quite impossible tomorrow as after this heavy rain there would be landslides all along the route and no local man would agree to act as guide in this sort of weather. Thus my last hope of visiting Jamlu was washed away.

Soon after dinner—for I think it deserved to be called that—I retired to my palatial bedroom, having first located the outside lavatory in a corner of the compound which consisted simply of a large *dalda* tin. It was by now pitch dark and still pouring with rain and I thanked God for my yellow sou'wester supplied by Zacharias of Oxford. My knees were black with mud from the kitchen floor and I could find no water to wash in, though had a bowl been handy I could very quickly have collected some of the torrential rain. I decided that if I tried to dust the *charpoy* the stuffy little room would be filled with a thick cloud and make me sneeze incessantly, so I lay carefully and gently down on top of my fleabag which I spread out on the bed, trying to disturb the dust as little as possible.

The rain, which sounded like a cloud-burst, continued all night and made such a noise on the corrugated iron roof that I hardly slept at all. Inhaling an unusual mixture of dispensary smells and dust I mused on my bitter disappointment over Malana after all the walking I had done to get into training for the trek. Evidently Jamlu was determined to exclude me from this theocracy. The precipitous path on the opposite bank of the Parbatti has a sinister reputation as the God is well known to pelt unwanted intruders with enormous rocks: a practice which he would certainly find only too easy in such weather. It would take days for everything to dry up and meanwhile I wanted to re-visit the upper Kulu valley and be back in Simla before the real monsoon broke: this was a foretaste and I certainly did not want to ride day after day in such rain.

Kulu: the End of the Habitable World

So I have been rejected by Jamlu! But I desperately hope that he will perhaps relent and allow me to visit Malana one day before I die: preferably before his March festival, for I greatly long to see the minute golden image of the Emperor Akbar which is only produced on that occasion, and the curious ritual connected with it.

At intervals during the night my dingy little room was lit up by lightning, followed almost immediately by great roars of thunder echoing through the narrow valley. The rain came down in unrelenting torrents until daylight when a sweeper woman appeared unannounced and proceeded to sweep the thick dust off the floor up on to me. Then a little man in a clean white overall with a broad grin on his face came to the door with a bright 'Good-morning Memsahib!'

'Are you the dispenser?' I asked.

'No, I am venereal diseases technician.'

* * *

During the early morning lull in the storm I decided to push off quickly while the going was good and get something to eat at a shack-shop on the way. But we had not been on the road for more than ten minutes before the rain came down again and the eider-down which formed my saddle was so sodden that I quickly dismounted and walked along in my long hunting mac and bright yellow sou'wester. I kept up well with the mules for the first three miles as it was all downhill. Then Shanti suddenly went lame. There was no stone in her near fore and B.R. thought she must have slipped in the mud and sprained her shoulder. Thus there was no question of riding today, but the walk from Jari to Bhuin rest-house is only twelve easy miles, a mere nothing compared to my scramble up to Khirganga and back. We stopped at the nice little shack-shop at Shat for tea and ate sickly sticky *jalebis* and I wished I could have waved a magic wand and turn them into toast and marmalade. Further on down the hill there were landslides right across the road in three different places and Durgi and Shanti had considerable difficulty crossing them. One blessing was that they prevented the nasty little Bunthar–Jari bus from running that day. After a bit I lagged behind and B.R. and the mules went on out of sight and when I finally emerged from the Parbatti valley I couldn't find the rest-house. Luckily I met a kind man who spoke good English and led me straight to it and said that I must be sure and come along to the Bunthar *mela* (fair) later on. We had got wind of this at Jari and several groups of gaily-dressed villagers had overtaken me on the way down, obviously fair-bound.

I was by now pretty tired of the usual dak bungalow diet and decided to have lunch at Bunthar. The rain had stopped at last and after a short rest B.R. and I walked along to the *mela* together, tacking on to a *devata* procession and following it over the Duff Dunbar Bridge to the fair-ground. Here the *rath*, the wooden litter hung with coloured draperies and stuck with metal masks, was put down and a middle-aged woman with long curly black hair squatted beside it and went into a trance, trembling and droning out jerky sentences. She was the *devata*'s *gur*, his oracle, and answered all the questions put to her in *pahari* dialect so, alas, I could not understand a word of what she said but having read a lot about these *gurs* I imagined it was chiefly to do with the weather and the probable yield of the crops. Sometimes, however, *gurs* are known to have identified thieves (who immediately confess their guilt when accused by the mouthpiece of their god) and very recently I heard of one who correctly predicted an exam result when questioned by an educated Hindu girl from Delhi. In my youth I often saw these *shamans* at work but this was the first time I had ever seen a woman *gur*. The men, when speaking for the *devata*, always go naked to the waist, never cut their hair or wear leather shoes, and are not allowed to plough or to spread manure; before specially important consultations they must also fast and practise sexual abstinence. I have read that some *gurs* beat themselves (but not very hard) with iron scourges before becoming possessed by the spirit of their *devata*, while others stick iron skewers through their cheeks, but I have never myself witnessed such devotional exercises.

Bunthar *mela* is a big fair combining religion and trade. Several *devatas* had come from other villages and were put on the ground while groups of men, mostly dressed in traditional Kulu clothes, danced slowly round them in a large circle. A man in the middle of the circle, apparently the Master of Ceremonies, gingered

up the dancers when their steps started to flag. I have never seen
women dancing in Kulu though I believe they do so on rare ritual
occasions. For them fairs provide the chief opportunities for
displaying their finest clothes and jewels. Then they wear their
best *puttoos*, some of check tweeds, others of bright plain colours,
but the smartest of all are plain white or plain black with brilliant
patterned borders. Their magnificent necklaces are made of large
flat plaques of silver, some of which have the outline of a god
or goddess traced on them interspersed with a few plaques of blue
enamel or Tibetan turquoise. The women's ears are adorned with
innumerable silver rings which hang not from the lobes alone but
all round the rims as well; the weight of these causes the ear
to bend over sideways in what, to me, is an unbecoming manner
but evidently not to the gentlemen of Kulu. To round off the
effect a large nose ring, four or five inches across, is always worn
at a *mela*. A complete set of such festal jewellery is now worth a
lot of money, yet according to the accounts of various travellers
the women have always been loth to part with it and few outsiders have succeeded in buying any. Incidentally I have frequently seen girls wearing everyday necklaces consisting entirely
of Victorian silver rupees with the image of the Queen Empress
stamped on each one instead of the Mother Goddess. These too,
must be increasing in value daily.

Outside the rings of dancers groups of skinny cattle were
standing around, white ones from the plains and the small
brown ones and black ones which are native to the hills.
There were also bunches of reasonably plump calves for sale, but
most of them had ringworm. Near the cows there were large
heaps of beautiful earthenware pots, the products of a form of
folk-art which, thank God, still flourishes all over India, and long
may the people prefer it to plastic. There were stalls selling Kulu
tweed, others selling toys, others displaying dozens of the little
pill-box Kulu hats with their broad velvet bands, and innumerable
food stalls, at one of which I treated B.R. and myself to a late
lunch of excellent hot *pakoras* and other delicacies.

For me the highlight of the fair, however, was the discovery
of a plump moustachioed travelling photographer with an
ancient plate camera on a tripod who was taking successive groups
of hill beauties in front of a wide backcloth stretched out on a

frame with a vast pink Rajput palace painted on it. I could imagine the girls looking at the finished prints and fancying they were princesses of Jaipur.

I returned alone to the rest-house leaving B.R. to disport himself further at the fair. Perhaps he would get merry on *lugri*, the local rice wine which is freely drunk at *melas*; if he did he showed no signs of a hangover later. This time I had the bungalow all to myself and passed a pleasant contemplative evening watching the dramatic stormy sunset and listening to the roar of the waters at the sacred confluence of the Béas and Parbatti rivers, both greatly swollen by the heavy rain.

CHAPTER X

A Hill Princess

Owing to little Shanti's lameness I decided it would be a good idea to give her two or three days' complete rest. Meanwhile I myself went down to Mandi, the former Punjab Hill State, just south of Kulu, to see the temples. I called on the Raja whom I had met in the old days and he very kindly asked me to stay in his little palace, which he told me had been remodelled in the early 'thirties by the late Mr. George, one of the New Delhi architects who worked under Lutyens. It is a long, low building of bluish-grey stone standing against the side of a well-wooded hill with terraced gardens rising up behind it, on the lawns of which you often met one of His Highness's sacred cows. The palace had Georgian-shaped windows and you could take it for a rambling early Victorian rectory were it not for the Indian-style columns supporting the two large porches in front. How I wish there were space to describe the little temple-strewn capital city of Mandi! But I must stick to Kulu where I returned three days later in the Raja's jeep, driven by an elderly chauffeur in an Eton-blue turban. The only other passenger was His Highness's sister, the widow of the late Rai of Rupi.

The name of Kulu is confusing because today it is used both for the whole district—now a part of the great Himalayan state of Himachal Pradesh—and for its small capital which can hardly be called a city. This comprises the modern section of Dhalpur, with government buildings grouped round a large *maidan* above the right bank of the Béas; the Dhalpur bazaar at the far end descending steeply down a rocky path to the Sarvari torrent at the bottom; beyond this there is a quarter of a mile of low-lying marshy ground criss-crossed by paths and streams; then the mile-long Akhara bazaar containing the principal shops and garages of Kulu standing on either side of the main road which runs northwards up the valley; and finally, on a hill above it, lies Sultanpur, the name given to his capital by Raja Jagat Singh (1637–72) when he moved the seat of government down here from Nagar in the middle of the seventeenth century, and which consists of the Rupi palace, several temples, and a long, narrow bazaar descending the hill. Up till the 1920's all guide and travel books refer to the capital simply as Sultanpur, but as in modern India the several separate sections of the town are collectively called Kulu, I will in future chapters refer to it as Kulu town to distinguish it from the district.

When we arrived in Kulu town in the Raja of Mandi's jeep we drove across the huge *maidan*, over the Sarvari river, and just before getting to the Akhara bazaar the jeep hair-pinned round to the left and chugged up a steep stony cart track which led on to a platform of burnt-up grass at the far end of which was a very fancy palace complex. In the centre stood a large mulberry-coloured gateway with a curved roof ridge and clusters of little pavilions, while on either side there were irregular groups of buildings. To the right a wooden chalet displayed a notice telling us it was the 'Office of the Potato Development Officer'. To the right of this there was an arched entrance affording cover to the Rai of Rupi's jeep so that the passage was blocked and we could not drive in.

We all climbed out of our own vehicle and walked into the paved courtyard which had open drains running along the sides and a further collection of assorted buildings grouped round it. On one of the verandas stood the heavily moustached Rai, the descendant of the former Rajas (Kings) of Kulu, dressed in what appeared to be a green boiler suit; then from a door just behind him emerged his wife, one of the most beautiful women I have ever seen, with perfect features, large liquid eyes, a rich olive complexion, her rippling black hair done up neatly in the nape of her neck. She descended from the veranda into the courtyard, went up to her mother-in-law, the old Rani, and stooped down to take the dust off her feet in the orthodox Hindu style. She was closely followed by her daughter, Princess Kiran, a tall, slim, shy girl of sixteen with gazelle-like eyes and a long, thick, blue-black plait down her back. She turned out to be the only member of her family then at home who spoke English and she invited me into the drawing-room, which we entered by walking across the courtyard, up a flight of steep stone steps to another veranda and through a door into a large square room with powder-blue distempered walls which had a dado consisting of a broad black line with a still broader band above it of red glossy paint. The low ceiling was painted a deeper blue than the walls and the three doors and two corner cupboards were also bright blue and the mantelpiece was faced with blue and pink tiles—a startling and original colour scheme. In each corner of the room there was a formal group of straight-backed chairs and a sofa; on the floor were a number of modern rugs, one with a life-size yellow tiger woven on to a blue ground and another with a design of bright red and orange Chinese dragons. The walls were hung with big tinted photographs of various members of the family, including one of the old Rani wearing an outsize silver nose ring which came well below her chin. There were also several portraits of the beautiful young Rani, who is a member of the famous Rana family—the former ruling family of Nepal—and of her father in the scarlet uniform of a Nepalese general including the magnificent jewelled helmet which, since the 1950 revolution, only the King is allowed to wear.

To my great delight Kiran invited me to stay as she said she loved to talk English. Accordingly it was arranged that the chauffeur should drive to Katrain, a village further up the valley, where B.R. had had orders to await me, and tell him of my altered plans.

After tea Kiran led me into the room next door which ran along the whole west wall of the drawing-room but was very narrow. At one end there was a bed against the wall and an old-fashioned marble-topped washstand, and in the middle there were four chairs round a square table at which I had all my subsequent meals alone with the princess. These turned out to consist of such hot vegetable curries that I could only swallow them by squeezing lots of juice over everything from my beloved little limes, the supply of which I had replenished in the Mandi bazaar.

My bedroom turned out to be next to the dining-room and was the same narrow oblong shape and size. At one end there was a tiny wash-room with a minute basin fixed to the wall but it had no stopper so that when you turned on the single cold tap the water ran straight through the hole on to your toes. There were two beds with mattresses and pillows but no bedclothes so I slept inside my faithful green fleabag. The walls were hung with the familiar modern colour-reproductions of Indian gods, and the one small window looked out through fine mesh wire fly netting on to a tiny courtyard with what appeared to be either a rabbit hutch or a meat safe in the middle of it.

I asked Kiran how she had learnt English so well when neither of her parents spoke it and she told me that she had a Parsi governess from Bombay who had been with her for nearly two years.

'Where is she now?' I asked.

'She stays with the Johnsons in Katrain at this time. You see when I have my monthly I am not allowed to touch anybody so I always send her away.'

'What do you do here when you are not doing lessons? Do you go for walks in the hills?'

'Oh no, I am not allowed out. I just stay in the palace. I read, and play badminton when my brothers are at home, and cards. I have my own walled garden where I play with my pets and sometimes my father takes me for a drive in the jeep. You see we can hang curtains up round it.'

'Have your parents chosen a young man for you to marry yet?'

'Yes, they have selected a boy of our own caste from Jammu.'

'Have you met him?'

'Yes, because he refused to marry me without seeing me first, so he was invited to tea in the drawing-room.'

'Did you like the look of him?'

'Oh yes! But, of course, I did not speak to him: to speak to him would have been shameless. He looked through some of our photograph albums and I saw later that he had removed one of me. He wrote to my father the next day and asked him not to give me to anyone else as he definitely wants me.'*

'Why do you have "Office of the Potato Development Officer" written up on the outside of your palace?'

'Oh, you see we are not such very big kings now so we have to let a part of it.'

We wandered through into an inner courtyard with carved wooden balustrades running right round the upper verandas with

* Kiran has since married a different young man, her cousin, the Raja of Mandi's second son, whom she knew well and with whom she was much in love.

great slices of precipice on the roofs, as on the farmhouses. This was undoubtedly a part of the palace which had survived the terrible earthquake of 1905, and may well date from the seventeenth century when Raja Jagat Singh moved his capital here from Nagar, higher up the valley. There were flat cakes of cowdung for fuel drying on the walls and I wondered why it was necessary to use them in a district where there is so much firewood. But the Forest Department is very strict about the felling of trees, and as the present Rai now only owns land in Waziri Rupi up the Parbatti valley it would mean carting his logs for thirty miles.

We walked on into yet another courtyard of the old *Shish Mahal* which also survived the earthquake and I asked Kiran who lived in the rooms round it.

'Oh, some elderly relatives of my father, and in that room over there a mistress of my grandfather's. She is a very old lady now.'

The royal concubine's apartment was fronted by a low wide veranda with cusped Moghul arches and on some of the inside spandrels and intradoses were painted medallions of Ravana fighting Rama and Lakshmana, Krishna flanked by adoring cows, the fish *avatar* of Vishnu, and Dhanu the winged cow giving milk to the *sadhus*.

Under a veranda on the opposite side of the courtyard I found a much more interesting wall-painting: the heaven of Tripura Sundari, one of the many forms of the Mother Goddess. She is here shown seated on the lap of a five-faced Shiva in the very centre of her palace which is on an island called Mani-dweep. The spectator looks down on the scene, as it were, from above, and can see that it consists of eighteen rectangular walls, one within the other, with a great variety of activities going on in the spaces in between. A large selection of strange reptiles and mythical creatures disport themselves round the outside wall; they are said to symbolise the ocean of nectar. Between some of the walls *sadhus* are meditating, while others do *puja* in front of small shrines. There are different forms of *Devi* herself—Kali, Durga, Lakshmi, Sarasvati—riding on their respective vehicles; there are processions of devotees, musicians, elephants and horsemen making their way to the centre of the palace to gaze upon the goddess. I quickly fished out my specs and spent quite half an

Bunthar *mela*. An itinerant photographer with customers sitting in front of a painted backcloth stretched on a wooden frame

Rupi Palace. Princess Kiran on the first day of the *Dussehra* festival, 1965,
wearing a mauve taffeta dress copied from a photograph of *Gone with the Wind,*
in a film magazine

hour of pure pleasure enjoying this wall painting while there was yet time, for the damp was fast seeping through the unmended roof and soon the heaven of Tripura Sundari will become invisible.*

Kiran said: 'Inside that room there are more paintings but it leads to our own family temple of Kali and I am not allowed to take you in, but if you follow me you can see it from the outside.'†

We retraced our steps, after which we walked along one side of the odd collection of palace buildings and then doubled back through an orchard into a small grass courtyard. Here I saw a pool of blood from a fresh sacrifice. While Kiran walked up some steps to a high veranda with three cusped white plaster arches along the outside, I stayed down below and peered in through the open temple door, but the mysterious darkness concealed the image within and there was no sign of the goat which must have been offered up to the Mother that morning. The Rupi Palace Kali temple was not in any of the main architectural styles found in the Western Himalaya, but in the Moghul style which became fashionable in the hill States fom the eighteenth century onwards. For this reason the architectural backgrounds of *pahari* miniature paintings are almost invariably in the Moghul style.

Kiran then took me to her own little walled garden which consisted of a lawn of rather rough grass, some rose bushes growing round the edges and a couple of almond trees in the middle. There were a few hens pecking about, two woolly lambs, nearly full grown, and a fluffy little white over-fed dog somewhat resembling a pom which bounced up to its mistress with great joy. Kiran told me how she loved animals and that her favourite pet had been a black lamb which followed her everywhere but it had died only last night and she had cried for two hours so her father procured these two white lambs to console her: but they did not know her and were too old to tame properly and anyway nothing could ever replace her own black lamb which was thought to have eaten a poisonous herb.

---

* I subsequently discovered an article on the Rupi Palace paintings in the June 1964 number of *Marg*, by Jagadish Mital. He thinks the Devi mural is early nineteenth century. Mr. W. G. Archer, on the other hand, thinks it is earlier. Since writing this the mural has been removed to the National Museum in New Delhi.

† When Nehru came to power he passed a law to allow everyone to enter Hindu temples but he had no jurisdiction over private family ones, and from these Europeans and low caste Indians are still excluded.

Kiran picked some almonds, removed the green outer skins, cracked them and gave me the delicious milky kernels. Then she took me to see what she called her nursery as it was still full of her old toys: literally dozens of dolls of all shapes and sizes arranged sitting on a shelf which ran all round the walls, and three clock-work trains set out on their rails which belonged to her brothers. Above the dolls the walls were again plastered with routine modern colour pictures of gods and goddesses, including several of Durga, eight-armed and sitting side-saddle on a tiger. In classical texts and sculpture her vehicle is always a lion: has she changed her mount in order to keep up to date? The lions which roamed over India in former centuries and were hunted by the Rajput kings and Moghul Emperors are now almost extinct and confined to a small area of Gujerat, the forest of Gur, but tigers are still fairly plentiful up and down the country and are, therefore, familiar to the Mother's devotees.

I felt compelled to bring up my persistent question about the worship of the Terrible and asked the young and gentle Kiran how she could love a goddess of destruction who demands continual blood sacrifices. She simply said: 'I call Durga my fairy godmother. I believe in her since I prayed to have an English teacher and very soon she sent me my Parsi governess, so now I have great faith.'

Kiran told me later that at last year's *Dussehra* festival when many animals were sacrificed according to custom, a visiting *sadhu* had protested to the priests and told them that they must not take life because there was nothing about blood sacrifice in the *Gita*. He said he was going to Delhi to protest to the Prime Minister but someone told him that Nehru knew all about it and that he would not interfere.

That night, surrounded by the same garish devotional colour prints as decorated Kiran's nursery, I reflected that their Indian Christian equivalents were every bit as repulsive: I had seen them in open-fronted shops in the bazaars of Kerala which sold Hindu and Christian religious pictures indiscriminately and there was little to choose between them. They were all on display together and you could take your pick of sickly sentimental Madonnas wearing sword-pierced immaculate hearts on the outside of their robes, sickly sentimental Durgas and Kalis smiling benignly through their tushes and wearing their severed head necklaces with complete unconcern; sickly sentimental heads of our Lord with blood pouring down his face from the crown of thorns; huge bullock hearts representing his sacred Humanity; Shiva as the great ascetic seated on a leopard skin with cobras twined round his neck and arms, raised eyebrows, and a sickly sentimental smile.

The next morning I longed to go for a walk in the surrounding hills and thought how sad it was for Kiran never to be allowed out of the palace precincts except with her father in a curtained jeep. But I did not want to leave her so we wandered about together with her little dog, whose figure would have been greatly improved by regular runs up and down the mountainside. Having paid another bewitching visit to the heaven of Tripura Sundari we went and sat in the brilliantly painted drawing-room and discussed her family gods.

'Three miles from here,' she told me, 'is our family temple of Neoli Rani. She was the senior wife of my ancestor, a former king of Kulu. I don't know exactly when she lived but she had no children so the king married another girl from the caste of the Chauhan Rajputs. When she became pregnant the senior Rani told her she would have a baby girl who would die. This sad thing happened. The young queen became pregnant again and this time the senior Rani told her that a baby boy would be born but that he too would die. When this prophecy also came true the young queen complained to her husband that the senior Rani was a witch. He agreed about this and decided to put his first wife to death so he took her with a manservant and a woman servant to a place called Ramghar in the hills near Mandi and left them all three in a valley where a giant was known to come down at night and eat people. But the Rani was very clever and when she saw the giant coming through the dusk she quickly cut her finger, rubbed it on his wrist and made him her blood brother. "Now I cannot eat you because we are brother and sister," he said, and he took care of her and the servants. The Raja returned in the morning to find them all three alive and well, so he decided to bury the senior Rani alive.

"If you leave me under the earth for twelve years then dig me up you will find me still living," said Neoli Rani.

'One day after some time had passed, god Jahanni Mahadev appeared to the Raja and said: "If you dig up the queen after twelve years as she has requested and she comes out of her grave then the people will worship her as a *devi* and will cease to honour me. But if you dig her up after ten years that will kill her effectively."

'So the Raja did what the god advised and though Neoli Rani seemed to be dead she appeared to her husband in a dream and he was very sorry for all the harm he had done her. He begged her to come back to the palace and live with him, but she refused. From then on whenever he sat down to a meal the food which was put before him was crawling with ants and the water which he wanted to drink turned to blood as he lifted the cup to his lips. Terrified, the king had a temple built in honour of the dead queen and elevated her to the rank of a *devi* whereupon she appeared to him again and told him to come to the temple every morning and drink blessed water after which his normal food and drink would no longer be polluted.

'An image of Neoli Rani was made and placed in the sanctuary and images of the two servants were put on either side of the temple door. Sometimes the *devi* likes to come to our palace and she expresses this desire through her *gur*. The image is then carried here in a litter and put down on the drawing-room floor. Last time she came in December 1963 and stayed six days and the members of our family all came to do *puja* to Neoli Rani and bring her offerings of flowers. She does not want blood sacrifices.'

I asked Kiran about the, to me, sinister Dunghri temple above Manali which I had seen as a girl and had heard that its demon Goddess Hidimba was somehow connected with the Rai's family.

'Yes,' said Kiran, 'we always call Hidimba grandmother because she gave the kingdom of Kulu to our ancestor Raja Sidh Pal. You see many hundreds of years ago my family was driven out of our country by the *thakurs*, local chieftains. Some time after that Sidh Pal, a grandson of the last reigning king, came up the Kulu valley from Mayapuri and settled in the village of Hat near Bajaura. He saw a temple on top of a big hill upstream and was told that it was dedicated to Bijli Mahadev and that if he took some water from the sacred *sangam*, the holy confluence of the

Béas and the Parbatti rivers at the foot of the hill, and poured it over the image of the great god, he would receive a wonderful reward. So he did this and, as it is a long climb of many hours to the top of Bijli Mahadev, he spent the night in the temple and the god appeared to him and told him to go to Jagat Sukh where he would get the promised reward. He therefore went on up the valley to this village which was our capital before Nagar, that is a long, long time ago because my ancestor King Jagat Singh again moved the capital from Nagar to Sultanpur in the seventeenth century. Well one morning as Sidh Pal was sitting in meditation outside the house of a potter where he had lodgings, a Brahmin saw the *padami*, the royal sign, on the sole of his foot and prophesied that he would become the king of Kulu.

'When the time of the annual *mela* came round Sidh Pal was on his way to the fair-ground when he overtook an old woman carrying a heavy *kilta* on her back which he offered to take for her. They walked on to Jagat Sukh together, but before they reached the village the old woman, who was *Devi* Hidimba in disguise, made him put down the basket and climb on to her shoulders. She then grew suddenly many furlongs tall and said: "You will rule over all the land you can see from here." So it was. After that all members of the royal family have called this goddess grandmother and often we go up to Manali to offer sacrifice to her.'

'Do you offer goats or buffaloes?'

'Mostly we offer goats. You see these days buffaloes are very expensive and now that my father is no longer a big king he has not so much money. There is a dip in the floor of the Doonghri temple where the blood flows from the goat offered up in sacrifice. If *Devi* accepts it the blood wells up and overflows: if not, you must bring another goat. Before the priest decapitates it you must put flour and water on its head. The goat must shiver all over before it is killed and if it does this it shows that Goddess Hidimba is pleased and the *pujari* can offer it up.* Its head is cut off and one of its front feet which is then put into its mouth and the priest takes these. The body belongs to the people offering the sacrifice.'

---

* 'The quivering [of the sacrificial victim] in the popular imagination, denotes the actual entry of the god into the body of the animal, and it is the divine spirit—and not the water as one might suppose—which is responsible for the animation.' *Tribes and Castes of the Punjab*, Lahore, 1911, Vol. I, p. 484.

Kiran, the hill princess, so young, so beautiful, so gentle, so loving, so deeply religious and so devoted to her pet animals: yet she takes blood sacrifices in her stride and sees nothing incongruous in them, just as, indeed, the Blessed Virgin Mary must have accepted them as a matter of course when she went up to the temple in Jerusalem.

That afternoon I enquired about Ragunath, the principal god of the valley.

'If you like I will take you to see his temple, it is very near.'

So we went out under the arch which shelters the Raja's jeep and walked diagonally across the small *maidan* in front of the palace and round the back of the buildings inhabited by Kiran's uncle and his family, and came to yet another courtyard on the far side of which stood a long low building with irregular slices of precipice on the roof. There was no carving on the wooden pillars of the veranda, in fact nothing to show that it was a temple at all, let alone the shrine of the chief god of Kulu.

Kiran disappeared inside, having first asked me to wait in the courtyard, and after a few minutes she reappeared with the *pujari*, who was all smiles and handed me some rose petals.

'In this temple,' announced Kiran, 'lives God Narsingh and also Ragunathji.'

'Is Narsingh the lion-headed avatar of Lord Vishnu?' I asked, 'who tore out the entrails of the demon king Hiranyakasipu?'

'No, God Narsingh has a small round black head but no body. At *Dussehra* time he rides on a horse.'

'And Ragunathji is Rama, isn't he?'

'Yes, and the very holy idol we have in our family temple was brought here about two hundred years ago by my ancestor Raja Jagat Singh.'

We walked slowly back to the palace and Kiran told me the story of the coming of the god to Kulu.

'The Raja greatly wanted some beautiful pearls which belonged to a Brahmin in the Parbatti valley but this man did not want to give them up. One day when the Raja was on a pilgrimage to Manikarn he again demanded the pearls and was told he could have them on his way back down the valley, but when the king and his courtiers came near to the house, the Brahmin set alight to it and died with all his family. It is a terrible thing to be responsible for the death of a Brahmin: for us it is the worst sin of all. After this the Raja's food always turned to worms whenever he tried to eat something, and his drink turned to blood.

'Nobody knew what to do until the advice of a very holy Suketi Brahmin called Damodar was asked, and this man told the king that the only way to make up for his very bad sin was to bring the sacred idol of Ragunath from Oudh and surrender the kingdom of Kulu to the God. The king begged Damodar to go himself to get it which he did and after many adventures he brought it back and Jagat Singh set it on the *gaddi* (throne) in his palace and made Rama the ruler of Kulu. Since those days our Rajas have always regarded themselves as his viceroys.'

The next day I reluctantly said goodbye to Kiran and her hospitable family, but as it happened this was only the first of three delightful visits to the Rupi Palace and I was soon to see her again.

CHAPTER XI

The Kulu *Dussehra*

In the autumn of the year following my mule trek I returned to the Rupi Palace for the *Dussehra*. No book about Kulu would be complete without a description of this famous festival. The *Dussehra* is among the most popular of India's many festivals and is celebrated up and down the country in a variety of ways. I am indebted to my learned friend Pandit Balak Ram Gaur of Katrain for an explanation of the Kulu ceremonies. He tells me that they are held in honour of Rama's victory over Ravana, the demon king of Ceylon, and that in the Kulu dialect it is called *dushet hera* which means 'the demon killed'. As Ravana was slain on the tenth day of the light half of the month the ceremonies start on that day and finish on the night of the full moon. The festival is also locally known as the *vijey deshmin*, the tenth day of victory. What is peculiar to Kulu about the *Dussehra* celebrations is the homage paid to Rama (alias Ragunathji) by the village *devatas* who come from all over the valley itself, from Inner and Outer Saraj and from the Parbatti valley. This custom was initiated in the seventeenth century as a way of taming the indigenous divinities: nature spirits of caves, trees, springs and mountain passes, the representatives of a more ancient and primitive religion than orthodox Hinduism. The only *devatas* who are exempt from such homage are deified sages (such as Vashist) who acted as tutors to Rama during their earthly lives; and of course the elusive, imageless Jamlu of Malana who is a law unto himself.

In a normal year between a hundred and fifty and two hundred *devatas* come to the Kulu *Dussehra*, but shortly after Independence the government removed their lands and their temple grants so that there was no more grain to fill their granaries and consequently no more money with which to pay their numerous attendants: the members of their private band, the standard bearers, *rath* bearers, priest and *gur*. Thus none but the villagers living in the immediate neighbourhood of Kulu town could afford to take their gods to the *Dussehra*. Now this was a serious state of affairs, not only spiritually but materially, because the festival had long attracted tourists, both Indian and foreign, to Kulu, and tourists bring cash. Eventually an excellent solution was found: the Indian Tourist Board agreed to pay the gods' annual *Dussehra* expenses so now everybody is happy again. Usually all the guest-houses, rest-houses, tourist bungalows, tents and aluminium huts up and down the valley are stuffed full for the festival, but in 1965, when I was present, only the Rai's family gods attended owing to the national emergency. The three-week Indo-Pak war had just ended and the government had requested the curtailment of *Dussehra* celebrations throughout the country. I was therefore fortunate in being present with less than half the usual crowd milling around and not a tripper in sight.

I was honoured at being invited to the Rupi Palace for the opening ceremonies as the arrival of the *devatas* in the principal courtyard and their reception by the Rai is normally never seen by English people. On the day before the gods were due to arrive, Kiran and I were strolling in the orchard where a nice dun hill-pony, about twelve hands high, was tethered to graze. At that time I was muleless and badly needed an animal to ride to outlying temples so I said:

'Do you think your father would lend me this pony to ride to the top of Bijli Mahadev?'

'No, I am afraid not. You see that is Narsingh's horse and only the god is allowed to ride him.'

On the opening morning of the festival there were great preparations at the palace for the arrival of the *devatas* that evening. From Kiran's nursery window I watched her father, the Rai, at his devotional ablutions. Wearing a pair of white cotton pants he first sat and shaved on the veranda outside his mother's apartments, then he poured cold water over his head from a brass *lota* which he refilled repeatedly from a large galvanised bucket. Then he got up and went inside and reappeared ten minutes later dressed in baggy orange trousers with a loose tunic of the same colour and a handkerchief tied round his head in the gipsy fashion of *pahari* women. Meanwhile the few decrepit old palace menservants appeared in the courtyard dressed in clean white cotton jodhpurs and pale blue waisted coats with matching *pagaris*. Most of them, Kiran told me, had retired years ago but returned each autumn to serve their master and their gods: and during *Dussehra* the two are closely identified. Kiran herself changed into a long flounced mauve taffeta dress which she proudly told me she had had copied from photographs in a film magazine illustrating *Gone with the Wind*.

I had always heard that the Kulu *Dussehra* cannot start without Hidimba, the royal family's demon goddess 'grandmother' about whom Kiran had told me. The idol has to be carried on a *rath* twenty-four miles down the valley from the Dunghri temple above Manali and spends the night beside the Ramshila bridge at the far end of the long Akhāra bazaar. On the opening day itself the Raja sends messengers down from Sultanpur to pay his respects to the goddess and invite her up to his palace. Hindu festivals, however, are invariably conducted in a haphazard manner, and on this occasion the first *devata* to enter the courtyard was Tripura Sundari of Nagar. She was preceeded by her private band, and her *rath*, stuck with metal masks, decked with flowers, and hung with brilliant draperies, was carried to the back entrance of the Kali temple where it was received and saluted by the orange-clad Rai. The men bearing her litter thereupon began to shake it up and down on their shoulders and tilt it over from one side to the other to show that it was indeed animated by the spirit of the goddess. She was then carried up the steep stone steps leading to the high veranda where I stood, and into the drawing-room where she was set down on the tiger-woven rug.

Next came *Devi* Hidimba, who by rights should have been first on the scene, with her band and her *gur* naked to the waist with long grey-black greasy curls falling to well below his shoulders. He shook violently, denoting divine possession, but smiled at the same time and appeared to be enjoying his festival duties immensely. While the *rath* of the demon goddess was oscillated in the customary fashion to the blare of her trumpets and the rhythmic beating of her drums, a live lamb was thrown up into the air and caught again by some of her devotees. This ceremony, Kiran told me, is known as *warna* and on the last evening of

Dussehra the lamb would be one of the five creatures to be offered up in sacrifice beside the river bank. After Hidimba had been received by the Rai she too was carried upstairs into the drawing-room and set down beside Tripura Sundari.

For the next hour or so other *devis* and *devatas* continued to arrive and the same ritual was enacted, except that no more *raths* were taken up to the blue drawing-room, but were set down in the courtyard instead, and none but Hidimba's followers threw up a live lamb. When the last of the *devatas* had been received by the Rai, all of the *raths* were lifted up on to the shoulders of their attendants and carried to the temple of Ragunath to do homage to the presiding deity of Kulu who would then himself be carried on a litter down to Dhalpur at the northern end of the great *maidan*.

After a seemingly interminable time in the temple during which I remained outside under a sacred *peepul* tree, the *devatas* at last emerged, their metal masks glinting in the setting sun. They were carried past me with their sovereign, Ragunathji, the great Rama himself, in their midst, incongruously represented by a tiny bronze image only a few inches high seated on a dark red velvet cushion in a gilt palanquin. He was preceeded by his vice-regent, the Rai, who had made another quick change, this time into the traditional ceremonial dress of the Indian princes: white cotton jodhpurs, a beautiful apricot brocade waisted coat, glistening with gold thread, and a *pagari* of the same delicate shade with a diamond cockade in front. For this short space of a few days every autumn the Rai of Rupi comes into his own again, for he is looked upon as the deified descendant of the Rajput kings of Kulu and entitled to veneration because of the ancient Hindu belief in the divinity of kings.

In the days of its greatness this Western Himalayan kingdom was no petty state. According to Hutchison and Vogel the total area was 6,607 square miles which was sometimes increased to as much as 10,000 by temporary acquisitions from neighbouring states. The last ruling Raja was Ajit Singh who ascended the *gaddi* in 1816, was deposed by the famous Sikh conqueror Ranjit Singh in 1839, and died under British protection in the small state of Shangri across the Sutlej in 1841. Four years later, at the end of the first Sikh war in 1846, large tracts of the Western Himalaya were ceded to the British, including the whole of Kulu and Saraj, and in 1852 the then Raja Gyan Singh was demoted to the lower rank of Rai because of his illegitimate birth. He was, however, allowed to live on—without sovereign powers—in the family palace at Sultanpur and to enjoy the *jagir* of Waziri Rupi, the tract of land between the Parbatti and Sainj rivers and bounded to the west by the Béas. Thus his descendant today is still known as the Rai of Rupi, his residence is the Rupi Palace, and he is the true representative of the old line of Kulu Kings and revered by the people as such, especially during *Dussehra*.

In front of the Rai walked his eighteen-year-old son, the *tikka sahib*, a medical student of Chandigarh University, but today a near-god, dressed in the same splendid style as his father.

Behind the palanquin of Ragunath pranced the pretty pony believed to be carrying god Narsingh, though not having the eyes of Hindu faith I was unable to see him. His miniature charger was led by a uniformed attendant who had considerable difficulty in controlling the animal which was overfed and under exercised, and matters were not helped by the fact that he was almost completely enveloped in a mulberry velvet rug, several sizes too big for him, with gold trappings trailing on the ground, because as Kiran explained later, the god's last mount had been an Arab, a considerably larger horse, which had unfortunately died.

The procession of gods crossed the flat *maidan* in front of the Rupi Palace, then wound its way down the steep paved stepped path through the narrow upper bazaar of Sultanpur to the motor road below, and from there through the beautiful alder groves criss-crossed with streams and over the wooden bridge which spans the Sarvari torrent near its confluence with the Béas. Meanwhile I was skipping along in front taking photographs at strategic points along the route which finally led up the hill through the Dhalpur bazaar to the northern end of the *maidan* where the large wooden *rath* of Ragunath, all hung with coloured draperies, was waiting to receive the chief god of the valley.

The word *rath* is really Sanskrit for a chariot, but in the India of today the term is chiefly used for the huge elaborately-carved wooden carriages of the Gods which are pulled along processional routes near the great temples of the plains by hundreds of youths at special festivals. In Kulu the word is confusing because it is used indiscriminately for both the carriages on wheels and the wooden palanquins of the village *devatas* to which the metal masks are fixed for *melas* and which have no wheels but are carried about on long poles. The wheeled *rath* of Ragunath is by far the largest one in the valley and is roughly made with no carving to decorate it. There are a few smaller versions of this *rath* in some of the bigger villages, but on the whole the wheel-less *raths* are far more practical in a mountain region and the vast majority of hill gods always travel in them.

Ragunath's great clumsy chariot runs on six solid little wheels and lies neglected and unprotected from the weather throughout the year, apart from the few days of *Dussehra* each autumn. As soon as the tiny image of the god was transferred to it, the bands of the *devatas* all blared forth together—the noise was terrific and thrilling—while the Rai and his son, led by the chief Brahmin priest from the temple, walked three times round the *rath* followed by crowds of devotees. The priest, together with several more Brahmins, then clambered with difficulty into the vehicle and sat cross-legged round a small wooden sanctuary in which the little image had been placed. Long thick ropes had already been attached to the front of the carriage and these were now picked up by some two hundred young men who started to pull the god with great glee across the huge *maidan*. But, alas, they were all too soon frustrated for the small metal umbrella protruding from the wooden spire of the *rath* roof became entangled in telegraph wires and for the next twenty minutes the boys pushed and pulled and shouted in their unsuccessful efforts to free it. At last one of their number, brighter than the rest, had the sense to climb up the nearest telegraph pole and carefully detach each wire one by one until the god was able to proceed. When the *rath* finally reached the high bank of the Béas at the far end of the *maidan* it was halted and remained there until the last day of *Dussehra* when the customary five-fold sacrifice was offered in honour of Durga and in the presence of the royal family. The victims all have to be provided by the Rai and consist of a buffalo, a goat, a cock, a fish and a fresh-water crab.

Nothing is more confusing to the uninitiated than Hindu ritual observance. Why should the Goddess Durga, who is the *Shakti* (female power) of Shiva, not Vishnu, be propitiated in a ceremony which is essentially Vaishnavite? Especially as the devotees of Vishnu (of whom both Rama and Krishna are *avatars*) hate blood sacrifice. But I was told that as the *Dussehra* celebrates the victory of Rama over Ravana, the demon king, offerings are made to Durga because she is the Goddess of Victory, having, with the aid of her faithful lion, slain so many enemies of the gods.

CHAPTER XII

Nagar

Returning to 1964, after my first stay in the Rupi Palace, B.R. and the mules were at the appointed place at Katrain dead on time and I thought what a brilliant second horseman out hunting he would make once he got to know a particular country.

From Katrain the old bridle road—now widened and open to traffic of all kinds—leads off the main road down to the river, over a suspension bridge, then southwards along the left bank of the Béas past a trout hatchery, after which it starts climbing very steeply, rising a thousand feet in a mile, to the large village of Nagar, a former capital of Kulu.* The first big building you come to is the castle, which is traditionally believed to have been built by Raja Sidh Singh in the early sixteenth century and was used as a royal residence and State headquarters until the middle of the seventeenth century, when Raja Jagat Singh transferred the capital to Sultanpur. It continued to be used as a summer palace, however, by subsequent rulers, until the British took over the whole of Kangra and Kulu from the Sikhs in 1846, when Raja Gyan Singh sold it to the first Assistant Commissioner, Major Hay, for a song. The latter converted the northern wing to the European way of living by putting in staircases, fireplaces and chimneys. He later sold it to the government when it was used as a court-house and as a civil rest-house for travelling officials and visitors. Today a part of the castle is used as an extension of the village school, but it is still possible to stay in Major Hay's wing when it is not occupied by officials on tour.

I found a very nice Indian lady, Shrimati Lal, the wife of the Commissioner of Agra, installed in the castle. She and her husband and their Labrador puppy occupied the principal suite while I had a bedroom at the back. She told me that her husband had set off for Malana that very morning: news that I could hardly bear

* There is now a well-graded motor road from Patlikuhl, near Katrain, up to Nagar, with daily buses running up to Manali.

to hear for had I arrived a day earlier I could perhaps have gone with him. However, having incurred Jamlu's displeasure and having been repulsed by him all along the line, perhaps it was as well I did not accompany Shri Lal. His wife told me that he had sent a coolie down to tell her that the ascent from Nagar to the Chanderkhani pass had been so steep, rising some 6,000 feet in seven miles, that he was camping on the downs just below the pass; being a bad walker myself I should doubtless have retarded his progress. Furthermore, the coolie had said that the clumps of rhododendrons near the top were so thick that the party had had considerable difficulty in forcing its way through them, and that Shri Lal, who was not carrying a gun, had seen a brown she-bear with two cubs but had most fortunately not been attacked.

Shrimati Lal told me during tea, which we had together in her vast sitting-room, that before going to Agra her husband had been dewan in Sikkim for five years where he was known as the Mountain Goat as he had climbed every peak in sight: so if he found the ascent to the 12,000 feet Chanderkhani pass tough, should I ever have made it?

Shrimati Lal was a Church of India Christian but also as *mandir*-mad as I am, and she described a stone *shikhara*-type temple some 500 feet above the village, which I did not remember seeing when I last visited Nagar in 1931. She said it was dedicated to Krishna and that the courtyard was so untidy that she had told the *pujari* that he ought to do something about clearing away the débris and keep the weeds in check. 'If you serve God he will serve you,' she had told him. And the *pujari* had replied: 'You speak the truth Memsahib.' But Shrimati Lal said she doubted whether he would ever bestir himself to do anything.

After tea she took me to see the large flat triangular slab of rock called Jagatipath which is preserved in an out-house in one of the courtyards of the castle. According to the local legend this was miraculously carried here from the cliff face of a hill near the base of the Rohtang Pass by *devatas*—in the form of a swarm of bees. A young Rani who had been reared in a village up there felt homesick when taken to live in the great sprawling castle at Nagar, so to comfort her the bees carried this slab of rock from her own native hills some fifteen miles further up the Béas valley. Jagatipath is given the same veneration as the image

The pony ridden by the god Narsingh in the Rupi Palace courtyard, *Dussehra* festival, 1965
The *rath* of a *devata* in the Rupi Palace courtyard, *Dussehra* festival, 1965

View of the Béas Valley at its widest point, taken from the ruins of Thawa, above Nagar

Nagar Castle, from a water-colour by Colonel Harcourt, *c.* 1870

of a *devata* by the local people and a story is told about a foolish British Assistant Commissioner who made fun of it and died within a week.

From there we walked about two hundred yards down the hill to see the *barselas*, the *sati* memorial stones of the royal family which are stuck in four irregular rows into the *khud*-side below the road. The carving is in the primitive folk style of the hills and depicts lines of wives, serving maids and concubines seated below their master, with whose body they were all immolated on the funeral pyre.

That night I spread out my old green fleabag on the wide veranda which runs along the north side of the castle, and wallowed in nostalgia. I actually spent at least an hour simply leaning on the balustrade and contemplating the moonlit view of the Upper Béas valley which had haunted me for so many years. There was the long white ridge at the head of the Solang Nala, and to the right of it, the twin Gyephang peaks of Lahul: no longer in my imagination at the end of a downland track, but here, in reality, in the Western Himalaya. I remembered how my mother and I and Gerald Emerson and our A.D.C., Geoffrey Kellie, had all spent the night on this very veranda by moonlight thirty-three years ago hoping to see the ghost of the poor young Rani who had thrown herself off at the far end and fallen down the steep *khud*-side to her death. Various versions of the story tell how some wrestlers or strolling players were performing before the royal family in the chief courtyard of the castle and at the end of their display the Raja turned to his youngest queen and asked her which man she considered the best. She singled out one whereupon the Raja had him beheaded before her on the spot, believing him to be her lover. In horror she rushed up to the veranda, ran along it and committed suicide. Her ghost has haunted it ever since, though the original wood of the veranda has been renewed several times since the tragedy. At Nagar I have always been lucky with marvellous moonlight nights, but have never seen the Rani, neither have I met anyone who has, but my old friend, the late Mr. J. C. French of the I.C.S., wrote: 'I slept in the western room of the castle, and shortly before midnight I awoke with a sense of uneasiness and oppression. I thought the night must have turned suddenly warm (it was cold when I went to bed) and I got up to open another window. As I stood up, swift and unmistakable as a gust of cold air or a drive of sleet came the sensation of fear. I went to the west wall of the castle and opened a window, and all the time I was moving there and back the sensation of fear was with me.'*

Next day I spent revisiting a few of the many temples in and near the village, including several I had never seen before. Nagar is the best village in Kulu for the study of Western Himalayan architecture. Its chief features were first noted and recorded† by Captain (later Colonel) A. F. P. Harcourt who was A.C. in Kulu from 1869 to 1871.

Accurate chronology is at present impossible when dealing with Himalayan architecture because of the almost complete dearth of inscriptions, but Harcourt's classification of the four different types of Kulu temple can hardly be improved upon and I shall use it here, only reversing his order of Types III and IV for reasons which I hope will become apparent.

Type I. The carved stone temple with characteristic curvilinear tower (*shikhara*), the style of which is not indigenous to the hills, but was imported from the northern Indian plains somewhere about the seventh or eighth century A.D. The best-known example in Kulu is the temple of Vishveshvara Mahadeva at Bajaura described in Chapter VII. At Nagar there is the exquisite little stone *shikhara* shrine of Gaurishankar just below the castle where I watched the elderly priestess performing the early morning ablutions of Shiva and Parvati, chanting as she removed their drab brown nightdresses, washed the deities, anointed them with oil and fixed on their day dresses of scarlet cotton striped with tinsel. Then she laid some freshly-picked flowers and small bowls of rice at their feet.

Among the ruins of the ancient city of Thawa, 500 feet above the present village, stands the temple of Murlidhar (Krishna the flute player), *Shaiva* in origin, with a late Gupta-style carved base, the upper part of the *shikhara* having been rebuilt after the 1905 earthquake. Close by lives the *pujari* who had been reprimanded by Shrimati Lal for failing to keep the sacred precincts tidy; and to the south stands a small *rath* on wheels (a miniature version of the

* J. C. French, *Himalayan Art*, O.U.P., 1931, pp. 26–7.
† *The Himalayan Districts of Kooloo, Lahul and Spiti*, London, 1871.

big one at Dhalpur), in which the idol is paraded at festivals.

In addition to the relatively few ancient, Type I, temples in Kulu there is a far larger number of much less interesting buildings in the same style but with little or no carving on the stone *shikharas*. Jagat Singh (1637–72), who popularised Vishnu worship in his kingdom through the theft of the idol of Ragunathji from Oudh, seems also to have been responsible for the revival of 'plains type' temples up and down the valley, a typical example of which is the large and uninteresting *shikhara* down in a dip to the east of Nagar castle.

Type II is the indigenous timber-bonded style of the Western Himalaya, which consists of alternate courses of dry stone and deodar beams. This style is used throughout the whole of the region in both sacred and secular buildings. It is said to be as earthquake-proof as anything can be because the absence of mortar between the dressed stones gives the walls a chance to quiver with the quake instead of trying to stand against the earthquake's movements.

One of the finest examples of this style is Nagar Castle itself, which stood up to the 1905 earthquake, though unfortunately its appearance has been spoilt by the substitution of corrugated iron roofs—painted a hideous green—for the original precipice-slice tiles. From the haunted veranda, however, you can look down on to plenty of private Type II houses in the village which still have their beautiful stone roofs.

In the case of temples built in this characteristically Himalayan style, the plan is in the form of a rectangular tower with a gabled roof topped by a great ridge pole; the latter consists of a complete tree trunk sometimes carved into animal heads at either end. Immediately under the roof, a wooden veranda, often with a carved balustrade carrying a row of cusped arches, runs right round the four walls of the building and is supported by the uppermost beams of the tower which run right through the building and project beyond it for this specific purpose. From the eaves of the roof, and sometimes also from the edge of the veranda floor, hang continuous fringes of wooden pendants. In Kulu such buildings are often several storeys high, each successive floor being reached by means of a notched log, for the staircase was unknown until the advent of European-style houses.

Type III is the Chalet Style. Harcourt refers to the little chalet-type temple in this class as 'being probably but a variety of the edifices of the second order'. For this reason I have put it in direct succession to the half-timbered Type II style, since I think it is clearer to keep them together. If, in your mind's eye, you black out the tower of a Type II temple and place the wooden top storey on a low plinth, you are left with a Type III summer-house or chalet-like temple, the commonest of the four types, found in assorted sizes all over the Western Himalaya and examples of which are still being built today.

Nagar has several small versions of this style, some of which are merely wayside shrines. The most beautiful of them is the tiny temple of Narsingh on the opposite side of the road, at the south-east corner of the castle, with its unbroken fringes of pendants rippling and rattling in the mountain winds.

Type IV, the Pagoda Style, is one for which historians of Indian art use various regional terms, though in this Himalayan region it simplifies matters if one sticks to the familiar term 'pagoda', by which is meant a building with a succession of super-imposed pent roofs, each one a little smaller than the one below it.

Of the four styles of architecture, Type I is now generally agreed to have originated in the plains: Types II and III are known to be indigenous to the hills, whereas about Type IV there is still considerable discussion, some authorities maintaining that it came to Kulu from Nepal, where it is very common in the valley of Kathmandu, others that it originated in the plains and was introduced into the hills during the reign of the Emperor Harsha (A.D. 606–47). Whatever decision art historians of the future may come to in the matter it is an interesting fact that the so-called 'Pagoda Style' is found as far apart as Kerala in South India, in various parts of the Himalaya, all over the Far East and, strangest of all, in the medieval mast churches of Norway. Seventy years ago James Fergusson wrote:* 'Whenever this chapter of Indian [i.e. Himalayan] architectural history comes to be written it will form a curious pendant to that of the wooden architecture of Sweden and Norway. The similarities between the two groups being both striking and instructive. It cannot be

* James Fergusson, *History of Indian and Eastern Architecture,* London, 1899 edn.

expected that any ethnographical or political connection can be traced between peoples so remote from one another which could influence their architectural forms; but it is curious to observe how people come independently to adopt the same forms and similar modes of decoration when using the same materials for like purposes and under similar climatic influences.'

Similar materials and climate may not be the only explanation. Since Fergusson's day a great deal has come to light about the movement of peoples backwards and forwards across the great Eurasian plains. The 'Animal Style' in art uses similar motives from Ireland to China, so the dragon of Scandinavia and the Far East, and its Indian counterpart the *makara*, may conceivably be culturally related.

In Kulu the Pagoda Style is a folk version of the much more sophisticated and highly finished Nepalese court architecture. At Nagar there is a graceful example of the former in the three-tiered temple of Tripura Sundari (the Mother Goddess under the title of 'The Beauty of the Triple World') built of deodar. As always in this region, the top storey is circular (whereas in Nepal it is square) and the two lower storeys are characteristically divided by squat wooden pillars through which you can see the landscape on the far side of the valley.

The Pagoda Style is the rarest of the four types of Kulu temple; Harcourt only knew of four examples, though the late Mr. Lee Shuttleworth, I.C.S. (A.C. Kulu, 1917 to 1919) lists seven. The British settlers do not seem to have taken much interest in Kulu temple architecture, but several of the Assistant Commissioners did, notably Harcourt, Howell and Shuttleworth. About the year 1912 Shuttleworth tried, and failed, to get transferred from the I.C.S. to the A.S.I. (Archaeological Survey of India), and had he been successful he would undoubtedly have written the classic work on the temple architecture of the Western Himalaya. As it is he only had the time to write the occasional article and his fund of knowledge must now be dug out of the learned periodicals of his time. He also wrote in a more popular vein in the *Times of India Illustrated Weekly*. Among his unpublished typescripts I found a useful list of villages in the Kulu and Parbatti valleys and in Inner and Outer Saraj which have good temples, all of which I plan to visit and to photograph.

In addition to the four styles briefly described above, you will sometimes come across a fascinating cross-breed, usually a fusion of Types III and IV. A beautiful example of such a hybrid is illustrated in Frazer's *Views of the Himala* [sic] *Mountains* though it is not, strictly speaking, in Kulu itself but on the opposite bank of the Sutlej somewhere below Narkanda. Owing to the curious transliteration of those days, however, I have been unable to identify 'Manjnee' on the half-inch Ordnance Survey map which, of course, one cannot consult *in situ* but only in a place such as the Indian Office Library.

I walked about a mile up a gully, through a deodar forest, to the mysterious, ramshackle 'chalet-type' temple of Jiri which is built against the side of a hill. Somewhere underneath it is said to be the entrance—now blocked—to a secret passage which connects this place with Manikarn in the Parbatti valley where I had seen the sacred boiling springs. In the gully below the temple lie huge fallen ramparts of black stone, and above it are vast heaps of similar stone, the ruins of the ancient city of Thawa, some 500 feet above Nagar. Kulu was visited in the seventh century A.D. by the Chinese Buddhist pilgrim Huien Tsang, and Thawa is thought to be the city to which he refers:

'This country [Kulu, which he calls Kiu-lu-to] is about 3,000 li in circuit and surrounded on every side by mountains. The chief town [Thawa?] is about 14 or 15 li round. The land is rich and fertile, and the crops are duly sown and gathered. Gold, silver and copper are found here, fire-drops (crystal) and native copper. The climate is unusually cold and hail and snow continually fall. The people are coarse and common in appearance and are much afflicted with goitre and tumours. Their nature is hard and fierce; they greatly regard justice and bravery. There are about twenty *sangharamas* and a thousand priests or so. They mostly study the Great Vehicle; a few practise the rules of other schools. There are fifteen *deva* temples: different sects occupy them without distinction.

'Along the precipitous sides of the mountains and hollowed into the rocks are stone chambers which face one another. Here the *arhats* dwell and the *rishis* stop. In the middle of the country is a stupa built by Ashokaraja. Of old the *tathagata* came to this country with his followers to preach the law and to save men. This stupa is a memorial to the traces of his presence.'*

On my way home down the hill to the castle I saw the tail half of a beautiful Himalayan grass-snake disappearing into the long grass. These creatures are light brown on top and pale yellow underneath and six feet long when fully grown. I have often seen dead ones lying beside a path and I can never understand why the local people kill them on sight when they are perfectly harmless and, incidentally, very sacred if one is to judge by the magnificent specimens carved on the deodar columns inside the temple of Bijli Mahadev and on the doorways of many another *mandir*.

That Nagar is certainly the best village in the valley for the study of Western Himalayan architecture with its four distinct styles was brought back to me when I thought how beautiful British hill stations could have been if only we had had the aesthetic sense to adapt the local styles to European living. But alas, this did not happen, and at Nagar, as at Simla, the former British settlers built themselves ugly nondescript-style houses roofed with corrugated iron. The chief of these is 'The Hall', built in the 1880's by the late Colonel Rennick, one of the biggest landowners and most influential of the settlers. His Nagar estate was subsequently bought by the present Raja of Mandi, who sold it during the twenties to the late Professor Nicholas Roerich, who left it to his son Svetoslav. The latter, together with his wife Devika Rani, the First Lady in Indian films (and a person of great intelligence and culture, unlike many film stars), is in the process of turning it into a centre of Himalayan art. She is building a museum above the house for the display of classical sculpture and *pahari* folk art of every kind: wood and stone carving, bronzes, *devata* masks and textiles.

The Hall is approached through an English-style garden still beautifully kept up; with its lawns and conifers, the wistaria and jasmin, and the beds of roses and dahlias in front of the villa, you could well imagine yourself in the suburbs of Reigate. But walk round the corner of the house and there, instead of the humble Surrey hills, you see the snow peaks and ridges of the great Himalayan range of Indian Tibet.

---

* *Buddhist Records of the Western World*, Samuel Beal, Trübner Oriental Series (2 vols.), London, 1884, Vol. 1, p. 177.

To the east of the road, above the temple of Tripura Sundari, stands Osborne House, a villa built for General Osborne who is buried in the garden. Today the house is used as a dispensary and cottage hospital. The General, a contemporary of Colonel Rennick, was a keen fisherman and did valuable work in helping the A.C., Mr. G. C. L. Howell, to establish trout culture in Kulu. The latter introduced brown trout from Kashmir in the spring of 1909, since when the valley has become one of the best centres for trout fishing in the hills.

About a mile to the south of Nagar lies the Kutbai estate, now the property of the great industrialist Shri G. D. Birla, but founded in the early years of this century by the late Mr. William Henry Donald, sometime chief P.W.D. engineer in the sub-division, and to whose pioneer work I have frequently referred in the preceeding pages, another of the many Europeans who settled in the Kulu valley in the late nineteenth and early twentieth centuries.

Type 1. The Classical Style of the northern Indian plains. Probably introduced into the hills somewhere around the seventh or eighth century A.D. and
consisting of a curvilinear stone tower (*shikhara*), richly carved and crowned
with the characteristic *amalaka* (imitating a segmented gourd). There is no
pillared hall (*mandapa*) attached, as there usually is in the plains. In the seventeenth century, Raja Jaggat Singh reintroduced this style into Kulu, but his
temples are not decorated with the excellent carving found on the early shrines.

Illustration: The little temple of Gaurishankar at Jagat Sukh, in the classical
style of the late Gupta period

Type 2. The indigenous timber-bonded style of the Western Himalaya consisting of alternate courses of dry stone and deodar or spruce beams. Sometimes whitewashed or thinly coated with mud plaster. Said to be as earthquake-proof as any building can be because the absence of mortar gives it the chance to quiver with the quake instead of fighting against it. A wooden veranda, often elaborately carved, runs right round the upper storey of the building. The roof is usually covered with enormous tiles, or rather slices of precipice, crowned by a roof ridge consisting of a single tree-trunk carved into a monster's head at either end.

This style is used for both sacred and secular buildings.

Illustration: The temple treasury at Sarahan in Outer Saraj

Type 3. The Chalet Style. If, in your mind's eye, you black out the tower of a Type 2 temple and place the top storey on the ground, you are left with a Type 3 chalet-style temple, the commonest of the four types, found in assorted sizes (going down to mini *mandirs*) all over the Western Himalaya, and examples of which are still being built today.

Illustration: The temple of Shring Rishi outside Sarahan, below the Bashleo Pass in Outer Saraj. Note the sacred pole (*dhoj*) to the left of the photograph

Type 4. The Pagoda Style, by which is meant a building with a succession of superimposed roofs, each one a little smaller than the one below it. The inside wall of the bottom storey is usually of timber-bonded stone, the remainder of the building being of wood. Sometimes, however, the eaves are covered with vast stone tiles in place of shingles. In Kulu this is the least common of the four types and I only know of eight recorded examples of which I have seen four.

Illustration: The temple of Tripura Sundari at Nagar in the Kulu Valley

CHAPTER XIII

British Settlers in Kulu

The Donald family, of Scottish descent, was one of those whose members served India in a variety of ways for several generations.

In the late 1820's Alexander Donald sailed out with the 10th Foot—now the Royal Lincolnshire—Regiment but after his marriage to a Miss Hackett he sold his commission and bought an indigo factory at Budaon, in the United Provinces (now Uttar Pradesh). This he ran until the Mutiny of 1857 (or the first War of Independence, whichever you prefer) when it was burnt to the ground and he and his second son were both shot whilst crossing the river Ganges at Cawnpore (modern Kanpur) by order of Nana Sahib.

Alexander's eldest son, Alexander John Stewart Donald, married a Miss Hilliard by whom he had ten children. Of his six surviving sons, John had a distinguished career in the I.C.S. and was awarded the K.C.I.E.; Ranald (Scottish spelling of Ronald), Douglas and Duncan went into the Indian Police and the latter, known in his family as Robin, was the origin of Kipling's Strickland in 'Miss Youghall's Syce'* being a gifted linguist who specialised in the dialects of the North-West Frontier; Charles Hilliard Donald, F.Z.S., a good field naturalist, was the first man on record to train golden eagles, but when they began to kill sheep he passed them on to the Lahore zoo. He worked for the big timber firm of Spedding's and later became Warden of Fisheries in the Punjab. Before all else, however, he will be remembered by grateful sportsmen for his little book, *Gundogs and Their Training*, about which letters still appear from time to time in *The Field*, expressing the view that it is the best book to have been written on the subject and should be reprinted.

The member of the family who most concerns us, however, is the second son, William Henry—always known as Willie—for it was he who spent the greater part of his life in Kulu. After leaving

* *Plain Tales from the Hills.*

school he could not make up his mind what to do, so his father, who finished up as a district judge, put him into a solicitor's office in Lahore to study law. But Willie pined for an outdoor life, took no trouble over his exams, and was ploughed. His father had by this time, the middle 'eighties, retired and settled in the Kulu valley where Colonel (then Major) Rennick was already a considerable landowner while following his career in the Indian army, and Mr. Donald got his son, Willie, the job of managing Rennick's Garh estate at Bajaura. This Willie did very efficiently, for he was by nature a farmer and gardener, and he quickly became one of the most successful and expert fruit-growers in the valley.

The land system in Kulu was similar to that practised in parts of Italy to this day: the tenants pay no rent but are bound to give the landlord half their produce. In addition to this, in Kulu certain obligations went with land ownership such as providing men for at least ten days' unpaid labour on the local roads each year; providing porters to carry the baggage of travelling officials (the system of forced labour known as *begar*, which continued into the 1950's but is now obsolete); providing a night's grazing for a huge *gaddi* flock on its way up to the summer pastures of Lahul: and into the bargain feeding the *gaddi* shepherd's ten or twelve dogs in return for the valuable manure left by the sheep.

After the British took over Kulu from the Sikhs in 1846 and established the first Assistant Commissioner, Major Hay, at Nagar, the sub-division became increasingly popular with British officers on leave in search of sport, and as the years went by some of them planned to settle there on retirement. They eventually formed a colony of planters, tea being the first crop with which they experimented. The Kulu Tea Company was founded in the 'sixties with gardens at Bajaura, Raison and Nagar, and was managed by a Mr. Minnikin from Ireland. But tea was never a success on a commercial scale, as it was in the neighbouring Kangra valley, partly because the latter province had less transport problems, bordering as it does, on the Punjab plains.

The Pioneer of the Kulu fruit industry was Captain R. C. Lee, who retired from his regiment, the Royal Sussex, in 1870, bought some land at Bundrole half-way up the valley, and built himself a comfortable house. He was a Devon man and noticed that the warm climate together with the heavy rainfall of the sub-division was not unlike that of the West Country in England, so he sent for fruit trees from his father's estate: apples, pears, plums and cherries. Though some of his land, according to the custom of the country, had to be worked by tenant farmers, he managed to cultivate a part of it himself and planted the first of the Kulu orchards, now famous throughout India.

A few years later an Irish friend of his, Captain A. T. Banon, retired from his regiment, the Munster Fusiliers, and also settled in Kulu, buying land in what is now the great tourist centre of Manali near the northern end of the valley. He, too, planted orchards and the example of these officers was soon followed by the British families already settled in the valley such as the Minnikin's and the Rennick's, by subsequent planters, and eventually by the Kulu cultivators themselves.

In those early days the favoured varieties of apples were Cox's, Blenheim orange, Newton and Russet; and Marie Louise and William pears. But in recent years in order to satisfy the Indian passion for bright colours such varieties as Red and Golden Delicious have been introduced from America and today it is difficult to find a Cox's orange pippin tree.

Once the orchards really got going the problem arose of transporting the surplus fruit to Simla, a hundred and forty miles away over the 10,000-feet Jalori range, down into the 2,000-feet Sutlej valley, and up again over the 9,000-feet Narkanda range. At first some consignments were sent there by coolies and some by pack animals, but the cost of transport proved too great to allow a fair profit for the growers. Then Captain Banon had the brilliant idea of sending the fruit by parcel post, which at that time was only two annas a pound, so that the postage on an 8 lb. parcel of fruit cost roughly a shilling! The postal route from Manali to Simla during the summer months in those days was by mail-runner for the first ninety miles via the Bhubu Pass (9,480 feet) to Palampur, and thence by *dak tonga* (mail pony cart) to Pathankot and up to Simla. From 1901 onwards, when the Simla mountain railway opened, the last stage of the journey was completed by train. The mail-runners did six-mile stages carrying five parcels totalling some 40 lb. in weight packed into their *kiltas*, the local all-purpose cone-shaped baskets in use in the Western Himalaya. At the height of the fruit season as many as two hundred runners were employed at each stage and by the relay system the first ninety miles of the journey were covered in under twenty-four hours. Today, when the fruit leaves Kulu in lorries by the Mandi–Larji gorge road, Willie Donald's daughters have told me that it arrives at its—now various—destinations in a far more bruised condition than it did when it went by mail-runner and pony cart.

In the heyday of the British settlers, that is roughly between 1870 and 1925, life must have been very pleasant for them. They lived in one of the most beautiful valleys in the world with a temperate climate in which they could grow all the fruit and vegetables and flowers that they were accustomed to in England, with the addition of apricots, pomegranates, tea and tobacco. Although the two latter crops were never a commercial success, most of the planters grew enough for their own consumption, with a bit to spare for sale to the Lahulis when they came down from their barren heights into the Kulu valley. The British also planted hops, from which they brewed beer, and some of them made cider from their apples. The sporting facilities were un-rivalled with plenty of big game, ibex, red and black bear, panther, burrhel, spotted, barking and musk deer; and small game in the form of several different kinds of pheasant and partridge, duck, snipe, quail, woodcock and teal. There was also good mahseer fishing in the Béas and its many tributaries and, after the intro-duction of trout in 1909, excellent trout fishing.

By the 1880's there were some ten estates up and down the valley on which the owners had built themselves ugly but comfortable 'Simla-Surrey style' villas. A few of the settlers, such as the Rennicks, Mackays, and later on the Donalds, had both summer and winter residences and when they were not shooting or fishing or attending to their land, their favourite recreation was tennis, although there are no vestiges of any courts left today. There is no church in the valley and I think that the reason for this may be that several of the planters married beautiful Kulu girls without religious rites. They simply entered into a legal contract for a certain number of years—or for life—according to the custom of the hills. This was known as a 'stamp marriage' because when a local *kutcherry* (court) was held the bridegroom got the magistrate to die-stamp the relevant document. Babies were baptised by the American missionary, Dr. Marcus Carleton, when he visited the valley, and later by visiting clergy from the Palampur mission in Kangra who also held occasional services in the houses of one of the settlers who had not married 'outside the church'.

What really broke up this little sporting and farming community was not so much the coming of independence in 1947, as the opening of the Mandi–Larji gorge road some twenty years earlier. Up till then the Kulu valley could be reached only on foot or by riding a hill pony up and down precipitous paths. But once the buses and lorries and private cars started pouring in and trans-forming Kulu into a popular holiday resort like Kashmir, the whole pattern of life changed for the residents. A few of them started to take in visitors during the tourist season and there are still some excellent guest-houses at Manali run by the descendants of the original Captain Banon; a few sold out and returned to England; a few still live in the houses their grandfathers built and run their orchards to this day.

To return to Willie Donald; soon after he was appointed manager of the Garh estate for Colonel Rennick he was given the Dobhi estate on the river, east of Katrain, by his elder sister, Mrs. Anderson, where he lived happily for many years and married the granddaughter of his neighbour at Aramgarh, the Mr. Minnikin who had originally come from Ireland to manage the Kulu Tea Company. Donald divided his time between managing his own land and Colonel Rennick's, a three-hour ride down the valley; and as a sideline he bred mules for the government. His daughters, Hilary and Barbara Donald, who now live surrounded by horses and ponies on the borders of Hampshire and Surrey, have lent me his surviving diaries which give a clear idea of the life of the British residents in Kulu in the 'eighties and 'nineties of the last century . . .

Dobhi. 2nd April, 1887. Fuel for tea completed by two men, three men worked at the potatoes and were helped by the two mollies [*sic, malis,* gardeners] after 12 o'clock. The two mollies cleaned out the hops which are finished today. Pulled out an enormous leech from the old grey's nose, which was the cause of his keeping so thin. Pobli returned at 12 o'clock to say that the leopard did not come to eat the sheep he had killed the day before, and found that the spring gun had not gone off and there were no marks of the leopard being close to the kill. Went over to Raisen at 1.30 o'clock and from there Minnikin and I went over to Bundrole to see Captain Lee. Discussed with Captain Lee about the fruit who said that his blossom both of pears and apples was good and thought if the fruit is a success we must make a reduction in the price of our fruit.

Manali. 5th April '87. All five of us (two Johnstones, two Mackays* and myself) left Dunbar house at 7.30 and went to a village called Kaneal. The road just as it leaves Mackay's house is steep for about $\frac{1}{4}$ of a mile and then is nearly level the whole way to Kaneal. The road to Kaneal is throughout picturesque and the hillsides are covered with violets and other pretty wild flowers. The two ladies and Johnstone rode part of the way going and rode back the whole way. Mackay and I walked both going and coming and were none the worse for it. After breakfast I read about 100 pages of *Treasure Island*, a book written by George [*sic*] Stevenson and just before we went into tiffin Mackay and Mrs. Johnstone had a set of tennis at which the former was ignominiously licked, getting only three games out of the set. After tiffin, Johnstone and I joined in the tennis and the sides were Mrs. J. and myself against Messrs. M. and J. but we were beaten, they having got two out of the three sets. Went for a walk in the evening towards Captain Banon's house but I did not see the Captain though I was anxious to see him for I heard he was growing an enormous amount of brushwood on the top of his head. Played whist after dinner and retired to bed at 10 p.m.

Dobhi. 23rd April. Set to work making a wooden box for 10 lb. of tea which was to go to Major Rennick, while the mollies and the two coolies worked at watering the apple garden. Kusro coolie left with the ten lb. of tea for Bajoura and should reach this evening. Minnikin sent over a coolie for the walnut plank which I made over to the coolie. The plank was 5 ft. 4 ins. long,

---

* Mr. Mackay was married to a high caste Brahmin girl called Baghti. She used to go about in a rickshaw with a man riding behind her on a white pony with a sword in his hand.

1 ft. broad and 4 in. thick. Minnikin wanted to make a tea drier, and if worthwhile I shall make one too. Received a letter from Captain Lee to say that he will be here for breakfast tomorrow so I wrote back to say that I would wait for him till 12 noon. Sent three cut glasses to Mrs. Johnstone for her picture frames, and also an iron curtain ring and some large wooden rings for curtains, as also some flowers, chiefly roses. Gave out a good many leases for land today. My drawing room was finished this evening. Retired to bed at 9.30 p.m.

Dobhi. 28th April '87. Got up at 5.30 a.m. and had *chota hazari* [early morning tea] out of bed. Put the men working at 6.30 a.m. During the day made up an estimate as to the amount of grain I should receive and find the amount of wheat I should get from Mandalgar Kothi should be 550 *bhars* [no one knows this measure], and about 260 *bhar* from Baragar Kothi. Sent two leopard skins for a reward and got 6 rupees for both notwithstanding both of them were full grown leopards, and I should have got 8 rupees each, 16 in all. Got a letter from Mrs. Johnstone asking me to send back the soda water bottles so shall send them tomorrow. The post came in at 2 p.m. with a letter from Robin [alias Duncan Donald, alias 'Miss Youghall's Syce] and some poetry. He rhymes the word month by the word front: thus . . .

> Thirty days had passed which counts a month
> Behind a tree she sat and he in front
> They were as lovers of the fondest kind
> With no defects in manner or in mind.

[Evidently Robin had more talent for speaking the dialects of the North-West Frontier than he did for writing verse.]

Manali. 13th May '87. Had a Europe morning [i.e. got up at about 7.30 a.m. instead of 5.30 a.m.] Began to play tennis about 8 o'clock and had three sets before breakfast. The sides were Mackay and Rennick against Miss Randolph and myself. After breakfast we went for a walk and saw Monali [*sic*] Fort which is about a mile and a half from Dunbar house and stands above the Monali village; There is a lovely view from the fort. There were a good many clouds about but it did not rain. In the evening we again played tennis and had some good sets. Retired to bed about 10.30 p.m.

Dobhi. 6th June '87. Got a report early in the morning to say that the leopard had been all about the place but did not let off the spring gun so I allowed the gun to remain there for the day and the following night. Dr. Carlton came here in the morning and remained to breakfast. At 1 o'clock Carlton and I left for Aramgarh where we met Messrs. Bateman and Harvey. After tiffin we went to Bundrole and had some pretty fair games of tennis. Just as we were to leave Capt. Lee asked for his second son to be baptised which detained us for another hour and Minnikin and I are the God Fathers, though the ceremony was done much against my wish. [Hilary Donald thinks this was because the unfortunate baby was born out of wedlock.]

Dobhi. 11th June '87. Went out and arranged some half produce in Mandalgar Kothi and have got a fair amount of wheat. Minnikin came over here about 1 o'clock and stayed to tiffin, then I returned with him, and when we got to Aramgarh both Lawley and Coates were in bed with Diarrhoea, so did not see the former but the latter appeared for dinner and is an old man and seemed to have done some travelling and is well informed. In the evening went up to a village close to Aramgarh where a lot of cattle had eaten the bowler grass and were dying off— Minnikin and I cured those that we took in hand by pouring apricot oil and chillies down their throat.

Manali. 11th July '87. Had a Europe morning, and as it was raining heavily I still prolonged my stay in bed. Had breakfast at 9.30 a.m. after which I had some games of tennis with Mackay and won a bet of 5 rupees which made us quits as I had lost 5 rupees the day before. There were heavy clouds at Monali about 12 o'clock but I did not pay heed to the weather and left Monali and did not get a drop on my way down. I had not been home an hour when Robin turned up and I was awfully glad to have him as a companion. I brought some apple cuttings from Mackay's apple trees and budded them which I hope will take. Robin brought four small tables from Suket which have quite set up my drawing room. Robin also brought some fine Bombay mangoes and didn't I enjoy them. The night had a few clouds and it was close.

The Hall, Nagar, built by Colonel Rennick in the 1880's; subsequently bought by Professor Nicholas Roerich and now used as an Himalayan Cultural Centre

Professor Nicholas Roerich with his two sons, George and Svetoslav, at Nagar, 1931

Miss Hilary and Miss Barbara Donald in their stable yard at Tignal's Cottage, near Borden, Hampshire

Dobhi. 4th August 1890. Sent off seven *kiltas* of fruit to Simla early in the morning. Went after breakfast to Raisen and then Wood and I went after four black bears but did not see them. Returned with nothing. Found Dyson here and we played cards (snap). It began to rain at 7 p.m. and flying foxes came in great numbers and destroyed a good many apples but very few pears. Shot one.

In the spring of 1893 Willie Donald applied for the job of P.W.D. engineer in charge of roads and bridges in the whole of the Kulu sub-division which included the Indo-Tibetan provinces of Lahul and Spiti. His daughters tell me that he had had no training for this class of work, merely a few years' first-hand experience of repairing mule-tracks and bridges on his own and Colonel Rennick's estates. But in those days you could often get government posts with good character references and Willie's daughters have preserved three chits by means of which their father landed the desired job, one of which says:

I have known Mr. W. H. Donald of Dobi, Kulu for some years.

He is thoroughly acquainted with the Kulu people and their language and, from what I have seen, appears to have considerable influence among them.

I consider that he would be well fitted for the post of Subdivisional Engineer in Kulu as he has had experience of the class of work required.

He is energetic and hardworking.

(Signed) St. G. Gore.*

Major R.E. In charge Himalaya Survey Party. Simla 21st April, 1893.

Thus for the next twenty-five years Willie Donald spent a good part of his life in remote rest-houses and under canvas, trekking from one road works to the next and supervising the maintenance of the innumerable bridges which, during the monsoon season, were frequently destroyed by floods. One of his greatest problems was the upkeep of the bridges in the virtually treeless highlands of

* This was the brother of F. St. J. Gore who wrote *Indian Hill Life*.

Spiti and Lahul, for some of which deodar planks had to be carried up by mule from Kulu. The traders from Central Asia, having safely crossed a bridge with their pony train, frequently turned round, pulled it to bits and used the precious wood for fuel! Willie Donald's diary entry of July 11th, 1894, records:

> Left Zinzinbar 14,000 feet 3.30 a.m. arrived on Bara Lacha Pass 16,047 feet 6 a.m. rode as far as huts Zinzinbar on Suraj Dal lake. Arrived Kenlung at 9 a.m. Had breakfast Kenlung—hired a pony from Kenlung to Sarchu 9 miles and walked back to Kenlung. Arrived in Kenlung 8 p.m. Inspected road and saw Sarchu bridge broken, only 4 pieces timber lying there. The rest of wood burnt by traders . . . coolies with headaches and two were snowblind for 3 hours.

At the beginning of the twentieth century Donald acquired land at Nagar and founded the Kutbai estate on which he built a house for himself and his family to reside in during the hot weather, that is when they were not on trek. In this most beautiful of all the Kulu villages the Assistant Commissioner lived in The Castle. Colonel Rennick in The Hall, so Donald called his new house The Manor, though anything less like an English manor house could hardly be imagined. It is simply an oblong bungalow with a corrugated iron roof and a one-room upper storey added as an afterthought, used as a schoolroom by his two daughters. Along the front of the house there is a narrow terrace with a mown lawn and flowerbeds; the view across the valley to the east and up to the snow peaks of Lahul to the north is magnificent. To the south stand the farm buildings: cowsheds, fruit stores and stables, where Barbara and Hilary kept their beloved ponies, which they not only used for transport but for polo as well, playing three-a-side on a small piece of flat land on their father's other estate, Dobi, with the Raja of Mandi and Pandit Balak Ram as well as various visitors who came from Simla. Now, sadly, the stables are put to other uses, for ponies have largely been replaced by beastly jeeps.

Below the garden, in a series of terraces, are the orchards planted and tended by Willie Donald with such expert care, for as well as leading a full life as the Sub-divisional Engineer, he still managed to grow some of the finest fruit in Kulu, as his trade card announces:

FINEST KULU FRUITS.

Cherries.	Plums.	Peaches.		Pears Apples.	Persimon & Fresh Walnuts
May-June.	*June-July.*	*July-August.*		*July to December.*	*October to December.*

5 lbs. nett in 6 lbs. basket by post @				8 lbs nett in 10 lbs. basket by post @ Rs	
„ ' „ „ Rail @					Rail @ „... ..
				14 „ 20 Cases	„ @ „ ...
				30 „ 40 „	„ ⁓@ „......

Grown from selected English, French, Italian and Australian. varieties. Different kinds of each available during summer, autumn and winter, sent by shortest route and at cheapest rate securely packed all charges paid by R.V.P. post or Rail.

Pears and Apples took all first prizes at **Simla** Fruit Shows and **Calcutta Exhibition** and will arrive in good order in any part of India and Burma.

Kindly get your order registered early to avoid disappointment.
Fresh Dried Apples and Pears @ Rs ......per lbs. all the year round.
Fresh chestnuts in October 8 lbs net. @ Rs.......

Apply—**MANAGER,**
Dobi-Kutbai and Naggar Estate,
Dobi, P. O. Kulu, Punjab.

Tele :—
Donald-Kulu.

CHAPTER XIV

The Donald Sisters' Narrative

For the past few years I have been paying regular visits to Willie Donald's daughters, Barbara and Hilary, in their Hampshire cottage, and tape-recorded their reminiscences which provide a vivid picture of day-to-day life among the British community in the early years of the present century—from about 1905 to 1920.

Hilary: One of my most vivid childhood recollections was of being carried up the Rohtang Pass with Barbara in a *dhooly* (litter). I suppose we must have been about five and six at the time, when without any warning a landslide descended from the *khud* above us and a human head rolled down with the snow and stones. We were accompanying father on a road survey expedition and he and mother had gone in front on ponies. The head turned out to belong to a mail-runner who had been murdered the previous winter and had been buried in the snow. When the snow melted and the usual seasonal landslides started the body rolled down and the head came first. I can see it now on the rough path in front of the *dhooly* and hear the shrieks of our *ayah* who was climbing up the pass beside us.

Barbara: We used to go on trek a lot with our parents as father's job took him all over Kulu keeping the roads and bridges in order. When we were very small we were each put in a *kilta* and carried on a coolie's back, or sometimes the *kiltas* would be slung on either side of a donkey. Our milch cows came too and our cook and sweeper, as well as the man in charge of the animals.

H: Do you remember how upset our poor sweeper was once when a tin full of kerosene was tied on top of his bedding on a pack mule and leaked so that his bedding smelt for weeks?

B: When we grew old enough to do lessons we had a series of governesses and we were usually very unkind to them. They were mostly very bad riders so we loved to canter on ahead and the governess's pony would follow and she would always fall off, so when we got into camp that night we would be sent to bed as soon as the tents were up.

We had one governess called Miss Oakley who always said 'That'll do, that'll do.' One evening Hilary for some unknown reason decided to set the drawing-room curtains on fire and the governess was in her bath-tub so I rushed off and banged on the door and shouted: 'Miss Oakley the curtains are on fire!' But all she said was 'That'll do, that'll do.'

But we had one governess we liked very much, Miss O'Donoghue,

H: Yes, but she didn't last very long with us because she bumped her head on a low doorway in one of the dak bungalows when we were on trek and collapsed, so she had to be taken back to Nagar where mother nursed her for six months. The Indian doctor said she must have a charcoal stove under the bed to keep her warm. Later on she married an Australian, I think he was a horse dealer. Anyway, they went out to Australia together where he died and left her penniless with a baby son. She returned to India and worked as a governess again in order to earn money for her son's education. She was employed by a very distinguished Sikh called Sardar Jogendra Singh—later on he was knighted. After his first wife died she married him, but on condition that she could go to England once every two years to see her son. It was a very happy marriage.

When we were about ten we began to learn to shoot with a 20-bore shotgun and we used to practise on the tennis court at The Manor. Barbara was a very good shot and when we were a bit older we used to go out on shooting expeditions with our parents. We rode ponies for ten or fifteen miles up or down the valley, camped for the night, and the next morning we would walk up the mountainside or along a *nala* looking for game. When we got back to camp at night complete with dogs and guns and lanterns there was always a good dinner waiting. It was a lovely life. But I remember doing a dreadful thing once: we were going after red bear, high up near the top of one of the passes, mother, Barbara and me, father wasn't with us that time. We carried 557 Schnyder rifles.

B: No, they were 555 Express rifles.

H: Oh yes! I believe they were, anyway we sighted a bear and my mother was crawling along in front and I was behind her getting ready to shoot when my rifle suddenly went off and the bullet went clean through mother's legs without touching her. The *shikari* was so overcome he just sat down and kept repeating 'Miss Sahib the Gods are with us! the Gods are with us!' Then we all recovered and Barbara shot the bear dead.

B: At one stage we had a tame *kakar*, a barking deer, which actually came shooting with us: when he saw us getting the guns out and the dogs getting excited he got excited too so we all went into the forest together, the deer together with the dogs.

H: Yes, one of the Forest Department coolies brought him to us as a baby, he said he'd found him deserted on a path. We called him Dickie and we reared him on milk in one of the bathrooms at The Manor. When he grew up we let him roam about the Kutbai estate but he never forgot his milk so when we wanted him to come in we would clink a cup and saucer together and call 'Dickie, Dickie, Dickie' and he'd come barking down from the deodars. He was a wonderful pet but after he grew his horns we saw less and less of him.

B: We didn't see him for some time and thought he was gone for good and only hoped he hadn't been eaten by a panther. Then we went down country to Amritsar for a week or so and got a wire from a *babu* at Katrain, saying 'Dickie deer found on the behind of Shim.' Shim is a village near Katrain. So we sent word to take him back to Nagar and afterwards we often saw him in the forest.

H: Do you remember that time we went pheasant shooting and couldn't hit anything? We were trying to get a couple of brace for the pot as we had friends coming to dinner later in the week. Barbara and I went into the woods behind The Manor and the dogs put up some birds and we shot and nothing dropped; then we walked on and again the dogs put up some birds and nothing dropped. After this had happened five or six times the dogs looked round with puzzled expressions on their faces as if to say 'What has come over you?' So in the end we just had to go home and tell the servants we couldn't hit anything and they said 'The Gods must be angry, take your guns to the *pujari* of Narsingh.' We thought it would be rather fun to see what he

said, so we went along to the little wooden temple near The
Castle and the *pujari* looked at our guns and said we wouldn't
be able to shoot anything with them until we had offered up a
sacrifice to *devata* Narsingh. We told our servants and they took
along a lamb and the next day we went back into the woods with
the dogs and we shot three or four brace in under an hour!

In those days doctors and nurses were very scarce in Kulu and
the local people used to come to us and expect us to cure them of
all sorts of ills. Barbara had a great reputation for cures. One
day a young man was carried to her by his parents who said
'Here he is: do something. He's no good to us, he can't work in
the fields and we can't afford to keep him. We can't just let him
die so do something.' The poor boy had terrible ulcers with a
huge hole in his leg the size of a saucer. But Barbara managed to
cure him after several months of treatment because he did what
she told him. She gave him various herb pills and dressed his
leg every day. He lived in the servants' quarters and after two
months he was able to walk and eventually got absolutely all
right and returned to his home. He used to come back every
rice season and bring us some rice and honey to show his
gratitude.

B: One summer we met his mother at a local *mela* and she was
covered with jewellery. She said '*Salaam Miss Sahib!* Thank you
very much for curing my son!' So we said to her 'But you told us
you were too poor to keep him! You don't look very poor!'
'But we couldn't afford to keep him doing nothing could we?
Now he can work, he is ploughing the fields so he's of use to us.'

H: I know you want us to tell you about some of the old Kulu
residents. Well, there was the mystery man, Mr. Theodore.
Nobody knew who he really was. I think he came to the valley
in the 'seventies. Anyway, he bought a lot of land at Dobhi, a
village near where the Phojal river runs into the Béas, and
converted a wool godown into his house and lived like a *zamindar*.
He did his own spinning and wore the real Kulu tweed suit
which the men don't wear often today, except at *melas*.

B: He spoke the local dialect fluently, but his English was very
broken. German was said to be his native language. There was
always a certain amount of speculation as to who he was: he
seemed to have plenty of money, and the rumour got round that

he was the vanished Duke of Hapsburg. At some time or other this duke reappeared in Austria at the very time when Mr. Theodore was absent from Kulu for about six months.*

H: Theodore himself left the Dobhi estate to our Aunt Nellie Anderson, father's sister. He wanted to leave it to her husband Alex Anderson but he was a government servant so could not accept. We still have a copy of the will which reads:

> This is the last Will of me J. Theodore, the present owner of Dobi estate in Kulu, Kangra District, Punjab.
> I give and bequeath, to Mrs. Nelli [*sic*] Anderson, the present wife of Alexander Anderson, Esq., formerly Assistant Commissioner of Kulu, Punjab, all my property, here in India (in India only) all my house and land, and all belonging to me, and all and every item of my estate, and all my money here in India (in India only). Whilst writing this Will, I am in full power of my senses and of sound mind. (Dated Koksar, 3rd August, 1883.)

B: You see he twice puts 'in India only', from which one gathers that he had property elsewhere. He died round about 1900 and was buried in the Dobhi orchard beside our Great-Grandfather Minnikin, who originally came here direct from Ireland to manage the Kulu Tea Company. The orchard was washed away in the dreadful floods of 1947 and the graves with them.

H: Our Aunt Nellie could not run the estate because Alex Anderson was stationed down-country when his time was up as the A.C. of Kulu, so she made it over to our father and her youngest sister. We inherited it in 1945 and sold it to the present Rani of Rupi's father, who gave it to his daughter as a dowry when she married the Rai.

B: We were always told that Alex Anderson was the only person

---

* A leading English historian of the Hapsburg family, Mr. Edward Crankshaw, wrote in reply to an enquiry from the author: 'I am not alas, very up in the personal ramifications of the Hapsburg family, and I can't for the life of me think who your Mr. Theodore might be. There *was* a missing Archduke towards the end of the last century. He was Archduke John Salvator, who quarrelled with his family and is officially supposed to have died off Cape Horn when a ship he had chartered went down with all hands. I have never been able to discover—though I haven't tried very hard—whether this was a fact or a convenient assumption.' 11.2.69.

who really knew who Mr. Theodore was but he was under a promise never to tell anyone.

H: The biggest English landowner in the valley was Colonel Rennick. He came here in the early 'seventies just when the Kulu Tea Company went into liquidation, so he was able to buy a lot of the company's land. He bought the beautiful Garh estate at Bajaura at the southern end of the valley where he lived in the winter, and the land in Nagar on which he built the house which he called The Hall you have seen, and the property has been known as The Hall estate ever since. He also had land at Narkanda where he grew potatoes on a big scale and started a factory to make potato flour. Colonel Rennick was one of the pioneer apple-growers and he made very good cider: friends who drank it at dinner always said they had seen the Rani's ghost when they rode past Nagar Castle on their way home afterwards.

B: When Colonel Rennick's regiment was on a campaign in Persia he eloped with a Persian Princess and married her. They had a son called Frank Rennick who was killed in the First World War in the famous charge of the 40th Pathans.

H: We only knew the Princess when she was an old lady but we loved her. She always spoke rather broken English and was very amusing. She had wonderful manners and was a very kind, really sweet person, and had quite a lot to put up with because the Colonel was irresistible to women and they to him.

B: The Princess had a companion called Miss Randolph and they built a house for her called Arcadia which is still a part of The Hall estate.* Poor Miss Randolph became very ill—it was cancer I suppose—and the Colonel who fancied himself as a leech used to bleed her and once we heard her scream 'Don't let him come near me!' She died at Arcadia during the First World War and is buried in the garden.

H: Soon after that a widow arrived in Kulu, a real adventuress called 'Midge'; everybody knew her as that and I don't know what her surname was. She succeeded Miss Randolph as companion to the Princess and one winter when they were living at Bajaura, old Mrs. Rennick died and everybody said that Midge had poisoned her, which is quite likely as the Princess was a very

* An oblong wooden chalet on a hill above The Hall, completely encircled by trees, so there is no view from the wide verandas.

healthy old lady. Of course the Colonel married Midge soon afterwards—I suppose he was nearly seventy at the time. They used to have awful rows. Midge went about in a rickshaw with four *janpanis* [rickshawmen] in very smart livery. When we heard a horse galloping furiously we would look over the edge of The Manor tennis court and see Colonel Rennick galloping like blazes, his horse's sides dripping with blood from the spurs, on his way to Bajaura, about twenty miles away. About an hour later down would come Midge in her rickshaw with all the bells tinkling and the *janpannis* running as fast as they could. 'Have you seen Bob?' she would ask us. 'He's not up at the Hall, he must have gone to Bajaura. I can't have it. I can't have it!' And off she'd go again. By the time she got there the Colonel was just starting to ride back to Nagar, but the poor *janpannis* were dead-beat and refused to go another yard so Midge was stuck down there until the next day and the Colonel had a little peace. It was quite like a musical comedy and happened again and again.

B: But Midge had some mysterious hold over him and in the end she made him take her to Europe. He sold The Hall estate to the Raja of Mandi in 1921 and the Garh estate at Bajaura to a Prince Effendi. I don't know what happened to the Narkanda property. He bought a villa in the hills near Florence where Midge got through his money very quickly and eventually he was picked up dying in a street in Florence and taken to hospital. All the money they found on him was about half a crown's worth of Italian lire.

H: Another well-known Kulu character was General Osborne who built Osborne House for himself, just above the temple of Tripura Sundari. He was a widower who retired to the valley in the late 'nineties. He used to go around followed by a high caste servant, a Brahmin I think he was, carrying a hookah for him. He was very keen on *mahseer* fishing—this was before the introduction of trout into the Kulu rivers. He and Colonel Rennick were always having rows over women and water. In the rice season there are always water rows: the villages on top take all the water for their crops and cut most of it off from the villages below so people go up and have a row with the men up the hill and there are free fights. Well, General Osborne had built himself a tank above his house but Colonel Rennick diverted all the water into his own fields and orchards so General Osborne went to see him and said he must let him have water according to the terms of agreement, but the Colonel said he was there first and had more right to the water than the General had and he would not let him have any. They shouted so loudly that Osborne's bearer rushed off to get the Assistant Commissioner as he thought they were going to shoot each other. In the end they had to have a court case. It was heard by Mr. Shuttleworth in Nagar castle, and finally the Colonel was ordered to let the General have a reasonable amount of water.

B: Then there were the Tyackes. They were stationed in Malta, and she was first of all married to a man who ill-treated her and one night she ran out of their house and took refuge with Colonel Tyacke who was a bachelor. Well, they ran off together which caused a great scandal at the time and they went all over Europe to try to escape the gossip-mongers and eventually came to Kulu where they rented a house at Raison from our Minnikin grandfather and lived happily ever afterwards.

H: They were both marvellous *shikaris* and spent all their time shooting big and little game of all sorts. She was a very small, pretty and incredibly tough little woman nicknamed 'Birdie', and she walked all over the mountains of Kulu and beyond dressed in an old-fashioned khaki suit with a tight waist and a long skirt with a red flannel petticoat underneath. She was a really brilliant shot and wrote a book called *How I Shot my Bears,** all about their shooting expeditions in Kulu and Lahul. The Colonel also wrote an excellent book about *shikar.*† I suppose nobody at that time knew the Western Himalaya better than the Tyackes: they went all over Spiti and Lahul and Chamba and Ladakh and Kashmir as well as Kulu. In spite of shooting so many bears and ibex and pheasants and other game, Birdie was mad about tame birds and animals and hated polo because she thought it was cruel to the ponies. She used to tell off any local people she thought were being cruel to animals and threaten them with the refusal of medicine if ever they were ill. But she

---

* Published in 1892.

† Col. R. H. Tyacke, *The Sportsman's Manual in Kullu, Lahoul, Spiti, etc.*, Thacker & Spink, Calcutta, 1893.

never minded shooting bears, even she-bears with cubs at foot, because they were cruel to other animals as well as dangerous to man. Barbara and I once saw a poor unfortunate bullock which had been let loose to graze come tearing down the hillside bellowing like blazes with a black bear perched on its quarters chewing hunks out of its back. Once they taste blood bears become flesh-eaters though their natural diet is vegetarian.

B: Black bears are specially dangerous at the time of the maize harvest when they like to gorge themselves with corn-on-the-cob all through the night and when daylight comes they fall fast asleep at the edge of the terraced field. A villager can easily trip over one mistaking it for a log, whereupon the bear wakes up and attacks. Bears tend to scalp people. Some of these poor men used to come to us with the most dreadful head wounds and expect us to cure them. We did what we could for them and sometimes got them right if they weren't too badly scalped.

H: Do you remember Colonel Tyacke's *syce* who got a great reputation as a weather prophet?

B: He was the *pujari* of the local temple and when the Tyackes left Raison and moved up to Nagar Colonel Tyacke gave the *syce* his barometer and the man hung it up in his house and did *puja* to it. The people said he was no longer the *pujari* of the Raison temple but kept his god in his house.

H: The Tyackes spent the last two years of their lives in Arcadia House at Nagar. I think Colonel Tyacke helped to run The Hall estate. When he died poor Birdie said 'Who will look after me now?' But she need not have worried for she was dead within a week herself and they were buried side by side in the garden. They were the most happy and devoted couple.

B: We could go on for hours talking about Kulu and the people we knew in the old days though, of course, we were away for five years at school in England. There were no aeroplanes then so you could not fly backwards and forwards for the holidays as European children do now.

In the late 'twenties Hilary and I decided to go to England and we started a riding school at Hendon which we ran till the beginning of the Second World War, when we went into the Army Remount Depot at Melton Mowbray. Then, in 1944, our father died and left us the Dobhi and the Kutbai estates, so the following year we got our release from the depot and went back to Kulu. As soon as we had probate we sold the Dobhi estate and lived up at The Manor, farming the Kutbai estate.

H: During the troubles in 1947 the Hindus started burning down Muslim houses and some Muslims from Katrain came and took refuge in our house. We had had warning from some refugees from Lahore that the older men could not control the young men and that they were determined to burn The Manor. All our servants left except the old sweeper and we thought the best way to protect ourselves was to take some of the calves indoors then we knew the Hindus wouldn't burn the house down. We kept them in the bathrooms.

B: We sat up for six days and six nights with our guns beside us and our six precious cartridges. It was impossible to get a licence for ammunition of any kind in 1947 because it was the policy of the British Government not to allow Europeans to have weapons —I suppose they thought we might cause more trouble. We sat up in the room at the top of the house which used to be our schoolroom and had a wide view up and down the valley and took it in turns to sleep.

H: We were very worried about the ponies; we thought the Hindus might come and pour kerosene over them and set them alight as we heard they'd already done this to some of the ponies belonging to Muslims.

At the end of six days things seemed quieter so we advised our Muslims to go to the *thesil* at Sultanpur [now Kulu] and ask for police protection while we rode down to Lerar, a small village beside the river, to get stores. There was a very anti-British schoolmaster there and the local village children stoned us which made us furious as we had always been on the very best terms with the Kulu people; we chased the children into the rice fields laying into them with our whips. They were terrified and ran away like blazes in all directions.

B: One evening a few days later, when we were feeding our dogs up at The Manor, the old sweeper came running in and said there were twenty or thirty men all armed with *lathis* coming up the road. We went out to meet them and they turned out to be the headman, *pujaris* and people of Narshala village and the head-man said 'Miss Sahib, we've come to protect you: there are a lot of bad men about. We will sit on your lawn from dusk till dawn and we will look after you and let no one near your house. We do not like to see old friends insulted.' And so at last we were able to go to bed and did not have to worry any more. At the end of a week they came and said: 'Things are all right now Miss Sahib, so we'll go.'

H: When we asked them what we could give them in return for their kindness they said 'Nothing at all: we could not possibly take any money from you, we came to look after you.' So we insisted on giving them each a basket of fruit and off they went. Meanwhile the Muslims who had left The Manor had divided into two lots: some of them thought of going for safety to the remote valley of Malana, but they never even got as far as the Chanderkhani Pass. The Hindus in one of the villages on the way up heard they were coming and took away the struts from an artificial path along the face of a precipice so that when the Muslims walked along it the path gave way and they all fell into the bottom of the rocky gorge and were killed.

B: The ones who took our advice and went to Sultanpur fared no better as the police picked them off one by one with their rifles instead of giving them protection. The police were just as bad as anyone else during the troubles. Up here they were all Hindus. They were mad, absolutely mad—and in Muslim centres it was the other way round, the Hindus were massacred by the Muslims.

After the change-over in 1947 things were very different in Nagar, many of our girlhood friends had died or had left India, and most of the educated Indians we met were visiting officials, not residents.

H: Then the trippers started coming up the valley, more and more of them every summer. They weren't really interested in the Kulu people at all but were simply in search of a good holiday. They fished or they shot, or they climbed, but they were just birds of passage. There was no real social life in the valley any more.

B: And it became increasingly difficult to get our fruit out of Kulu. It all had to be packed in boxes to go by lorry and there were never enough lorries and you could never get them to come just when you wanted them. In the old days it was so much easier as the coolies came to the orchards and the fruit was packed in *kiltas* which they carried on their backs, 40 lb. to each man. But with the coming of motor transport everything became so complicated: one was frustrated at every turn.

H: So the long and short of it was that we decided to sell the Kutbai estate in 1952 and return to England for good. We bought this cottage with a twelve-acre field and have been living here ever since breeding hunters, taking horses at livery and giving riding lessons to the local children.

CHAPTER XV

Nicholas Roerich

'In the history of the fine arts certain individuals have appeared from time to time whose work has a unique, a profound and indeed mystical quality which differentiates them from their contemporaries, making it impossible to classify them in any known category or to ally them with any school because they resemble themselves only—and one another—like some spaceless and timeless order of initiates. Such were Leonardo, Rembrandt, Dürer, Blake, and in other fields Beethoven and Balzac. . . . Their work shows flashes of that daemonic and eerie beauty which is the sign whereby they may be identified as belonging to that mythical mystical brotherhood. Roerich in his life, in his character and in his art reveals himself as a member of this fraternity.'*

'Through the societies dedicated to him in all countries the name of Nicholas Roerich is so universally proclaimed and impressed upon human hearts, not only as master of the brush but also as a thinker and builder of life.'†

'Like a great reverberant note, the voice of Nicholas Roerich —master of our day—has penetrated into all countries and resounded in the spirit of all peoples.

'His paintings are treasured in the greatest museums and collections of the world, and America has dedicated a permanent monument to his art in the Roerich Museum in New York, devoted to his works.

'As his latest step Roerich has turned towards the East. There, facing the white ramparts of the world, the Himalayas, his genius sounds a cosmic note, and he fulfills that magnificent panorama of art to which this Monograph is devoted. Transmitting for us the beauty of those summits which surmount the heavens, Roerich

---

* From Claud Bragdon's Introduction to *Altai Himalaya*, by Nicholas Roerich, New York, 1929.

† From the Introduction to *Realm of Light* (6th volume of the American edn. of Nicholas Roerich's *Works*).

Mrs. Tyacke, 1892. A picture entitled 'My Trophies' from her book *How I shot My Bears*

Dashal, Shaivite temple of Gaurishankar, and a carving of the female doorkeeper, possibly the Goddess Yamuna

proclaims his message—the message of the victory of the spirit of man, and of the approaching unity of all peoples in the name of Beauty and Truth.'*

Nicholas Roerich was the only European settler in the Kulu valley who, for a time, achieved world fame. Today, outside of India and Russia (where he has recently been culturally rehabilitated) it is rare to find anyone who has heard of him.

Nicholas Konstantinovich Roerich was born in St. Petersburg in 1874 where, as a young man, he first fulfilled his father's wishes by studying law, but switched over to painting as soon as he had graduated. He was also deeply interested in prehistoric Russia and took part in a number of digs including the excavation of tumuli on his father's estate, and made a name for himself as an archaeologist by his contributions to learned journals. To these rapidly developing and versatile talents he added an intimate knowledge of Russian folk-art derived from the museums and workshops of Abramtsevo and Talaskino, two centres for the revival of cottage industries, where many professional artists used to go and work at wood-carving and design stage sets for Vasnetsov's private opera theatre. The latter activity was to prove a revolution in theatrical history as it soon led to the replacing of the traditional craftsmen stage designers by professional artists throughout Europe.

In October 1898 the first number of *Mir iskusstva, The World of Art*, appeared. This was a journal edited by Diaghilev to which Roerich was a regular contributor for the six years of its short but influential life. It sought to express the ideal of Art for Art's sake: 'Art was seen as a form of mystical experience, a means through which eternal beauty could be expressed and communicated—almost a new kind of religion.' And Bakst, who designed the magazine's emblem, wrote: 'The World of Art is above all earthly things, above the stars, there it reigns proud, secret and lovely as on a snowy peak.' These words might just as well have been written by Roerich himself who was a complete child of his time, a *fin de siécle* idealist whose visionary view of the world persisted throughout his life.

In the summer of 1903 he travelled extensively in Russia paint-

* From the Introduction to *Roerich—Himalaya*, A monograph, Brentano, New York, 1926.

ing and recording churches and other monuments, in the process of which he became a passionate conservationist. 'Learning persistence from the stones,' he wrote in *The Renewed Earth*, 'I preach continually about the beauty of the national heritage. I repeat it in the most varied publications before the most varied public.'

The seventy-five oil paintings which he brought back from his Russian journey were exhibited in 1904 and seen by the Emperor who said he wanted the whole collection to go to the museum of Alexander III. War with Japan unfortunately interfered with the realisation of this plan and the collection went to the St. Louis exhibition after which the pictures were sold and dispersed throughout the United States.

Early in the twentieth century Russian decorative art came into its own and Roerich turned his attention to theatrical design which attracted him by the opportunities it gave for work on a monumental scale. Several members of the 'World of Art' group had continued to collaborate for some years after the journal had died a natural death and undoubtedly the greatest fruit of their labours was Diaghilev's Russian Ballet Company which had its first season at the Thèatre Châtelet in Paris during the summer of 1909. Here the demanding French public was able to judge the best of contemporary Russian art for the first time. And what a feast they were given! The music of Rimsky Korsakov, Moussorgsky, Glinka, Borodin, Tchaikovsky and Glazunov; the dancing of Pavlova, Karsavina, Fokine and Nijinsky; the décor of Bakst, Benois, Korovine and Roerich. During the season Roerich enjoyed the highest praise from the critics for his décor and costumes for the Polovtsian dances from *Prince Igor*, a success which he was to repeat with a new set of designs for the same ballet a few years later. In 1919, when the five hundredth performance was reached he received the following telegram:

Te félicite gros succès 500me spectacle Igor, ton décor a enthusiasmé public de tous pays. Amitiés. Diaghilev.

But among his many commissions for stage design before the First World War probably none gave him greater pleasure than *Le Sacre du Printemps*. The subject, the heathen cult of earth worship, was just to his taste because of his study of prehistoric Russia. This marvellous ballet was the result of a close collaboration between Roerich, Stravinsky and Nijinsky, and as well

as designing the décor and costumes Roerich was largely responsible for the libretto and the composer dedicated the work
to him. The world première took place in 1913 at the Thèatre
Champs-Elysée in Paris and immediately caused a great sensation.
The sound of whistling and roaring at times drowned the or-
chestra for the performance called forth rapturous praise from
some quarters and angry protest from others. Since those far-off
days *Sacre* has taken its place as one of the great masterpieces of
the Diaghilev Ballet.

At the time of the Russian Revolution, Roerich had to decide
whether or not to clear out. On March 4th, 1917, Maxim Gorky
called a meeting of people involved in the arts and a committee
was elected named the Council of Art Affairs which met at the
Winter Palace. For two months Roerich worked as its chairman,
after which he took his family to Finland. That autumn several
people came to Serdobol to beg the artist to return to St. Petersburg, as he and Benois were candidates for the Portfolio of Minister of Fine Arts. But he decided against returning and, after
wintering in Finland, made his way to England where Diaghilev
suggested that he should hold an exhibition of his paintings.
Accordingly one was arranged at the Goupil Gallery in the spring
of 1920 under the title 'The Spells of Russia', the sponsors of
which included H. G. Wells, Frank Brangwyn, Lord Glenconnor
and Sir Samuel and Lady Maude Hoare.* Two paintings from it
were presented by the Comité d'Honneur to the Victoria and
Albert Museum, 'A Sketch in the North', and 'The Polovetzky
Camp', a stage design for the Diaghilev Ballet.

At this time Albert Coates, who had been conductor of the
Imperial Opera at St. Petersburg, introduced Roerich to Sir
Thomas Beecham who gave him several commissions to do stage
sets for Covent Garden. Later that year he sailed for America at
the invitation of the Chicago Art Institute to exhibit his works
throughout the country. For the succeeding decade he became an
international figure because of his aim to unify humanity through
art. This was the sort of ideal which appealed greatly to the more
starry-eyed type of American and Roerich soon collected around
him a devoted circle which developed into a cult, with himself as *guru*.

* For a review of this exhibition see N. Jarintzov, 'A Russian Painter: N. K.
Roerich', *Studio*, Vol. 79, No. 325, April 15th, 1920, p. 60.

The following year, 1921, he founded the Master Institute of United Arts with the ambitious programme of establishing 'faculties for piano, organ, harp, violin, violincello, voice, ear-training, theory and composition, orchestral, instrumental and church music; painting and drawing, applied design, theatrical décor, interior decoration, illustration, etching, sculpture, architecture, ballet, Dalcroze eurythmics, drama, journalism and languages'.

In the same year, in the month of June, Roerich and his wife joined the Theosophical Society but remained active members for only two years. They never resigned, but simply allowed their membership to become inactive. Presumably the *guru* preferred to be boss of his own esoteric group whereas the remarkable Annie Besant was already leading the Theosophists.

In November 1923 Professor—as he was now known—and Madam Roerich and their two sons sailed for India and went on the first of their trans-Himalayan expeditions. On their return to the States in the following year a museum was founded in 'the Master's' honour to house his own paintings and the treasures of Himalayan art which he had collected. From 1926–8 the Roerich family, financed by American admirers, embarked on a longer expedition to many remote parts of central Asia including Tibet, the Altai mountains and the Gobi desert. Apart from being able to indulge his passion for art and archaeology the explorer also conducted research into the mystical cults of these regions and became convinced that the Second Coming was to take place in Mongolia. In Tibet he claimed to have discovered an ancient Buddhist chronicle which stated that Christ had spent the 'hidden years' partly there and partly in India. This, in fact, was nothing new as there has always been a strong tradition that these were spent in Kashmir where a collection of Our Lord's sayings from this mysterious period of his life is still preserved: one of them was quoted by Akbar on his Victory Gate at Fatehpur Sikri: 'Said Jesus, on whom be peace! The world is a bridge, pass over it but build no house there. He who hopeth for an hour, may hope for eternity; the world is but an hour, spend it in devotion; the rest is worth nothing.'

After this Roerich lived largely in Kulu for the remaining eighteen years of his life, apart from one more Central Asian expedition in the mid-thirties. From The Hall estate in Nagar which he bought from the Raja of Mandi, he wrote regularly to his followers in New York who, in return for his greatly sought after spiritual advice, sent him handsome monthly payments so that he was relieved of all financial worries for the rest of his days. He and his family do not seem to have mixed with the English settlers in the valley and Hilary Donald recalls:

The fruit-planters of Kulu did not care for the Roerichs as they considered themselves V.I.P.'s and the planters well beneath them, so I don't think anyone ever saw the inside of their house who was not a government official or visitor of standing. So of course we neither knew nor cared how important the outside world considered them.

Knowing very little about the artist-writer-explorer-archaeologist-*guru*'s distinguished career we visited the Roerichs in Nagar in September 1931 with instructions from Simla to try to form an opinion as to whether or not the Professor was a spy. I presume his wanderings in Central Asia had brought him under the suspicion of playing a late round in the Great Game, especially as he was known to have gone to Moscow during the course of his travels in the 'twenties. Anyway, I had not the slightest idea how to conduct a spy test, and when we called at The Hall, I simply engaged in a fascinating conversation on Indian philosophy in which Nicholas Roerich was deeply versed. He was then in his middle fifties, completely bald but wearing a white two-pronged beard. Had he been dressed in silk robes instead of tweed breeches and a Norfolk jacket he could easily have passed off as a Chinese sage. He presented my mother and me with his most famous book, *Altai Himalaya*, about his Central Asian explorations. This, I confess, I have never found easy to read. Instead of being a direct account of the fascinating places he saw it is a series of vignettes, anecdotes, legends, reflections, and passages of theosophical jargon often unconnected and jumping about from one place to another so that you never know where you are. But here and there some interesting comments stand out: 'Over the mountains rings out the forging of the sword, and the call of the Valkyrie, and the magic fire music and the roar of Fafner. I remember Stravinsky once was ready to annihilate Wagner. No Igor, this heroic realism, these harmonies of achievement are not to be destroyed. And the music of Wagner is also true and rings remarkably in the mountains.'*

It is completely consistent with his character to learn that Roerich was a keen Wagnerian.

With the Professor on the occasion of which I write, were his two sons, George with a pointed golden beard, and Svetoslav with a pointed black one. George became a distinguished orientalist and Svetoslav† a good painter whose portrait of Nehru hangs in the Indian Parliament building in New Delhi. Madame Roerich we did not meet. It was rumoured that she was anti-British: a dedicated spiritualist and a fine handsome woman judging by her son's portrait of her which now hangs in the New York Roerich Museum. She was a grand-niece of Field-Marshal Kutuzov who, in a sense, defeated Napoleon through his brilliant strategy of indefinite retreat.

Meanwhile the combined Roerich Museum and the Master Institute of United Arts had been housed in a twenty-nine-storey skyscraper on Riverside Drive built in honour of the artist-sage and designed by the architect Harvey Wiley Corbett. Over a thousand of his paintings were hung in a special gallery designed for them in the new building, including a cycle of five hundred executed during the artist's Central Asian expeditions. Roerich was nothing if not prolific. The financial side had been arranged by Louis L. Horch, one of the Master's leading devotees who regarded him as an incarnation of a great World Teacher on a par with Christ and the Buddha, and who believed that his pictures had divine healing powers.

The laying of the corner-stone of the 'Master Building' on Riverside Drive had been performed with great éclat on March 24th, 1929, before several hundred distinguished guests, who included the official representatives of twenty foreign countries and of the leading museums and universities of the United States. Roerich himself was in Kulu at the time but sent a long message

* Letter to the author, May 20, 1969.
† He is also the author of *Art in the Kulu Valley*, published by the Roerich Museum, Nagar, Kulu, 1967.

which was read out after the delivery of several laudatory speeches. The message opened:

> Greetings to the Master Building!
> White, never surmounted rises the mountain, full glimmering with snow and icy its rocky ridges. . . . Beauty is the conqueror and knowledge the invincible shield. . . . Let these, the Precious and the Beautiful dwell unextinguishably within these walls. Let the united thoughts, as a creative stronghold lend their power to the beneficent beginnings.
> Hail to the builders! Hail to the building! Its very name is adorned by that conception, precious to the world, that of the Teacher.

At the conclusion of the Master's message, Mr. Horch placed a sixteenth-century Rajput casket in a specially prepared cavity in the cornerstone.

* * *

It was some time during the late 'twenties that Henry Agard Wallace, one of the most controversial politicians in America's New Deal government, became involved with the Roerich cult. He visited the Master at the original Roerich Museum (before the erection of the Master Building), studied his writings and wrote regularly to him and to some of his leading disciples, one of whom was Miss Frances Grant. A few years later, in 1933, when the *guru* was living in Kulu with his family and Wallace had been appointed Minister of Agriculture in Roosevelt's New Deal government, Miss Grant asked him to help her publicise the Master's scheme for the protection of cultural treasures and the promotion of world peace, to be known as the 'Roerich Pact'. The praiseworthy idea was that all the nations of the world should agree not to attack churches and museums as well as hospitals. Just as the latter already flew a Red Cross flag in time of war so the former should fly Roerich's 'Banner of Peace', a red circle enclosing three spheres symbolising past, present and future. Wallace loved symbols and the 'Banner of Peace' appealed to him greatly. He organised the discussion of the plan by the League of Nations and in time his efforts resulted in the signing of the Roerich Pact at the White House by the representatives of twenty-two countries in April 1935.

Wallace, a mid-Westerner of Scottish-Irish descent, was brought up a United Presbyterian but became a high church Episcopalian when he grew up. He also studied eastern religions and eventually worked out a pantheistic synthesis for himself, believing that nature, science and religion are one. In spite of what some might call these spiritual fantasies, Wallace was a brilliant experimental farmer and plant geneticist who developed new strains of hybrid corn and strawberries. He was also a good businessman and ran his family's prosperous weekly *Wallace's Farmer*, the motto of which was 'Good Farming, Clear Thinking, Right Living'. It had been founded by his grandfather and was one of the most influential farming journals in the United States. In addition Henry Wallace was President of the Hi-bred (a play on hybrid) Corn Company, also founded by his family, the income from which enabled him to provide well for his wife and three children throughout an active political career of some fifteen years.

When Wallace is mentioned today many middle-aged Americans immediately recall his early policy of killing off millions of piglets to raise pig prices; but he soon came to realise that both this practice and that of ploughing-in excess crops was crazy, and he later created a food bank for peace with the object of exporting farm surpluses to starving countries: a noble idea which is now taken for granted but which, in those days, was uncharitably referred to by his detractors as 'milk for the Hottentots'. He was also the author of several New Deal slogans, the most famous of which, 'The Century of the Common Man', has passed into the English language on both sides of the Atlantic.

But undoubtedly Wallace's greatest work for American agriculture was in the sphere of soil conservation. In the early 'thirties large areas of the United States were developing into dust bowls through bad farming and Wallace introduced contour ploughing and deep-rooting grasses to counteract this menace. A fellow New Dealer, Thomas Corcoran, wrote of him: 'Every time you ride or fly over this country and see the condition of the land—the ploughed contours, the bulging granaries, the neat productive look—you think of Henry Wallace. He saved the land and then made it possible for this nation to feed the whole world.'

Arthur Schlesinger has summed up the two sides of Wallace's character, the practical and the mystical, very well in *The Coming of the New Deal*, 'The concrete and utilitarian mingled in Wallace with much that was vague and dreamy. His interest in crop genetics, in agricultural prices, in banking credit were the expression of a practical and exact intellectual curiosity. Yet, at a certain point, his mind seemed almost to break through a sonic barrier and transform itself, so that hard-headed analysis passed imperceptibly into rhapsodic mysticism.'*

One can see how greatly Roerich appealed to Wallace, for Roerich was a modern prophet both in appearance and in his utterances, and the Minister of Agriculture had a passion for prophets and a deep knowledge of Old Testament prophetical literature. 'Micah and Jeremiah, Elijah and Amos were almost as real to him as Senator Norris. He cited their views as he might those of the elder liberal statesmen with whom he lunched the day before.'†

Wallace was also absorbed with the symbolic content of much of Roerich's teaching and it was due to this that America had the Great Pyramid, with the All-Seeing Eye in the floating apex, printed on her one dollar bills from 1935 onwards. At the time he told the Secretary of the Treasury, Henry Morgenthau, that it would be most appropriate as *Novus Ordo* was the Latin for New Deal. *Novus Ordo Seclorum* is written underneath the pyramid in the Great Seal of the United States. I wonder how many Americans today think of Nicholas Roerich when they look at their one dollar notes?

In 1934 Wallace sent a scientific expedition to Mongolia to look for deep-rooting drought-resisting grasses to help him in his fight against soil erosion. He appointed Roerich as the leader, ostensibly because of the Professor's previous experience of travel in Central Asia but also, so it was rumoured, to look for signs of the Second Coming.

* Arthur Schlesinger, *The Age of Roosevelt*, Vol. II, *The Coming of the New Deal*, Boston, 1959, pp. 30-1.
† Ibid.

Kulu: the End of the Habitable World

The expedition was not a success. The scientists fell out with the leader; the Russians thought that Roerich was a secret agent spying for the Japanese, the Japanese that he was spying for the Russians, and the Chinese that he was spying for the Americans. Wallace was forced to recall him and in 1936 Roerich's service with the United States government officially came to an end. He never returned to America but spent the remaining years of his life happily in Kulu, painting and writing and collecting works of art, surrounded by primitive cults with strange rites and music which must have reminded him of *Le Sacre du Printemps*.

Simultaneously with the Master's dismissal, the richest and most influential of his disciples, Louis Horch, turned against him and won a lawsuit in New York whereby he and his wife gained complete control of the great skyscraper on Riverside Drive. From that day to this it has been known as the Master Institute of United Arts and Riverside Museum and all connections with the name of Roerich have been permanently severed. This was quite contrary to the resolution signed by the directors of the original Roerich Museum on July 24th, 1929, which states that:

We the trustees of the Roerich Museum, which is devoted to the art and ideals of this master, do hereby proclaim the museum as the property of the people of the United States of America. In proclaiming the Roerich Museum as the property of the American nation we do hereby declare it an unalterable condition thereof that the museum shall never be dissolved, sold nor change its name or its original purpose as a monument to the art of Nicholas Roerich, nor shall the walls ever be used for any other purpose than the exhibition of the paintings of this master.

Part of the collection of Tibetan art which the Master brought back from his earlier Central Asian expeditions is still housed in the Riverside Museum, but the majority—a thousand or so—of his own paintings were moved by his still-faithful followers to a small Victorian house now known as the Nicholas Roerich Museum, at 319 West 107th Street in New York, where selections of them may still be seen. The house is not big enough to show them all at once but different cycles of his works are on view at different times of the year. I was fortunate to see some of his early oil paintings of old Russia, and some of his sketches for *Prince Igor* and *Le Sacre*, which I much prefer to his later and largely mystical works in tempera. These give me the impression of having been 'knocked off' at a great rate and indeed he is said to have executed over seven thousand paintings in his lifetime: but they are still highly prized by members of the cult for whom, of course, they have an inner meaning.

Poor Henry Wallace never lived down his association with the Roerich cult and his subsequent political career was dogged by what became known as the '*Guru* Letters'. These were believed to have been written by Wallace to his *guru*, Roerich, and to a few of his leading disciples. Some of them fell into the hands of his Republican opponents who planned to use them as campaign ammunition when he stood for the Vice-Presidency in 1940. Fortunately this was stopped by Wallace's agents who threatened Wendell Wilkie, the Republican candidate, and several other leaders of the party with startling revelations about their private lives if the '*Guru* Letters' were published. In the end both sides decided to call it a day and Henry Wallace was duly elected Vice-President.

Seven years later, however, Wallace had left the Democrats and was actually standing for the Presidency as a member of what was believed to be the communist-dominated Progressive Party, when up popped the '*Guru* Letters' again. This time it was Westbrook Pegler, the most merciless columnist of his day, who got hold of them and published a selection in seven issues of the *Journal American* in March 1948. He admitted that there was no absolute proof that Wallace had, in fact, written the letters and that he had tried repeatedly—and failed—to get a direct answer from him. In the first devastating column attacking the Presidential candidate he wrote: 'I believe it would be a violation of the obligation of a reporter of our free press to withhold information which may bear on the mentality of one who, in conceivable circumstances, might become President next January 20th.'

The letters refer to the Buddha, Maitreya, Krishna, and others as the Great Ones, to Roosevelt as the Flaming One, but sometimes as the Wavering One; to Churchill as the Roaring Lion; to

Cordell Hull as the Sour One; to the British as the Monkeys and to the Russians as the Tigers. They are written in a sort of theosophical jargon, doubtless pregnant with meaning to the initiated, but boring bilge to outsiders, such as:

Dear Guru, I have been thinking of you holding the casket—the sacred and most precious casket. And I have thought of the new country going forth to meet the seven stars under the sign of the three stars. And I have thought of the admonition: 'Await the stones.'

We await the stones and we welcome you again to this glorious land of destiny, clouded though it may be with strange fumbling fears. Who shall hold up the compelling vision to those who wander in darkness? In answer to this question, we again welcome you. To drive out depression. To drive out fear. We think of the people of Northern Shambhalla and the hastening feet of the successor of Buddha and the lightning flashes and the breaking of the new day.

The Progressive party never had the remotest chance of winning the election, but owing partly to Pegler's campaign, poor Henry Wallace only got 1,150,000 votes out of a possible 49,000,000 and did not carry a single State.

Meanwhile the '*Guru*' had died peacefully in Kulu the previous year and his corpse was disposed of by Hindu rites. His *samahdi*, a large block of undressed stone, may be seen on a terrace below The Hall with the following inscription engraved upon it in Hindi:*

15th December 1947

Samvat 30 Magh 2004 Vikram Era
The great Friend of India
Maharshi Nicholas Roerich
The Last Rites were performed here
OM RAM

* *Samvat 30 Magh 2004 Vikram* indicates an Indian era—The inscription's end is a salutation to Rama, one of the most popular of Hindu gods.

CHAPTER XVI

From Nagar to Manali and Beyond

The twelve-mile walk or ride from Nagar to Manali is among the most beautiful in the world. To begin with the fertile valley is nearly a mile broad, but it gradually narrows as the mountains close in on either side. Torrents tumble into the alder-shaded river in a series of waterfalls and the track leads over frequent bridges through several villages with step cultivation in between and occasional deodar forests. At the northern end there is a great mountain wall, topped by the snow ridge above the Solang *nala*, to the right of which is the 13,400-feet Rohtang Pass.

In September 1965, accompanied for part of the way by my friends the Sinhas, I went on a temple tour along this track. Kiran (both men and women are called by this name) Sinha is a Bengali artist who has settled at Nagar where he has built himself a bungalow. His wife Gertrud is Austrian and they have a grown-up daughter nicknamed 'Bulbul' (nightingale) because of her beautiful voice. When Kiran paints the Mother Goddess she does not trample on a buffalo demon but on a Chinaman.

The track leaves Nagar below The Hall and descends into the spectacular Chhaki *nala* with a great waterfall above the *sangha* bridge and below it a lot of little stone water mills. Up this gorge runs the footpath which eventually brings you out on to the Chanderkhani downs some 7,000 feet higher up, and the pass leading to Malana, the remote stronghold of *devata Jamlu*.

The Manali road then winds up through deodars on the side of a hill to a wide stretch of gently terraced paddy-fields—greeny-gold in September—among which sits Sarsei, a village with a seventeenth-century *shikhara*-type temple dedicated to Krishna, and a chalet-shrine with three iron peacocks along the ridge pole. But under a deodar in the village street I found a stray sculptured panel which must once have formed part of a far older temple: pilasters supporting a triple Kashmiri style arch, beneath which stands a nine-inch figure of Shiva flanked by larger *chauri* bearers.

We asked the way to Dashal which stands about half a mile back from the Nagar–Manali road and where my good friend Pandit Balak Ram had told me there was an ancient stone temple still standing. We were directed eastwards along a footpath beside a little stream which meandered through paddy-fields across which we could see the village of Dashal with the roofs of its houses orange with maize cobs laid out to dry. To the south of it, on a high platform, we found the little temple we were looking for, in the classical style of the Indian plains, with the hideous blue tin notice-board planted beside it—a legacy I must shamefacedly admit of British rule—declaring it to be a protected monument. The tower, about 30 feet high, is slimmer and more elegant than that at Bajaura but the sculpture, though classical in style has, nevertheless, a far more *pahari* flavour. The temple probably also dates from around the ninth or tenth century though the dating of monuments in the Western Himalaya is still in the conjectural stage. The two enigmatic female figures facing one another on the entrance slabs with their freely flowing lines and swelling curves, partially concealed by pillars with pot and foliage capitals, are among the most moving pieces of sculpture I know, not only in the hills but anywhere in India. I call them enigmatic because their iconography is puzzling: they have not got the attributes of the river goddesses Ganga and Yamuna who so often face one another at the entrances to shrines in northern India. Instead they carry the trident of the Mother Goddess, and yet their position leads one to assume that they are more likely to be *dvarapalas*, doorkeepers or guardians.

The temple is dedicated to Shiva and Parvati under the form of Gaurishankar and stone slabs representing these deities with their sacred bull Nandi, lean up against the back inside wall. In front of them is the chief object of worship, a *linga* in a *yoni*, above which sits a curious devotional device consisting of an earthenware pot resting in a wooden framework on three legs. At the bottom of the pot a wick runs through a tiny hole and drips water on to the phallus night and day, for the *linga* of Shiva is believed by certain sects of Hindus to generate great heat which could easily burn up the whole universe if it is not kept cool.

I dearly wanted to photograph this little-known and beautiful classical temple in great detail but just as I was about to click my fourth shot the village headman came rushing up a side path and told me to stop, as all photography was prohibited during the Indo-Pak war.

My friends the Sinhas—I am eternally grateful to Gertrud for introducing me to the excellent watercress of the Kulu streams—left me and returned home to Kalpatoru, their bungalow in Nagar, and I walked on alone to the village of Haripur where I was anxious to see the temple of Dochamucha, one of the family goddesses of the Rai of Rupi, containing two standing images which Dr. Goetz believes to represent Scythian donors but which are now worshipped as *devis*. I subsequently learnt that this temple is not in Haripur at all but in the hamlet of Gajan, a few furlongs to the north-west. Because, as usual, I was mapless, I never succeeded in finding it; instead, I was wrongly directed eastwards up a steep pine-clad hill and after about a mile of puffing and panting I came upon a wooden mini *mandir* in a grove of deodars, a tiny chalet-type shrine containing no image of any kind. Having examined it carefully for folk-carving, of which there was none, I went out on to the open hillside and had my lunch of Kulu apples and a hard-boiled egg, looking towards my favourite view, the Solang *nala* at the head of the valley. I had barely finished eating when an unpleasant youth of about sixteen came up and shouted at me in his own peculiar Kulu dialect. I pretended to take no notice and began to walk off down the path to Haripur as quickly as I could, but was hotly pursued by the boy who started to throw stones at me. Thank God some older men suddenly appeared from the hamlet above and caught up with us and stopped the stoning—the ancient Hebrew punishment for blasphemy and adultery—and the headman asked me who I was. Owing to the war I took the precaution of carrying my passport everywhere so I produced it and having satisfied himself that I was not a Pakistani lady spy (there were said to be some about disguised as Europeans) I was allowed to proceed down the hill unmolested. I was told later that the mini *mandir* was in point of fact dedicated to Jamlu (who is never represented by either an image or a symbol) my Public Enemy Number One, and as I was wearing leather shoes this, rather than my possible prowess as a female spy, may have infuriated the youth, for Jamlu will not tolerate leather in any form near his temples.

Once back on the main track I continued northwards through Sajala where there is a small stone *shikhara* shrine containing images of Shiva and Parvati and a very pretty chalet-type temple dedicated to Vishnu with three tall sacred poles planted beside it; then on to Gojra, where there is a large stone tank—full of watercress—to the right of the road, with carvings of the god Narsingh along the back wall. On either side are small sculptured panels showing the lion *avatar* of Vishnu and a lively *nag* (serpent) scene, while a vigorous *pahari* stone lion stands astride the spout which feeds the tank. Above it stands the chalet-temple of Sitaram.

Eventually I reached Jagatsukh, one of the most interesting villages in the Western Himalaya which, under its old name of Nast, was the capital of Kulu before Nagar. It was here that, in the early sixteenth century, Sidh Pal met the goddess Hidimba, under the guise of an old woman, who prophesied that he would recover the kingdom of his ancestors [see Chapter X]. And it was here too that the dynastic name was changed from Pal to Singh, for when Sidh Pal was one day holding a calf for his Brahmin hostess while she milked the cow, a lion suddenly appeared which he killed on the spot and was from then on given the name Singh—lion—which he passed on to his successors.

At the southern end of the village there is a small white bunga-low, now the property of Pandit Balak Ram, which was originally built in the eighteen-eighties for the great father figure of Indian archaeology, General Sir Alexander Cunningham, who used it as his base for an expedition to Ladakh. In the early 'twenties an eccentric English woman artist, called Mrs. Budd, occupied the bungalow; she wandered up and down the valley on sketching expeditions with a large dog carrying saddlebags containing her painting things.

A few steps further on, to the right of the road, there is an open courtyard with a beautiful small *shikhara* temple about eight feet high on its far side; it is said to have been buried by a landslide many centuries ago and to have been dug out by order of Mr. Howell the Assistant Commissioner (1907–14) who introduced trout into the Béas in 1909. The shrine, like so many

Jagatsukh, detail of Sandhya Devi temple. The lower stone part is carved in the classical style, the upper part (where the grain of the wood is clearly visible) is decorated with nineteenth-century wood carvings

Jagatsukh. Durga slaying Mahisha, the buffalo demon; a stray image slab, about three feet high, in the classical style, leaning up against the base of the small temple of Gaurishankar. (See photo facing p. 126)

of this type, is dedicated to Gaurishankar, the popular *pahari* combination of Shiva and Parvati, of whom there is a carved stone slab leaning against the back wall of the interior in what I would call the local—and undateable—*pahari*, as opposed to the classical style, though the latter is in evidence on the exterior of the temple. Leaning up against the plinth are several image slabs of the same presumed early period—seventh to eighth century—as the carving still *in situ*, except for one icon of Durga killing the buffalo demon which may be of the eighth or ninth century. She wears the same triple crown as her counterpart at Bajaura but her body is less elongated and she has fuller rounder breasts. She is four-armed and carries a *trishula* (trident) in one of her right hands which she is sticking into Mahisha the buffalo demon, whose tail she grasps in one of her left hands. The forepart of the animal's body is unfortunately broken off as are the lower halves of the Devi's legs. Squashed into the bottom right-hand corner of the composition is a stiff and stylised, almost Achaemenian, lion, the animal which carries her into battle. Sculpturally speaking this is one of the most rhythmically pleasing images of the goddess in Kulu, and reminiscent of the best work on the Kailasa at Ellora.

To the north of the courtyard stands what, at first sight, appears to be the usual chalet-type temple, but on closer inspection turns out to be a fascinating hybrid. It is dedicated to the goddess under the title of Sandhya Devi. An inscription records that it was built in A.D. 1428. A subsequent fire, however, must certainly have destroyed the upper part, for what exists today is a nineteenth-century wooden superstructure built on to an ancient stone base and enclosing a stone sanctuary with a Gupta-style doorway, consisting of three recessed jambs and lintels, which probably served as a model for craftsmen designing the doorways of the indigenous wooden temples. In the centre of the lower lintel there is a carving of Ganesh, and the sanctuary contains two stone images, but as they both had their tinsel day dresses on when I saw them it was impossible to appreciate their aesthetic qualities.

If you stand on the plinth in front of the Sandhya Devi Temple you will see, if you look carefully, that the grain of the wood suddenly stops about two-thirds of the way down the outer walls, and that the lower third is in fact stone and carved in the classical manner, as opposed to the folk-style above it. This element of the unexpected, this curious jumble of ancient and modern shrines, is what makes Kulu such a happy hunting ground for the amateur archaeologist.

It is no exaggeration to say that Jagatsukh is stiff with the remains of classical carving and I pottered about for nearly an hour, though one really needs days, searching it out, finding slabs of it built into the courtyard walls of the eighteenth-century *shikhara* temple of Jagannath and on either side of the nearby Hanuman shrine, also in many other walls up and down the straggling village. I admired ancient *makara* fountain-heads and stray images of familiar gods with their various animal vehicles, and tried to imagine what this little capital of a remote mountain kingdom must have looked like in its heyday over a thousand years ago.

On the spur of a hill to the east of Jagatsukh are the crumbling remains of a fifteenth-century fortress built by the Piti *thakurs*, Lords of Spiti (a part of Indian Tibet), who for a time ruled some of the territory along these upland frontiers and had a penchant for offering up human sacrifices and for drinking human milk.

About a mile north of the old capital a wide stony track branches off to the right with an intoxicating notice board at its junction with the main one—'Jagatsukh/Hampta Pass Road. Road length 14 miles. Height of Hampta Pass 14,500 feet'— on the far side of which lies Spiti.

Further along the main track at the hamlet of Aleo there is a group of ten very rough memorial stones almost devoid of carving and vastly inferior to the *barselas* of Mandi and Nagar. But the story of their origin is interesting.* Sidh Singh was the Raja who came to Kulu about the year A.D. 1500 and gradually recovered the kingdom of his ancestors from the *Ranas* and *Thakurs* who had divided it up amongst themselves. He had difficulty in subduing a popular chieftain named Jinna Rana who lived in the fort of Mandankot above Manaligarh, and ruled the top end of the valley. Eventually Sidh Singh bribed a treacherous groom to shoot him. As soon as the ladies in the fortress

* See G. C. L. Howell, I.C.S., F.Z.S., 'Some Notes on Ancient Kulu Politics', *Journal of the Punjab Historical Society*, Vol. VI, p. 74.

heard of their master's death the senior Rani ordered a funeral pyre to be prepared and the fort was set on fire. Thus all the Rana's wives became *sati*, except for one who was pregnant at the time and who was therefore sent out of the fort by the senior Rani. In due course the young woman gave birth to a son. Some years later when the boy was herding buffaloes near Manali, Raja Sidh Singh went to the Dunghri temple to offer sacrifice to Hidimba. The victim—a buffalo—escaped and was shot by the young herdsman with his bow and arrow—or according to another account caught by the horns. The Raja rewarded him with a *jagir*—a grant of land—but on learning of his parentage decreed that it should be 'a place with the river in front and a precipice behind', which is the Kulu idiom for a tight fix. Howell thinks that the Raja was actually hinting that the boy might be conveniently removed, but as Jinna Rana had been a well-loved ruler of the Upper Béas valley no one wanted to kill his son. So the boy was given land round Aleo in a situation which answers well to the above description, and he grew up and founded the Nuwani family. Assistant-Commissioner Howell records that members of this family, although working as ordinary farmers, had never forgotten their descent from Jinna Rana and had assumed the royal right to erect *barselas* at Aleo like the ones at Nagar.

From this group of standing stones it is only a mile through terraced paddy-fields to the bridge over the Béas leading to Manali, the present-day Mecca of holiday-makers, though in my opinion it is not so beautifully situated nor so interesting as Nagar. It is normally reached by bus or by private car along the motor road running beside the right bank of the river, but nowadays it can also be reached by bus along the left bank, for since my last walk along it the ancient track has been converted into a partly tarred motor road.

Manali is not really Manali at all. If you can get hold of an old half-inch map of the upper Béas Valley—I have the 1921 edition open before me—you will see it is called P.O. Duff Dunbar, and just above this is written *Dana*, which means fodder, the name of the original hamlet which used to be the last place where muleteers could get fodder for their beasts before crossing the Rohtang Pass.

The true Manali, after which the modern tourist centre is named, is a big village across the Manalsu river at least a mile to the north-west of Dana. To distinguish it from the new Manali it is always known as Manaligarh because of the ruined fortress on its citadel.

Duff Dunbar was Deputy Forest Officer in Kulu during the early years of the British occupation—that is the 'fifties and 'sixties of the last century—and he evidently made such an impression on the residents of the Upper Béas Valley that the postal district was called after him. He was among the first of many Englishmen to develop a deep-seated love of Kulu and the only one with the aesthetic sensibility to build himself a house in the local *pahari* style. This, still known as Dunbar House, stands in a glade in the deodar forest near the hamlet of Dunghri a good mile up the hill to the west of new Manali. It is built of alternate courses of dry stone blocks and cedar beams in the true Himalayan style, but instead of the lower storey being a cattle byre as in the *zamindar*'s farmhouses, it has dining- and sitting-rooms complete with fire-places together with a kitchen and offices at the back. A wooden veranda runs right round the upper storey which contains the bedrooms and Duff Dunbar employed a local craftsman to carve traditional patterns on the balustrade and on the sets of receding jambs and lintels round his front door. The roof has unfortunately had its original slices of precipice tiles replaced by the inevitable corrugated iron which seems to have become a modern Himalayan status symbol.

Mr. Dunbar, who had the materials for the first iron suspension bridge in the valley, at Bunthar, sent out from England at his own expense, cared lovingly and skilfully for the forests in his charge and many of those which now clothe the mountainsides were planted by him just over a hundred years ago. Had he not inherited an estate in his native Scotland he would undoubtedly have settled permanently at Dunghri. As it was, he returned to his family inheritance near Caithness in the early 1860's after presenting Dunbar House to the Mr. and Mrs. Mackay who figure so frequently in Willie Donald's diary. Through Bhagti, Mackay's Brahmin wife, the property eventually descended to my friend Pandit Balak Ram of Katrain, the hereditary *pujari* of the Dunghri temple and one of the few present residents in the valley who takes a learned interest in the temples and religion of his native land. For most of the year Dunbar House is now let to visitors but during the fruit season of August and September (apples ripen more than a month earlier than do similar varieties in England) the Pandit's son, a keen politician, lives in it while supervising the picking and despatch of fruit from the orchards founded by Mr. Mackay.

About a quarter of a mile to the north-east of Dunbar House stands the mysterious Dunghri temple dedicated to the demon goddess Harimba, also called Hirma Devi, the Hidimba of the Mahabharata, who was lucky enough to make an excellent marriage, far above her station, to no less a person than Bhima the Pandava. Since then she has never looked back and is still the most influential goddess in the valley, though together with the other indigenous *devis* and *devatas* she has to pay yearly homage to the imported god Ragunathji at the *Dussehra* festival. Unfortunately Hidimba recently inspired such devotion in Renu, her hereditary drummer—and one of the most brilliant *shikaris* in Kulu—that he painted all the wood carving on the temple bright red and blue and green and gave her four red and green concrete columns ranged along the principal veranda—all as a thank-offering for the safe delivery of his first-born son.

The temple stands on a little hill in a grove of magnificent cedars. 'The deodars round the temple of Hirma Devi must be over a thousand years old,' writes Judge Khosla in an entertaining and informative travel book.* 'Some of them were cut down and removed for timber a few years ago but a somewhat eccentric Scottish member of the I.C.S. fortunately stopped further depredation by issuing an order that the deodars were ancient monuments and, therefore, protected under the Ancient and Historical Monuments and Archaeological Sites and Remains Act. No one challenged the legality of the order and the trees were saved.'

Below the great cedars huge smooth boulders bulge out of the brown earth and in the monsoon season the clearings are carpeted with short green grass spangled with the brilliant blue flowers of dwarf gentians (*argentea*) and the brilliant red fruits of wild strawberries.

* G. D. Khosla, *Himalayan Circuit*, London, 1956, p. 28.

The temple is in the Pagoda style (Type IV) with four super-imposed wooden pent roofs considerably out of the perpendicular. The top one is circular and crowned by a brass ball and trident, the *trishula* of Shiva which is also an attribute of the Mother Goddess. The total height is 80 feet but the surrounding deodars, whose shape the temple echoes, are taller still. It is the only *mandir* in the whole of the sub-division which can be accurately dated from an inscription A.D. 1553, though there was certainly a sacred shrine on the site long before that. Close by there is an oblong half-timbered *sadhu* house, and it is the *sadhus*, the wandering holy men, who so often set fire to the very buildings where they have come to worship. They go round with their begging bowls, collect lots of rice and vegetables and spices for a good curry from the nearest hamlet, light a fire in or near the shelter and cook themselves a delicious meal. Meanwhile the wind only has to be in the right direction for a spark to set light to the dry and brittle shingles of the nearby *mandir* and it is soon a heap of ashes. Throughout the centuries many a hill temple has thus been burnt to the ground, only to be quickly rebuilt in the same style as before. Sometimes the wood simply rots and the roof or roofs have to be renewed, an operation which is accompanied by a set religious ritual.

During the medieval period parts of the Upper Béas Valley were under Tibetan domination and there was a Buddhist monastery at Dunghri: the present *sadhu* shelter may even have formed a part of it and the monks may well have meditated in an earlier edition of the present temple. In any case there is a tradition that towards the end of the last century a Buddhist monk came to Kulu from Lhasa bringing with him an old map of the country round Manali by which he was able to identify the site of the monastery. He maintained that the former occupants, being driven away in a hurry, had been forced to leave their valuable library behind, but that they had concealed the scrolls in a cave, the entrance to which they had sealed with a curse. The monk found a log pile near the temple of Hidimba which he suspected was blocking the mouth of the cave, but so effective was the curse that he was unable to touch it. This seems odd, as one would have expected it to operate only against those of another faith. A more satisfactory dénouement would surely have been that the monk, being a Buddhist, would have had the power to lift the curse, retrieve the manuscripts and take them back where they belonged.

The present temple at Dunghri was put up by Raja Bahadur Singh, the son of Sidh Singh who reputedly built Nagar Castle. The façade is decorated with elaborate carving and a recurrent Indian legend—also attached to the Taj—recalls that the King ordered the sculptor's hands to be cut off so that he could never repeat such work. The carving is in the folk style of the area, as opposed to the classical tradition, but one of the most interesting things about it lies in the choice of subjects: in addition to the customary gods and goddesses, elephants, *makaras* (very stylised crocodiles), and the pot and foliage motif which is common all over north and central India, there is the ancient Scythian figure of the stag looking back over its shoulder and spouting forth foliage, and the familiar Mediterranean theme of confronting birds drinking out of a large pot which represents the water of life. Such themes, including knots, scroll and plaitwork, are common in the folk-art of the Western Himalaya because of the many different tribes—some of them Celtic—which came down into northern India on successive waves of conquest and were eventually absorbed into the local population, chiefly of the Punjab hills and Rajasthan.

Attached to the woodwork above the door and windows of the façade are the horns of ibex and other wild animals of the region—a usual form of offering to the hill gods, members of the temple staff often being themselves great hunters; Renu, for example, the aforementioned hereditary drummer of Hidimba, is booked up for months ahead by sportsmen after big game during the summer and autumn.

The interior of the temple is dark and mysterious and as your eyes become accustomed to the dim light you see a rope hanging from the ceiling over large natural boulders enclosed by the four walls. One of the boulders partly overhangs the sacrificial stone which is smooth and slopes down to the right and has a dip in the middle into which the blood of the animals flows, the goats and the buffaloes which are offered up to the demon goddess, as described to me by Princess Kiran. The *rath* and processional masks of the *devi* are all kept in a temple at Manaligarh and the only idols in the Dunghri temple are two small brass images of Durga—

with whom Hidimba has inevitably become identified—killing the buffalo demon, and a carving in dark grey stone of the same subject. To see them you must seek out the old *pujari* who lives in the beautiful nearby hamlet of Dunghri and who wisely keeps them hidden in the deep recesses of the interior to protect them from art treasure thieves.

Although a number of villagers in the more tourist-ridden parts of Kulu are in the process of lapsing from their ancestral religion, Hidimba still seems to inspire great devotion and it is touching to watch the local girls pass by in the morning and lay an offering of flowers in front of the closed doors of the temple and stand for a minute in silent prayer before walking on to their work in the fields. Among her other virtues Hidimba is the bearer of rain and when there is a drought in the Upper Béas Valley it is still the custom to carry the mask-covered *raths* of neighbouring *devatas* to Dunghri and to shut them up in the temple in an attempt to force them to send rain down on the particular crops for which they are responsible.

It is curious to think of all those sets of tennis being played and all the games of whist in the evening up at Dunbar House so near to this ancient shrine of the demon goddess. And when today you walk down from the sacred grove to modern Manali you enter a different world: a world of hideous bungalows with red tin roofs and aluminium huts and paying-guest-houses with holiday-makers of many nationalities walking up and down the main street, buying unbleached wool sweaters in the Tibetan refugee bazaar. There is even a little public garden with flower-beds and seats among the primeval boulders, which insist on pushing up from the earth all over the place in the Western Himalaya, and behind it a thick plantation of specimen trees, including English oak as opposed to the three varieties of ever-green oak which grow naturally in the temperate zone of these mountains.

A little further up on the same side of the road is the well-appointed forest rest-house where Pandit Nehru stayed on the brief visits he allowed himself away from the affairs of state; and further up still, on the opposite side of the road, is the excellent John Banon Guest-house where I have spent so many happy days at various times, and met so many interesting people. It

Dhungri, above Manali, temple of the demon Goddess Hidimba dated 1553, from a water-colour by Colonel Harcourt

Sangha bridge over the Manalsu between modern Manali and the ancient village of Manaligarh

The Banon Memorial at Manali

Manaligarh, stray image slab, eighteen inches high, of Durga and her lion in a pacific mood, leaning up against the base of a small modern wooden shrine on the citadel

Manaligarh. Interior of the shrine on the citadel showing cult objects including tiny primitive image of the Mother Goddess leaning up against the *linga* of Shiva

stands in its own orchards and, close to the front door, boasts one of the only Cox's orange pippin trees left in the valley. The apples are ripe in early September and guests are allowed to pick them *ad lib*, a privilege of which I availed myself with great delight when I stayed there in 1965, for in my opinion there is nothing to equal a Kulu Cox.

On this visit I also had the pleasure of meeting the famous dancer Indrani Rahman, who is the daughter of an American mother and a South Indian father. She was staying in John's guest-house with her young son and she told me that when she had performed the dance of destruction during the Indo-Pak war, members of the audience got so excited at the moment of the conch blowing that some of them jumped up and shouted '*Devi Durga Ki jai!*'—'Victory to the Goddess!' She found the spirit of destruction in the dance was having a bad effect on her so she started doing the *Uma* dance instead, stressing the gentle, benevolent and compassionate aspects of the Mother.

John Banon is the grandson of the Captain Banon who settled here in the 'seventies of the last century and became the un-crowned king—'the white Raja'—of the Upper Béas Valley. He married a girl from Garhwal, by whom he had four sons, Henry, Herbert, Harold and Hugh, all of whom fought for the allied cause in the First World War. Henry was nicknamed 'Sugar' by his mother and was consequently always known as Chini Sahib. He became a major in the 18th Royal Garhwal Rifles and when he retired from active service he stepped into his father's shoes and ran Manali, becoming president of the bank and chairman of the *panchayat*, the village council. Herbert was the father of my friend John, the owner of the famous Manali guest-house. John is tri-lingual with English, Hindi and Kului (the local *pahari* dialect) and is married to a woman of extra-ordinary charm from Goshal, a little village some three miles up the valley. Harold was killed in France in 1915; his memorial is inscribed on a giant boulder beside the road leading uphill out of Manali to the north-west. Recently, his nephew John commissioned some local Tibetan refugees to frame the carved inscription with gaily-coloured Buddhist paintings and prayers in their beautiful script. The result is very striking—and ecumenical. Hugh, the youngest of Captain Banon's four sons, fought in both

World Wars and his two sons run first-class guest-houses in Manali today.

More or less in the centre of new Manali stands the Lady Willingdon Hospital, opened by the Vicereine on behalf of the Church Missionary Society in 1936. It is a small affair with beds for only twenty-three patients but, as in all well-run Indian hospitals, accommodation and cooking facilities have to be provided for the patient's family as well as for the patient. The compound contains staff bungalows, including that of Dr. Peter Snell, who runs the establishment, and his wife Margaret, a State Registered Nurse whom he first met when they were both training in the Radcliffe Infirmary, Oxford. Their patients include nomads, such as Gujars and Gaddis, as well as the local hill people, Tibetan refugees from several nearby camps and now the hippies, who have made Manali a summer resort, moving down to Goa for the winter. In the summer, when they can get sufficient help to leave the hospital in good hands, Peter and Margaret's chief delight is to tour round the villages in a large Land-Rover fitted up as a dispensary. They both speak Hindi fluently and Margaret sometimes wears a *puttoo*, the three-yard length of hand-woven tweed draped in a special way and held in position by two silver safety pins—resembling Scottish kilt pins—fixed close to the collar bones on either side. This garment, which appears to be confined to the Kulu valley, bears no relation to the Indian sari and may be a legacy from a tribe of central Asian or even of European origin, members of which settled here after the subsidence of the barbarian invasions of the fifth and sixth centuries A.D.

To the north-east of the village there is a beautiful deodar forest, bordered to the east by the Béas and to the north by its foaming tumbling tributary, the Manalsu torrent. The clearings are carpeted first with iris and later with wild columbine, and in the monsoon season the little streams which intersect them are full of water and the emerald grass is studded with the brilliant blue flowers of the dwarf gentian. It is well worth making a detour through these enchanted glades in order to reach the wooden *sangha* bridge over the Manalsu which leads to old Manali. On the far side of the bridge there is a cluster of little water mills with dry stone walls and rough stone tiles, and past them, a track leads up to the village dominated by its ancient citadel—Manaligarh—where the fortress has long since fallen into ruins which have been used as a handy quarry for building the local houses.

A climb to the top of the citadel is well worth the trouble. On the western edge of it stands a very new-looking mini-*mandir* (Type III) complete with a mini-*dhoj* planted at the rear. At first glance it does not promise to be of much interest but if you kneel down and look inside the tiny open door there is a fascinating set of cult objects on the mud floor: an incense burner and spoon, a bell, a crooked candlestick, and, leaning against a squat, almost circular *linga*, a minute folk-type stone carving of Devi with very low-set breasts as on prehistoric statuettes of the Mother Goddess. Lying around outside this little wooden shrine are four stone fragments of a far older temple: a large lion-like face known in Indian art as a *kirtimukha*, the top section of a window frame, a beautifully decorated lintel built into a nearby modern dry-stone *sadhu* shelter, and, leaning against the plinth of the mini-*mandir* a well-preserved image, about three feet high, of a four-armed goddess wearing the tall triple-crown with beaded edges characteristic of hill *devis* and framed in pilasters supporting an odd-shaped triple arch recalling Kashmiri architecture. For once she is not engaged in killing demons, though an adoring lion looking up into her face from the left-hand corner of the slab confirms that she is the goddess Durga.

On the top of a mountain some 3,000 feet above Manaligarh stand the ruins of Mandankot, Jhinna Rana's fort (referred to in the previous chapter) up to which I admit I have never yet climbed. The sad *sati* spirits of the immolated women are still believed to haunt the place, and the chief Rani herself inevitably became a *devi* with a shrine among the ruins.

A footpath leads across fields up the right bank of the Béas to the little village of Goshal where I saw a god's garage. If you turn left off the main path and walk up the hill through the hamlet you will see a chalet-type wooden temple with carvings of snakes on the outside, and inside, resting on the rafters, sits a row of bare *raths*, the wooden palanquins carried on poles which are decorated with scarves and flowers and hung with the metal *devata* masks displayed at religious festivals and fairs.

The road along the left bank of the Béas from Manali to Rahla at the foot of the Rohtang Pass has not only been made jeep-able but also bus-able during the course of the past few years. When I was a girl, Manali was the northernmost point in the valley which could be reached by car and we rode our ponies to Kothi along the ancient route to Central Asia which was then a mule-track free from the dust and the poisonous gasses which come in the wake of the internal combustion engine. First we rode up to the big village of Vashisht (then called Bashisht) to see the hot sulphur springs. Vashishta was a celebrated Vedic sage who later—a matter of a few hundred years, for time means nothing in India—became the teacher of Rama, the Ragunathji of Sultan-pur who is nominally the chief god of Kulu. A large black stone idol, with glinting silver eyes, represents him in his little chalet-type temple in the middle of the village, the door jambs and lintels of which are carved in the local folk-style including the Scythian motif of the stag looking back over its shoulder. Beside the shrine there is a stone tank fed by a sulphur spring which gushes out of the hillside. The water is very hot, not boiling as at Manikarn, and the tank is enclosed by four stone walls with a niche in one of them surrounded by classical-style carvings. Several local *devatas* are brought here for an annual ritual bath and many pilgrims come to bathe in the healing waters. In 1931 I photographed a *sadhu* sitting cross-legged, apparently in deep meditation, beside the sacred spring and was very dis-illusioned when he suddenly sprang up and asked me for his bus fare from Manali back to Delhi.

The village houses in Vashisht are beautifully grouped against the now close background of the Solang *nala* at the head of the valley. The roofs are covered with a succession of crops put out to dry and some houses have carved balustrades running right round the verandas of the upper storey. But some do not, and Peter Snell told me that nearly every week children from different villages fall off the unprotected verandas and are brought along to the hospital with broken limbs.

High up on a yellow precipice beyond Vashisht there is the clean triangular patch from which the bees are believed to have removed the flat slab of rock, Jagatipath, which they carried down the valley to Nagar to please a homesick princess, and which I saw preserved in a shrine in Nagar Castle: it certainly appears to be the same shape as the patch on the precipice.

At Pulchan, a village a few miles further up, the Solang joins the Béas so that the latter really has two sources: Béas Rikki to the north-west from which flows the Solang; and Béas Kund at the top of the Rohtang Pass to the north-east. Just beyond this fork, and below Kothi rest-house, the Béas rushes through a gorge a hundred feet deep and three-quarters of a mile long and in places the cliffs at the top nearly meet, so that it is almost like an underground river. There are many legends about this eerie chasm connected with the plant of immortality which is said to grow in caves in the rock face, and of *sadhus* hundreds of years old who live in them. I was told about one *sadhu* who was let down on a rope but found a huge serpent at the mouth of a cave so quickly signalled to be hauled up again. But to me the most macabre of all—and this is a true story—is about three Japanese friends who had driven to the top of the pass in a jeep a few years back and were returning to Mandi in the evening. The Indian driver was racing along from Rahla in order to reach Aut in time for the last stream of south-bound one-way traffic of the day when he ran off the road into the terrible gorge. One of the Japanese jumped clear at the top and photographed the jeep in its fall.

The contrast between this northern extremity of the Upper Béas Valley in the 'thirties and 'sixties was extraordinary: in the old days the traffic consisted of pack mules and ponies and little pack sheep bearing salt and borax; the bridges were all of the old *sangha* cantilever type not more than a few feet wide; in the 'sixties there were buses and military lorries and jeeps racing along the motor road, and huge yellow bulldozers on their way to and from their work on the pass. And to support this heavy traffic, wide modern metal bridges have been built alongside the now rotting wooden ones.

Parts of the Solang *nala* are suitable for ski-ing and various plans have been proposed for 'developing' it with ski-lifts and skating rinks and luxury hotels. But happily nothing that man is able to do can destroy the wildness and beauty of scenery on so vast a scale—unless perhaps a multi-storey Hilton Hotel springs up as high as the Rohtang Pass.

CHAPTER XVII

The Rohtang Pass

Kulanthapitha, traditionally the original name of the Kulu valley, is translated as 'the end of the habitable world', or 'the end of society', which is appreciated by anyone who has stood at the top of the Rohtang Pass, the boundary between Kulu and Lahul. Behind lies a thickly inhabited, fertile valley where almost any sort of corn, rice, vegetables, flowers and fruit can be grown, and a never-ending supply of timber is to be had from the forests. In front is a desolate, windswept land, framed in mountains and glaciers without a tree or a house or a human being in sight.

The first time I came to Kulu in 1931 we rode to the rest-house at Kothi and only went a little way up the pass on the following day to see the sacred snakes which live there under two flat stones. Sometimes they can be tempted out with saucers of milk, but on that occasion they did not oblige, and the only person I have ever met who has actually seen them is John Banon, who told me they are very small, not more than a foot long.

I have only once been to the very top of this great pass: in September 1965 on the day before the outbreak of the Indo-Pakistan war. I was staying in John Banon's guest-house at Manali and he arranged for four ponies to meet us at Rahla, by the bottom of the pass, at 7 a.m. We caught the early bus from Manali, but needless to say on arrival at Rahla there were no ponies to be seen. There is now a considerable encampment here owing to the construction of the motor road, which is to lead over the pass right across Lahul to Leh, the capital of Ladakh, so a number of shack-shops have sprung up selling stores, as well as several tea-houses with roughly constructed dry-stone walls. We passed the time in one of these until eventually our ponies appeared, having been rounded up and driven down with some difficulty from one of the high grazing grounds, known as *thaches*.

Our party consisted of eight people: the English Air Force attaché from Delhi with his wife and two daughters, a young

Indian couple, an American lady doctor from Ludhiana and myself. We took it in turns to ride and walk, except for the young doctor, only two days up from the plains, who absolutely declined the offer of a pony but strode ahead of everyone and reached the top first.

I agreed to walk up the first half of the pass and then to ride a pony to the top. But before proceeding we had to get past the 'check-post', consisting of three officials—a clerk and two policemen—sitting outside a tent. It took a full fifteen minutes of polite arguing before we were allowed to go up.

The stony zigzag track ascends from 9,000 feet at Rahla to 13,400 feet at the top of the pass. It is now wide enough for jeeps and small lorries, but they have to go into reverse two or three times to get round some of the more acute hairpin bends and progress is so slow and bumpy that it is simply a form of torture to travel by them. The only advantage of making use of the internal combustion engine, to my mind, is when you want to get quickly from one place to another, but if you are going to have your inside turned upside down by jolting and be in a perpetual state of tension for fear of going over the *khud* and, if after all this you are only climbing at a speed of five or six m.p.h., then give me a pony or my two feet every time.

The scenery at the far 'end of the habitable world' is so spectacular that you want to be able to give it all your attention and to be able to stop when the spirit moves you to contemplate a particular view. On this occasion, added to the wild grandeur of the landscape, there was the thunder of blasting, echoing and re-echoing around, and the roaring of the great yellow bulldozers scooping out the new thirty-mile motor road. I could not stop thinking about the incredible courage of their drivers: the slightest error of judgement would send them and the monsters they controlled hurtling through space into the rock-lined abyss thousands of feet below. Much as I hate to see the wild places of the world 'opened up', I must confess that this road, when completed, will be a triumph of Indian engineering.*

Half-way up the pass there is a wide, flat, barren open space known as 'Murree', with a military camp at one end and a stone-

* Now completed and since 1969 buses take parties of tourists to the top during the summer. And with a special permit it is possible to continue by the road all the way to Kyelung, capital of Lahul, and stay a week there.

built hut beside the track with a tarpaulin roof and a wooden notice-board announcing 'Chamba Hotel and Restaurant'. Here we all stopped for half an hour and refreshed ourselves with syrupy tea and took endless photographs of the landscape and of each other standing beside the Tibetan-run Rohtang 'Ritz'.

I rode up most of the second half of the pass and consequently did not suffer any breathlessness from the unaccustomed height. In several places there were jets of water shooting out of the *khud* forming a series of arches right over the track under which it was fun to ride and in spite of getting well splashed by the spray it was not uncomfortable as my shirt dried very quickly in the hot sun.

At the top I dismounted and walked half a mile across the broad flat ridge, at the far end of which I stood and gasped out loud at the view before me. The track drops steeply down to a gorge through which runs the 'River of the Moon', the Chandra, though it is invisible from here. Beyond lies a vast amphitheatre of the eternal snows of the great Himalayan range. Now at last I seemed really close to the 19,000-feet twin Gyephang peaks which had so tantalised me as I rode up the Kulu valley. Here they were, only eight miles away and unable to hide from me any more, scintillating in the sunlight against a perfect background of deep blue sky. I got out my camera, screwed on the wide angle lens and tried to open the lever for an exposure. It was firmly stuck at number twenty. Then the awful truth dawned upon me. I had been recklessly photographing all the way up under the impression that I had a thirty-six exposure film. It was a twenty exposure film. Of the many idiotic mistakes I have made in my photographic career, this was the crown of them all.

So, for at least an hour, I just sat and contemplated what the ancient chroniclers of Kulu regarded as the uninhabitable world, this barren treeless landscape of great glaciers and snow peaks. I could carry no image of it away on film so I was determined to impress it upon my mind's eye for ever. As I gazed I thought of the three young Moravian missionary brides who rode to the top of the pass in the middle of the last century and got their first view of this strange land where they were to spend the better part of their lives. I thought also of the Ladahki and Tibetan traders who had passed along this ancient route with their pack-ponies and pack-sheep carrying salt and borax down to Kulu and re-

View of the Solang *nala* at the head of the Kulu Valley, from the village of
Vashisht. To the right of the long snow ridge lies the Rohtang Pass

Vashisht, village houses; note the *kilta* (cone-shaped basket) on the veranda and the hay drying on the roof

turning with rice which cannot be grown at this height. While musing thus I was distracted by a great mass moving up from the Chandra valley which slowly materialised into a vast flock of sheep and goats with their *gaddi* shepherds and ten or twelve dogs. The *gaddis* must surely be one of the hardiest races in the world, for they carry no tents but sleep on the ground beside their flocks. They wear short, kilted unbleached tweed tunics stopping well above the knee—mini-skirts in fact—and yards and yards of brown woollen rope wound round their stomachs to protect the most vulnerable part of their bodies from the wet and cold.

The Moravian missionary Heyde told Mrs. Tyacke that when they kill a sheep for food and can find no fuel on which to roast it, they simply tear it apart with their hands and eat the raw flesh. They also frequently puncture a small hole in the side of a goat, near the kidneys, insert a straw and drink the fat. My vet tells me that it would in fact be possible for an animal to suffer no ill effects in spite of such extraordinary treatment.

The *gaddis* come mostly from Kangra, Mandi and Chamba, where they pasture their flocks during the winter and spring, then move gradually up the valleys and over the high passes into Lahul and Spiti for the late summer grazing. Now it was mid-September and the flocks were starting to go down again.

It is extraordinary that Moorcroft in 1820 calculated the height of the Rohtang to within a hundred feet: 'The ghat or pass of the Ritanka Joth', he writes, 'which is above 13,300 feet high forms a gap in the most northern and elevated mountains of Kulu . . .' Dr. J. G. Gerard, who followed this route on a geological expedition ten years later, is the first writer to call the pass by its present name, the Rohtang, but his estimate of the height was 13,000 feet, 400 feet out.

Near the top, to the right of the track as you face Lahul, is Béas Rikki (from the Sanskrit Vyasa Rishi, the famous sage, to whom the authorship of the *Mahabharata* is attributed), the spring which is the principal souce of the river, the other, Béas Kund, is at the head of the Solang *nala*. I am ashamed to say I was so absorbed in the view that I forgot all about going to see Béas Rikki. Not so Moorcroft who records that 'our people constructed a small pile of stones as a memorial of the first visit paid by a European to the source of the Byas'.

At last my reverie was rudely disturbed by a member of our party coming to inform me that it was time for us all to start on the downward trek in order to catch the last bus from Rahla back to Manali. Fancy having to think of such mundane things as catching buses when contemplating the mountains of the central Himalaya at close quarters! Really, at the rate everything is being 'opened up' in this part of the world there will soon be a jeepable road up Everest.

It was now about mid-day and as I reluctantly started to walk down the track I thought how lucky we had been with the weather. So many writers of guide and travel books since Moorcroft have warned of the icy winds and sudden blizzards which may arise at any time of the day even during the summer. Mr. Tyson records that 'in 1862, seventy-two coolies, returning from bridge work in Lahul, lost their lives. The sky was cloudless when they left the first village beyond the summit on the banks of the Chandra, but when they reached the top of the pass a furious gale and blinding snowstorm suddenly developed and drove the snow over them in great drifts.' Forbes records that on another occasion 'Over four hundred coolies who were returning from Lahul at the end of October, were caught in the *bianna* as this icy blast is called, and perished almost to a man.'

This day the sky was cloudless from start to finish, the sun pleasantly hot, and there had been no wind even on the Lahul side of the pass. I walked the whole way down in just under three hours whereas the ascent had taken a good four.

There are now three distinct routes up the pass: the zigzagging mule-track which has probably been in existence for thousands of years but was built on its present alignment and completed in 1871, by the mysterious 'Mr. Theodore', who among his other occupations found time to carry out the duties of district engineer; the 'short-cut' route which is to be found on all mountain passes, but which in this instance has steps cut out of the living rock up much of the ascent: Moorcroft records that 'it is a rude but useful work and deserves a tribute to the name of the constructor, Killat Bhagt, the *guru* or religious head of an establishment of mendicants at Bonua, a small village between Gosala and Phulchan.'*

And lastly, there is the new motor road, still in the process of

* William Moorcroft, op. cit., Vol. I, p. 188.

construction, which is planned to rise the 4,500 feet from Rahla in thirty easy miles, whereas the gradient of the present track is six times as severe, rising to the same height in only five miles. Being on my feet I kept mostly to the steepest roughest and short-est path—that favoured by the *gaddis* and their flocks—which cuts out all the loops on the mule-track, but I followed the latter for an occasional half mile when the pain in my calves became acute. The way in which unladen hillmen negotiate this 'short cut' route must be seen to be believed: they actually run the whole way down and can do it in under an hour from top to bottom. At one point near-ing Rahla where the rough stone steps are particularly steep, I was foolish enough to try to imitate them and almost immediately fell headlong, which was extremely painful, and I was lucky to break no bones. As it was I remained bruised and sore for a week.

We caught the bus home to John Banon's guest-house in time for supper, and that night in bed I could not stop kicking myself for having made such a stupid mistake about the film. The next day the three weeks' war broke out and I knew perfectly well that there would be no further chance of going up the Rohtang for some time to come. And yet, and yet . . . surely anything was worth trying for the sake of that view? To be able to stand and stare once more at the unearthly beauty of the semi-circle of snow peaks beyond the 'River of the Moon': to be able to photograph them with Kodachrome II for the delight of the ladies' luncheon clubs and group meetings of the W.I. . . .

And so it was that two days later I told John Banon I was going to the top of the Rohtang again and not to expect me back that night as I intended to spend it in the Chamba Hotel half-way up the pass. On the following morning I planned to walk up to the ridge at daybreak, take my photographs in the early light and then climb a further 600 feet to see the sacred lake of Sarkund.

But in my heart of hearts I knew I would never get past that beastly check-post at Rahla—and I didn't, not by the official way. While drowning my sorrows in sickly sweet tea in a *chai kana* I decided to try and dodge past the official-ridden tent by way of the great boulders below it. This proved exceedingly easy to do for any noise that I made was drowned by the roar of the lusty young Béas tumbling down from its sacred source 4,500 feet higher up.

Once clear of official vigilance I crossed the foaming torrent by a wooden bridge and walked up the left bank for about two miles to photograph a forty-foot waterfall. Then I had to make one of the greatest decisions of my life. I had only to recross the Béas in order to join the regular track leading up the Rohtang. I could see it barely a quarter of a mile away from where I stood and was sorely tempted to walk up to Murree, spend the night on a wooden bench in the Chamba Hotel hut, and proceed to the top at daybreak to take my photographs as originally planned. But it would be impossible to avoid being seen by the military police patrolling the route, who would arrest me and lodge a complaint with the British High Commissioner in Delhi and then there would be a fearful row all round: so in great agony of mind I resisted the temptation.

I ate my sandwiches at 2 p.m. shaded from the hot sun in a wonderful pre-historic-type shelter: a colossal rock of ages jutting out from the side of the mountain with an overhang of at least twenty feet. Underneath, on the level platform of earth at the back, there was an oblong enclosure of loose stones filled with dead leaves which had obviously been made by a *sadhu*. John Banon was not expecting me back till the next day, so why shouldn't I spend the night in the ascetic's empty bed? Nothing would ever compensate me for the loss of the view from the top of the Rohtang but at least it would be a new experience to spend a night in a cave on a Himalayan hillside.

So I staked my claim by leaving a mac, sou'wester and brown canvas satchel on the bed while I went off exploring. There were no trees within a mile, by which I calculated that neither bears nor panthers would come to share my hideout. I also presumed that the daily blasting would have driven most of the wild beasts away. It was a dramatic landscape of huge smooth boulders with the roaring river rushing among them and in some places it was possible to cross from one side to the other by giant natural stepping stones. About a thousand feet further up the rock-face behind the waterfall I could clearly see a bright yellow bulldozer going backwards and forwards cutting out the new road; and frequently I heard loud booms and saw puffs of white smoke where the precipice was being blasted away.

The sun disappears early and very suddenly behind great

mountains and there is a quick drop in temperature and I soon realised that without a sleeping bag I was in for a cold night. I was wearing jodhpurs and a cotton shirt and had suffered from the intense heat reflected off the rocks all day. But now I felt chilly and pulled on my old red sweater, sat on a still warm stone, and ate the remains of my lunch for supper: two mutton sandwiches, a hard-boiled egg and two delicious Cox's orange pippins from the old apple tree in John Banon's garden. When it grew dark I lay down on the *sadhu*'s bed, covered myself with my heavy hunting mac and tried to go to sleep. The deep leaf mattress was comfortable enough and not in the least damp but the cold was intense as I was about 10,000 feet up. I wished I had mastered the yoga of the psychic heat. Failing that, if only I had been a smoker I would have had a box of matches in my pocket with which to light a fire, as the *sadhu* had tantalisingly left a considerable pile of dry sticks handy in the shelter. I sat up and frantically rubbed two of these together hoping to ignite my sandwich paper, but I had not got the knack and failed. So I got up and went outside and walked up and down reciting all fifteen decades of the rosary: then I did violent physical jerks, including flinging my arms round my shoulders as I had seen the London cabbies do in the old days when they were standing beside their horses waiting for a fare. In desperation I rubbed sticks together again but I knew in my heart of hearts that my efforts were doomed to failure: though they got very hot the paper remained unlit. Late in the night a waning moon appeared but clouds soon overshadowed it and rain came down in torrents. I had a great feeling of satisfaction sheltering under my huge stone umbrella. If I couldn't be warm, at least I was perfectly dry and I spent the rest of the night alternately lying down in my leafy bed and stamping around doing exercises. Sleep was out of the question and the dawn seemed an eternity away. But at last it came and the rain stopped and the magnificence of the stormy sunrise compensated just a little for what should have been the most spiritually inspiring night of my life but which had, in fact, turned out to be a spiritually barren physical endurance test.

CHAPTER XVIII

Retracing My Steps: the Bashleo Pass

From my digression forward in time I return to B.R. and the mules to make our way back from Kulu to Simla.

An excellent feature of modern India is its tourist service. The young man in the office at Sultanpur was always charming and helpful and gave me consistently good advice. He had planned my highly successful tour up the Parbatti valley and now, knowing my desire to avoid jeep-able roads, he suggested that I should return to Simla via the little-frequented Bashleo Pass and Rampur Busahr. He accordingly wrote out all the relevant rest-house passes—those magic chits to wave confidently at the *chaukidar*.

How lovely it must have been riding quietly down the valley in the heyday of the English settlers! But now that 'progress' has transformed the main Kulu valley road into such a busy, dusty highway I decided to travel the eighteen miles to Aut by bus and to send B.R. on ahead with the mules.

Dependable as ever, he was waiting for me on arrival and I climbed on to little Shanti and rode her the three miles to Larji rest-house where I had slept out on the veranda on the way down and had parted from my two young A.D.C.'s, Krishan and Rajinder. I strolled on up the road towards the Jalori range before supper and saw a milestone stating we were 101 miles from Simla, i.e. by the direct route, whereas this time we were embarking upon a considerable detour. Although India has officially gone over to the metric system in her weights and measures it will take a generation before it is popularly adopted. Shopkeepers still talk about eight annas when they should say fifty *neue paise*. I never yet heard anyone, either young or old, refer to kilometres when you ask him how far away such and such a place is, and he is far more precise than we are in his directions, for where we only use the term furlong—an eighth of a mile—in horse racing, an Indian uses it daily in measuring distances and will tell you that a certain village is, say, two miles and three furlongs distant.

Across the Tirthan *khud* at Larji is stretched a *jhula*, a wire cable from which an iron seat, enclosed by three bars, is hooked on to a small grooved wheel. I watched a man pull himself across from the far side by putting one hand in front of the other along the cable. When another person from the far side wants to cross, he can pull the chair back from the opposite side by a rope attached to its back.

I remembered that the Larji *chaukidar* made a good egg curry so I ordered the same again for supper and greatly enjoyed it. Before retiring to bed I saw the same little black scorpion motionless on the veranda where I had previously slept—or could it have been his wife? I cannot imagine how you tell a lady from a gentleman scorpion. Anyway he or she was doing no harm so I let it be, carrying the doctrine of *ahimsa* perhaps a little far?

We set off at 6 a.m. on the following morning, Tuesday, June 3rd, and as usual I walked for the first two or three miles, enjoying the cool of the early morning. On this march the myriad oleander shrubs, covered with pale pink flowers, are a great sight on both banks of the river and running up the lesser *khuds*. These hot June marches through the almost treeless foothills of the sub-Himalaya are very trying and I well understood why the occasional spreading peepul tree—*ficus religiosa*—with its God-given shade, is regarded as sacred.

I mounted and rode through the large village of Mangalaur by a short-cut I had cleverly spotted, thus cutting off at least four furlongs, as an Indian would say. At Mangalaur we crossed over the suspension bridge, dated 1941, from the left to the right bank of the river Tirthan, where I presume there must have been a *sangha* bridge when we crossed it in 1931. About two miles below Banjar, B.R. shouted out his by now familiar battle cry '*Mandir Memsahib!*' And I looked up and saw a little summer-house-type temple on a ledge above the road: but I was so hot and tired that for the first time on my tour I did not dismount to look at it. This I think B.R. regarded as nothing short of a betrayal for he looked bitterly disappointed. I felt very ashamed and tried to explain that I would return *rat ko*—tonight.

By now we were climbing all the time and would soon be back

in the aforested area. Facing us there appeared a large circular hill, the upper part of which was covered with chil pines. To the right of this the deep wide *khud* of the Bamhara torrent descended from the Jalori range, and to the left the narrower *khud* of the Tirthan river came down from the Bashleo.

Banjar rest-house stands on a grass ledge about half-way up the side of the circular hill and commands a magnificent view down the valley towards Larji. It is actually a mile below the important village of Banjar, the metropolis of these parts and the capital of Inner Saraj. This rest-house is a real credit to the P.W.D. to whom it belongs: it is quite the most superior one I have stayed in up till now, bar perhaps Narkanda: there are only two bedrooms, one on either side of an oblong central dining-room, but everything is very clean and I found a foam rubber mattress on my bed! The washroom has an easy-to-wipe-over composition floor and the lower half of the walls are of the same material with the upper half white-washed. An efficient sweeper emptied the thunder-box regularly and kept the two large buckets filled with cold water. There is also a neat little garden with large clumps of hydrangeas on either side of the veranda steps, and beds of cabbage roses and dahlias on the little front lawn, and, most welcome surprise of all, there is a very nice and honest *chaukidar* who only charged me Rs. 1.25 for three hard-boiled eggs and two pots of tea. I was very much in a non-rice-and-dal mood and enjoyed an egg for supper with two sardines and some bread I had bought in the Dhalpur bazaar, all eaten together with wild apricots, which the ever-attentive B.R. had picked on the way.

In the evening I tried to fulfil my promise to B.R. and for over an hour I searched up and down the Larji road for the little *mandir* he had so triumphantly spotted for me. It was nowhere to be found. The Aut to Banjar mini-bus clattered past me in a cloud of dust but there was not a single pedestrian to ask where it was so I comforted myself by indulging in flights of imagination—obviously the *jognis* had transported it temporarily elsewhere so that it should not be defiled by an unbeliever.

The following morning, June 24th, we stopped retracing our steps and branched off to the left up the part of the Tirthan *khud* which I had never explored before. The first stage as far as

Bandal is said to be jeep-able but it is extremely steep and rough in places and far narrower than the Jalori Pass road, and I would rather die than drive up it thank you: give me a riding animal any day, which does not jolt you mercilessly about and disjoint all your bones, and from whose gently rocking back you can enjoy the flora and the ever-changing views.

I walked for the first two miles leaving B.R. to tie the baggage on to Durgi and to bring my modest mule train along at his leisure. Thank God no jeeps dashed past me but I exchanged greetings with several village children on their way to school in the great one-street metropolis of Banjar. Just before I reached Bandal I saw a track leading through a pinewood up to the Forest Department bungalow and noted that it would be a lovely place to go and spend a week—the maximum period allowed in any rest-house.

At the next village, Gushaini, there was a little timber summer-house-type temple with some of the best *pahari* folk-art carving I have yet seen in the hills. On the four square posts supporting the ceiling of the wide veranda there were panels of confronting peacocks, Celtic-type knots and scrolls, little imps in what my gym mistress called 'the curtsey sitting position', and a spectacular *Hanuman* (monkey-god) with his tail curled in a large coil above his head. There was the usual low entrance to the sanctuary with the five receding lintels and door jambs, the *nag* motif prominent on some of the latter, and the principal lintel having the frieze of dancers, musicians and bowmen which always characterises it. The villagers told me it was the temple of Gara-Durga and inside I saw a statue of the goddess about three feet high, in black stone, only the head and arms being visible, the body veiled in the *devi*'s day dress of red cotton with silver tinsel stripes.

The *Kangra District Gazetteer* gives the story of Gara-Durga and is yet another example of a local character becoming identified with a major goddess of the Hindu pantheon.

This *devi* was originally a lovely girl, the daughter of a *thakur* of Dethua in Kothi Kot. A mason of Bandal did such good work for the *thakur* that the latter made him that foolish promise which has got so many men, such as King Herod, into trouble down the centuries: he said he would give him whatever he wished. The mason asked for the *thakur*'s daughter, Gara, and was allowed to take her home. She went, in duty bound, but was so unhappy in the company of her low-bred husband that as she sat weeping one day by the bank of the Tirthan near Bandal the river drew her down into its cool depths and she became a *devi*.

Approaching Bathad, the village where I was due to spend the night, I saw numbers of *excelsa* pines tapped for resin. A slice of bark is cut out and an earthenware pot attached into which the sticky resin drips. Shanti grazed on the fallen pine needles which I thought very eccentric of her.

Bathad turned out to be a hamlet of some half a dozen houses with a tiny pillar-box fastened to a wooden post supporting a veranda. Evidently the post here is carried by mail-runners as the track is mercifully quite unjeep-able. The rest-house turned out to be a minute bungalow perched on a small ledge a hundred feet above the river. It contained two little rooms with a single bed in each. Two scrubby pear trees grew on the scruffy lawn with a few dahlias round the edge of it, though what the site lacked in elegance it more than made up for by the splendour of its views up and down the valley, with numbers of little stone water mills worked by the torrents which tumbled into the river.

For lunch I ate the sardine sandwich I had prepared the day before at Banjar rest-house, with a pot of reasonably strong tea, provided by the *chaukidar*, into which I squeezed fresh lime juice from my treasure-trove of little *nimbus* from Sultanpur—they were always unobtainable in the villages. This was one of the rare cases where a rest-house *chaukidar*'s wife lived with him—in a squalid godown at the back; their three children with runny noses played on the lawn in front. I gave each child a ten paise piece and hoped the baby wouldn't swallow his. To my great delight I saw dozens of *varanus* lizards, quite up to Luri rest-house standards, running in and out of holes under the bungalow. I wonder if they have no ears? They never seem to mind noise but the slightest movement causes them to vanish like lightning which is why they are so difficult to photograph.

After lunch I sat on the veranda and wrote a letter to Miss Douglas—former receptionist at my publisher's. I was determined to test the little dented pillar box and see if a letter would reach its destination in Albemarle Street posted from this remote Himalayan hamlet. It did not.

Then I went for a botany walk but found nothing new: there were dwarf primulas, white night-shade plants, and a large variety of beautiful ferns and lichens the knowledge of each of which forms a specialised study of which I am, alas, ignorant. Bathad is only 6,000 feet above sea level and yet in late June the great horse-chestnut trees were still in flower, and there were also giant alder and walnut trees growing up the *khud* on both sides of the foaming river, mingling with the pines and cedars on the mountainside. I noticed a wide slit in the roof of one of the houses made by pushing aside the large irregular precipice slices to let the smoke out; and the next morning they had been pushed together again in case of rain. Evidently the influence of the good Moravian missionaries with their German stoves had not penetrated up this valley.

Inevitable rice and D.D.D. for supper, but I was lucky to find the *chaukidar* had any stores at all in such a small place and I felt I must conserve my own already depleted stores for even remoter villages.

I went on writing by candlelight till 10 p.m. and was about to go to bed when I heard the sound of footsteps on the veranda followed by a knock on the door so I called 'Come in!' In walked a heavily moustached young Indian in pyjamas. He told me that he and another man were employed by a Swiss firm called Sandoz Swiss-India Ltd., with its head office in Bombay, to dig up *podophyllum* plants. Their roots are used in cancer relief. The firm has a hundred acres of this herb planted in Chamba and a second plantation in Kashmir; they are now anxious to get a third going in Kulu. I said I wished he had called earlier in the evening when he and his companion could have shared my rice and D.D.D., but that I must now ask him to return to his hut as I wanted to get up at 5.30 a.m. to start my climb up the pass, and therefore hoped to get to sleep early.

The visit to one's bedroom after dark of a young man in pyjamas might well be misinterpreted by the uninitiated; but Indians often wear pyjamas all day, especially when off duty, as did the young doctor and his brother on Sunday at Jari, while workmen sometimes have no other clothes.

B.R. brought the mules round to the veranda on the dot of 6 a.m. next morning and I had my bags all ready for him to tie on and left him to it while I walked on ahead. I crossed a beautiful *sangha* bridge over the main torrent after which the path led along the bank of a smaller stream descending the mountain in a series of waterfalls. Then I noticed a flag sticking up above a boulder so I left the track to investigate. I found a most curious shrine: on a flat rock were lots of old rusty pots and pans and tins, while stuck into the ground nearby were two *dhoj* poles bearing pennants and a short post to which one large and several tiny *devata* masks were attached. Was this where cooks came to pray? I could not believe there were many in the humble hamlet of Bathad at the foot of the Bashleo Pass. Evidently the place was not big or rich enough to support a structural temple, and these curious platform shrines—known as *thairis*—are often found in tiny villages.

I returned to the track again, which very soon started to climb steeply so that my progress was extremely slow and B.R. soon caught up with me. I rode Shanti for a bit but felt sorry for her so dismounted and held on to her tail instead and let her pull me along, which was very much less effort for her and a considerable help to me. Neither horses nor mules object to this practice which I had first observed in 1932 when riding a Tibetan pony over the Chandragiri Pass into the valley of Kathmandu. On that occasion I had a leather saddle, weighed much less and the pony was a lot stronger than little Shanti, so I had stayed aboard while my *syce* held on to the pony's tail and was pulled up in the manner I now imitated.

From Bathad at 6,000 feet the track to the top of the Bashleo Pass rises nearly 5,000 feet to 10,750 feet in a little under five miles and I think it is a tougher climb than the Rohtang where you climb from 9,000 feet at Rahla to 13,400 feet in five miles. Both tracks are stony, but the Bashleo is strewn with large boulders near the top, over which you have to scramble. On the other hand, the Rohtang is completely exposed for its whole length whereas the Bashleo is pleasantly shaded. In the deodar belt there were masses of mauve columbine, *aquilegia atrata*, growing in the virgin forest and higher up large clumps of yellowy-green sunspurge in the grassy glades among the fir trees.

It was somewhere along this wild precipitous path that Raja Ajit Singh, the last king to rule Kulu, was rescued from his Sikh captors. In 1839 the forces of the great Sikh conqueror Ranjit Singh occupied Mandi and the Kulu valley with little resistance, and in the spring of 1840 proceeded to take over Inner and Outer Saraj. They made the Raja of Kulu accompany them to order his people to surrender their forts. On their way back they crossed the Bashleo Pass and were walking down the steep boulder-blocked track when a party of Sarajis who had been lying in ambush rushed out, seized their king, and carried him up the mountainside from where they fired at the surprised Sikhs and rolled rocks down on to them. The soldiers took temporary refuge in the nearby fort of Tung but after two days they had to leave owing to lack of food and tried to make their way down to the Tirthan valley. The Sarajis, who knew every inch of these mountains and could dance up and down them as only hillmen can, plagued the Sikhs every inch of the way by loosening the rocks above to create landslides and driving any stragglers over the nearest precipice. The few soldiers that remained alive at the bottom were made to surrender: four or five low caste men disguised as Brahmins entered their camp with a cow, put their hands on its tail and promised the Sikhs a safe passage back to Kulu if they would lay down their arms. As soon as they had done so the Sarajis massacred them to a man. Meanwhile Raja Ajit Singh was taken across the Sutlej to Shangri State, which was under British protection, where he lived until he died in September 1841, the following year.

Our progress was very slow up the pass and we frequently paused for breath so that we did not average more than one mile an hour from Bathad to the summit, but in our defence we were rising a thousand feet in each mile; I am a very slow walker and if it had not been for Shanti's tail I would never have got up at all. How useful animals' tails are in India for purposes of haulage as well as the taking of oaths.

Near the top we met a train of about eighty unladen ponies, mules and donkeys, for on these splendid unjeep-able routes pack animals are still the only means of transport. The five men in charge of the train, who were all dressed in blue striped pyjamas, told us that there were Gujars on the Bashleo grazing grounds who would give us milk. The Gujars are a most mysterious race for whom I have long had a passion since I first encountered them among the ruins of Tughlakabad, the third city of Delhi, many years ago. They are supposed originally to have entered India in the sixth century with the Barbarian invaders who eventually broke up the great Gupta Empire. From then until the middle of the eighth century they ruled their own kingdom of Brahmapura after which they seem to have merged with the Rajput clans. But the fascinating thing is that the lower orders of this race—or collection of tribes as it probably was—have preserved their identity as nomadic herdsmen right up till today.

At last we reached the top of the Bashleo Pass which is like a large grass-covered Andalusian saddle, the high pommel and cantle at either end consisting of two 12,000 feet peaks. Across the middle runs the track which is level and smooth for about a quarter of a mile. The snowpeaks of upper Bashahr, which I knew lay to the north-east, were hidden in the great blue-black clouds of the approaching monsoon; but below the clouds the view down towards Rampur was clear and beautiful, framed in wooded hills with a stream, seemingly miles below us, meandering through a *maidan* to the little village of Sarahan where we were to spend the night.

I told—no this is not quite true as my Hindi was not advanced enough—I indicated to B.R. that he was to remove my baggage from Shanti and let the animals graze while he rested and I went to look for flowers. I walked off across the meadow to the right which was full of beastly bulbous buttercups, the sort I am for every uprooting at home and putting on the bonfire because they choke the grass. Among the buttercups some of the Gujars' beautiful beige, blue-eyed buffaloes were grazing, magnificent specimens of the *panch kalyani* breed which I had learnt about in Mandi from a brilliant young Sikh vet, Sardar Sarchan Singh, in charge of the herd of the Indo–German Agricultural project. I remembered him telling me that a good animal gives between three and four gallons of milk at its peak period and has a lactation of 370 days and continues to produce profitably for nine or ten lactations. Yet the Hindu cow, which gives so little milk, is sacred and never allowed to be put down, whereas the productive water buffalo is identified with the demon Mahisha and offered up in sacrifice to Durga the slayer of demons. Father Delevry, S.J., thinks this may be because buffaloes love swamps, and swamps—

although nobody knew anything about the malaria mosquito in ancient times—have always been associated with disease.*

Close to the brown oak and silver fir trees at the edge of the meadow were two Gujar tents so I walked across and sat down on the ground and said to two beautiful dark-skinned women *'Dudh hai?'*—'Is there milk?' One of them went to a large shallow pan in the shade and filled a tin mug with lovely cold unboiled milk, the first I ever remember drinking in India. I so hate the taste of boiled milk and still more the skin on it that at that moment I did not care how badly I got T.B. because it was such a rare treat to drink it fresh. Several small children sat round and watched me, including two obviously M.D. boys, aged about ten and twelve, with almost no crowns to their heads. How much happier they must be living this gipsy life with their families than in an institution.

I walked on towards the western peak of the saddle—the cantle—and passed the Gujar men cutting wood in the forest at the edge. Climbing up the hill there were clumps of rhododendron *campanulata*, all windswept one way, just as I had seen at the top of the Jalori Pass. Then I started climbing the southern slopes of the peak which were out of the wind and covered in lush long grass starred with wild flowers. The most prominent were the potentillas, mostly with dark red flowers, but some (*Nepalensis*) a much lighter pinkier-red, while others were bright yellow. Then there were dwarf iris I had not seen before, only six to eight inches in height but having a large mauvey-blue flower quite out of proportion to the size of the plant; masses of blue and white anemones, sunspurge, puce-coloured orchids and other flowers, which in my ignorance I could not name. How I wished I had had the great Doctor Randhawa with me who had helped me so much with my down-country botany. I remembered him telling me that up here in what are known as 'the Alpine meadows' of the Himalaya, of which the average height is 12,000 feet, the plants have to complete their cycles of growing, flowering and seeding in three months, that is between June, when the snows melt at that height, and September when snow starts to fall again.

* *Religious Hinduism*, by Jesuit Scholars, St. Paul Publications, Bombay, 1964, p. 99.

On the way down I saw some of the 'buffalo demons', lords of the swamp, wallowing ecstatically in a muddy round pond in the middle of their meadow. I returned to the Gujars' camp and had a second mug of lovely fresh creamy milk for which the young woman would not accept a *paise*. I really think I ought to look after M.D. children as they always seem to like me: the elder of the two boys came and sat down on the ground close by and smiled delightedly as he watched me drink and I could have kicked myself because I had nothing to give him. Then I had a bright idea: I would give him my rosary, so on the spur of the moment I did and he beamed all over and went and showed it to his mother. It was not till months later that I learnt that the Gujars of the Punjab hills are all Muslims: still, I am sure they are neither orthodox nor fanatical and would not regard a tiny crucifix as an idol.

But I was not the only bearer of gifts. When I returned to B.R. and the mules, he came forward and presented me with a real Victorian posy! An orchid in the middle surrounded by a circle of buttercups, another of red potentilla and an outer one of iris, the stalks all wrapped in silver paper from his cigarette packet. I was deeply touched and said 'Many thanks: many, many thanks' several times.

At the top of the Bashleo Pass we passed from Inner to Outer Saraj, both of which districts are administered by the Kulu Assistant Commissioner. The track descending to Sarahan was so steep that I walked the two miles down to the level stretch of grass with the brook running slowly through it which you can see from the top of the pass. First the path led through clumps of brown oaks, then over bare rocky ground, till it plunged into the deodar forests so that I knew we were round about 8,000 to 9,000 feet. Through the trees to our left I could see a narrow waterfall about a hundred feet high. Had I kept to the mule-track on these steep descents I should have been quickly out-distanced by my 'train' but I always slid down the precipitous footpaths, made centuries ago, found on mountain passes all over the world, which cut off nearly every loop of the tracks.

About half-way down we met an old man driving up two browny-black yearling heifers. They turned and fled at my mule's approach with their loud jingle of bells, much to the con-

Half-way house on the Rohtang Pass. We have now left Kulanthapitha 'the end of the habitable world', and come to—to the ancients—the uninhabitable world of Indian Tibet

Gushaini temple in the Tirthan *khud* leading to the Bashleo Pass between Inner and Outer Saraj. Chalet-type village temple with folk-art carvings

Left: detail showing Hanuman, the monkey god

Right: detail showing confronting peacocks, an imp, and Celtic scroll-work

sternation of the poor old man. B.R. was very naughty as he obviously thought it a great joke to chase the heifers further and further down until I called a halt and let the owner round them up and drive them safely past us.

When we reached the valley at the foot of the pass I mounted and rode the remaining mile or so to the Sarahan rest-house. It was one of the flattest rides of the whole tour along a widish valley carpeted by burnt-up grass and very different from the lush pastures of the alpine meadows 3,000 feet above us. The brook, fed by the tall narrow waterfall I had seen from above, flowed quietly along in the manner of English brooks, and as we approached the village there were willows and poplars growing beside it.

We finally reached the rest-house at 2 p.m. having spent exactly eight hours on a journey of eight miles, but it was worth every minute of the time and it is not given to everyone to wander knee deep in potentillas and to drink demon's milk with Gujars on Himalayan heights.

The rest-house at Sarahan is dramatically perched on a ledge above the *maidan*, a few hundred yards from the village of Sarahan with a marvellous view up the valley to the top of the Bashleo Pass. At the back of it an ancient deodar forest climbs up the *khud*. I was dying of hunger having breakfasted at 5.45 a.m. off two *chapatties* spread with pineapple jam: but I could not face watery rice and D.D.D. so I told the unusually decrepit old *chaukidar* to heat my last tin of Indian tomato soup; and a little later I walked into his godown as I thought he would be certain to let the precious liquid boil over. Sure enough it was about to do so. There was the maddening old man sitting on his haunches with his back to the mud stove smoking his hookah, completely unconcerned. In a rage I seized the tongs—which are always used for cooking pans, since they have no handles—and tried to remove the pot, but the tongs slipped and the crimson soup ran all over the mud floor. In the *chaukidar*'s defence I must admit that he did not laugh triumphantly. I only saved about three tablespoonsful and retired much mortified to my room where I opened the inevitable tin of sardines and ate the lot without bread or *chapatties*. It was on such occasions as these that I suffered from a deep longing for the past when our own *khansama* accompanied us on Himalayan treks and at every rest-house produced excellent meals from the lavish stores our pack mules carried, supplemented by game shot en route and occasional generous presents from local Rais.

The corrugated iron roof of the Sarahan bungalow, painted an unusually brilliant red, can be seen from the top of the Bashleo Pass. Being in such a prominent position I wished more than ever that the British authorities had had the taste to build it in the local style, but so far the one at Pulga is the only one so built that I came across on my tour. The scant furniture in my bedroom at Sarahan was thick with dust, and the floor had not been swept for weeks as few travellers take this route. There was a good-sized washroom complete with commode, but the old *chaukidar* made it quite clear by waving his arm towards the forest that I was not to use it on any account as there was no sweeper to empty it. Of course a *chaukidar*—with nothing to do all day but sit on his haunches—could not possibly lose face by performing such a degrading task. The unkempt rest-house lawn was bordered by narrow flower beds with a few courageous marigolds struggling through the weeds. 'Why does the *chaukidar* not pass the time of day by doing a little light work in the garden?' I thought to myself; but recollected that he is, of course, a *chaukidar* and not a *mali* and would supposedly lose face if a passing villager were to see him pulling up some groundsel. But one thing I tend to forget when Indian servants drive me mad by their incompetence and lethargy, is that for countless generations they have existed on an insufficient and thoroughly unbalanced diet, which accounts for their lack of vitality and enthusiasm.

After an hour's rest on my bed I walked into the village and tried to buy eggs and milk but nobody would sell me any. The people appeared very poor and were mostly dressed in torn clothes, as in the Parbatti valley. Again I wondered why they should be so poor in this temperate zone at 8,000 feet where the same crops and plants flourish as in England—wheat, barley, potatoes and vegetables of all kinds. Why can't they keep chickens properly? Why can't they make silage out of their luscious *bathu* (goose-foot, *chenopodium*) plots to produce winter milk? But one comes up against the same problems every time: the minute size of the holdings, the sanctity of the cow, the natural sloth of the *pahari* people, and their lack of ambition which makes them seemingly content if they have just enough to keep body and soul together, plenty of time to sit under trees and gossip, with an occasional *mela* where they can get pleasantly drunk on *lugri*.

Sarahan is a beautiful village with no modern building to dis-figure it, the rest-house being right outside. The houses are all built in the traditional timber-bonded style; the roofs consist of the familiar precipice slices and the doorways leading into the cattle byres on the ground floor are in the same Gupta style as the temple doorways with three receding jambs and lintels, but painted terracotta red, yellow and white in traditional patterns, instead of being carved. On the unenclosed veranda of the upper storey of one such house, I saw a poor woman lying and groaning in pain. She was not big with child but obviously suffering from some internal complaint, and I realised that there were drawbacks to living in such an out-of-the-way place. To reach a doctor she would have to be carried twenty-one miles down the valley to Rampur in a *dhooly*.

In the middle of the village there is a beautiful tower-type temple with an enclosed balcony of carved deodar running round the four sides of the upper storey. A solid deodar bell is fixed under each corner of the eaves between which hangs the usual fascinating fringe of tinkling wooden tassels. The gabled roof of precipice slices is tied by a huge cedar beam coarsely carved at each end into a monster's head.

I asked some nearby villagers if I could go in and to my surprise a key was produced and the door opened to let in the light as well as me which was useful as there were no windows. I came to the conclusion that this was not the temple proper but the temple treasury (*bhandar*) where the *devata*'s masks and band instruments are stored from one *mela* to another. The villagers told me that their *devata* was Shring Rishi, whose headquarters I had already learnt are at Banjar, the capital of Inner Saraj. His two highly-polished brass masks were fixed to the stem of a red wooden umbrella (*chhatri*) about three feet high and the same in diameter, which was fixed to a block covered with hideous modern floral chintz; this in turn stood on a low platform painted bright blue. Several garlands of dead flowers hung from a low ceiling beam near by. On the floor close to the *devata*'s platform stood a long-handled brass bell, a conch shell, a flute, a vast brass cauldron and a skeleton umbrella with not a shred of cloth adhering to it. Two huge drums with brass sides hung from a beam in the back wall and other instruments of the band leant against the wall, among them the eight-feet-long silver trumpets and the curious 'serpents'. A step-ladder led up to the next floor but I was not allowed to go up it. Although this was so obviously the temple treasury and store-house, a tall and splendid upright pole, the *dhoj*, was fixed in the paved courtyard outside the door.

On the way back to the rest-house I noticed many little sheaves of wheat drying on the sun-soaked slices of precipice which roofed the houses. When the path left the village it led through flourishing fields of barley, *bathu* and *bhang*; yet the small black hill cows which were being driven home through this land of apparent plenty were scraggy, miserable-looking specimens with hardly a bag between them and from which the owners would be lucky if they could squeeze a thimbleful of milk. No wonder none was forthcoming for my supper. So milkless, eggless, sardineless and soupless I had to be content with rice and D.D.D. again.

It was the night of the full moon and as I stood on the terrace outside the bungalow looking up at the pass I wondered if my good friends the Gujars were asleep in their tents and whether the M.D. boy was holding my rosary. A curly fleecy white cloud sat in the Bashleo's saddle and the clumps of brown oaks looked like beetles crawling up its flaps. The steep, narrow waterfall was hidden by the great cedar forest lower down and because it was so small it did not roar, but it kept up a ceaseless sighing sound all through the night.

The next morning I walked across the valley to inspect a little summer-house-Type III temple which I had noticed as I rode into the village. The carving on the pillars and round the cella door was in the primitive folk style with camels, elephants and horses included in the designs. There was also a seated ogre holding human heads under his arms in a panel to the right of the door, and a large freestanding figure of a man—reminiscent of Nuristani wood-carving—squashed into the gable above the cella door. A beautiful carving of the goddess Durga in dark grey stone, and curiously enough in the classical style, was the object of worship, and for some mysterious reason she was surrounded by votive offerings of rusty keys and padlocks. Were these from thieves who had successfully broken into houses? Or from householders who had successfully kept thieves out?

Behind the temple stood the village school, but the seventy-nine pupils, boys and girls, were sensibly being taught in the open air outside the modest wooden building which looked as if it could not possibly have contained them all. They sat in rows on their haunches on the grass; some of them had reading primers in the difficult *Devanagari* script while others were writing it on those curious boards with handles which I had seen the children carrying on their way to school at Khanag.

By a great piece of good fortune the school-inspector, Shri H. D. Kohli, who spoke excellent English, happened to be there. He told me his official title is the Banjar Block Educational Officer, that he has twenty-six schools under his jurisdiction and that he either rides or walks to inspect most of them, though a few are accessible by jeep and by the little hill bus which crosses the Jalori in the summer months. He said it was still difficult to persuade *pahari* parents to send their children to school: 'We require their services at home,' is the stock answer, as in Spain.

The pupils study the three R's but I am sure Europeans do not realise how much more complicated it is for Indian children to learn to read than it is for ours. For instance, these sons of the Himalaya speak a western *pahari* dialect which varies considerably from region to region and has never been a written language. When such a boy comes to school he is first taught to read and write in Hindi, the lingua-franca of northern India, using the *Devanagari* script with an alphabet of forty-six letters. When he reaches the fourth class between the ages of nine and ten he starts to learn to speak and read Urdu which employs the beautiful but very difficult Persian script, and as a third language he must study English, through the medium of the Roman script. Besides reading, writing and simple arithmetic, the children are taught a little general science and 'social science' which I presume means personal hygiene.

Shri Kohli told me that he, too, had drunk milk with the Gujars and had learnt that they stayed up on the Bashleo for three months every summer so that their beasts had the benefit of the rich grass between the melting and the falling of the snow. He said they take their milk to sell in Banjar every day. It is seventeen miles from there to the top of the Bashleo Pass which comes to thirty-four miles a day carrying down heavy cans of milk, though naturally they would take all the innumerable short cuts. However, as it nearly killed me walking eight miles from Bathad to Sarahan—and that was with the aid of little Shanti's tail—the daily journey of the Gujars, laden with the milk of Mahisha, is dreadful to contemplate.

I left the school and walked up the hill past the rest-house into the great deodar forest which the *chaukidar* had designated as my lavatory. There were almost as many giant boulders as giant trees, with columbine growing freely between them and even a few of the tall iris still in flower, while the grass of the forest glades glittered with the tiny stars of the blue dwarf gentians.

CHAPTER XIX

The Last Lap

After a rice and D.D.D. lunch we left Sarahan and set off along the track down the valley, which started to fall steeply, and the river was transformed from a meandering brook into a raging torrent called the Karpan Khud. When we got down to about 7,000 feet the little terraced paddy-fields reappeared and in one of them I counted ten women in a row planting out seedlings, singing as they worked. We stopped at a shack-shop beside the track where I treated B.R. to tea and custard creams, and ate some myself seated outside on a rickety wooden bench under a *ficus pommatus* with lovely thick shady foliage. The proprietor of the *chai khana* cum stores actually had—and used—a fly spray.

After crossing a *sangha* bridge to the left bank of the Karpan, the track led slightly uphill so I was able to ride. Summer travel in the Himalaya would be very pleasant if one never had to go below 6,000 feet, but unfortunately you cannot reach the heights without first descending into the depths.

We were now leaving the temperate zone and the following day we would reach the sub-tropical region of the Sutlej valley where the June heat is intense and the flora largely similar to that of the plains. Meanwhile our path was cut out of the side of a brown hill sparsely wooded with chil pines. There was no shade to speak of but mercifully the sun was clouded over most of the time and there was a delightful breeze blowing. I saw a seed-bed being prepared with an enormous seven-pronged wooden rake a yard across, pulled by a yoke of tiny oxen which, together with the driver, were plastered with mud.

B.R. had been in a bad temper with the mules most of the afternoon and when we got to our destination, the village of Arsu, and were climbing the steep path to the rest-house above, he got really angry with poor Durgi and hit her savagely. Whereupon she—quite rightly—kicked up her heels really high and got him full in the chest: then she swung round and ran away down the path up

which we had come. I instinctively leapt off Shanti knowing I had
no control over her. I was only just in time, for she did a perfect
turn on the hocks and fled down the hill after her companion in
less time than it takes to tell. I prodded B.R.'s breast-bone which
thankfully was not broken; he was only a bit winded. I tried to
make it clear to him that it was entirely his own fault and that he
had asked to be kicked by continually hitting and kicking Durgi.
I did not feel a bit sorry for him. He soon recovered sufficiently
to run down the hill after the terrified mules. I was tired and
cross and inwardly swore I would never again go on a riding tour
unless the complete care and control of the animals was in my own
hands.

I continued the climb up the zigzag path to the little rest-house
on my own two legs instead of on Shanti's four. It was locked
and no *chaukidar* came to my loud call. I asked a woman working
in the field below where he was and she made me understand by
clear gestures that he was in the next village but would return
to Arsu that night. It was now near 5 p.m. so I prayed he wouldn't
be long. While I waited I explored the rest-house outbuildings and
to my delight found a door open which led into a tiny square room
with a window on one side and a four-burner mud stove at waist
level on the other: my Himalayan kitchenette! On the way through
the village we had passed a shop so I decided on the spur of the
moment to cook my own supper and make a *pahari* version of
pôtage paysanne. I took my thermos down to the village store
where I got it filled with milk; then I bought 250 grams each of
potatoes and onions, 100 grams of rice and of *dalda* at a total cost
of one rupee; after which I borrowed a saucepan from the old
woman in the store.

Returning uphill with my shoulder bag full of these treasures
I picked up sticks as I went. It was a bare bit of country with
no cedar or pine trees near so timber was scarce and I had to resort
to pulling some of the thicker bits out of the little thorn hedges
built up along the sides of the path. Back in my kitchenette I got a
fire going under one of the burners of the stove by poking sticks
in through a hole at the side and melted some *dalda* in the saucepan, then I added the sliced onions and potatoes and simmered
them together; when the vegetables were tender I poured in the
milk, brought it to the boil and added rice and salt (which I always

carried in my bag together with my metal spoon) but, alas, no lovely freshly-ground black pepper because I did not carry a pepper-mill around.

Eventually, after about half an hour B.R. reappeared leading my rebellious mule train; Durgi with a gash above her nearside hock which had obviously been inflicted by B.R. This made me very angry so that when at last the *chaukidar* arrived I started ordering him about like a real old *ao* and *jao* Memsahib.

> My Hindustani words are few
> They hardly could be fewer
> It's *idder ao* and *jaldi jao*
> And *kubberdar you soor.**

'*Idder ao*,' I commanded imperiously, '*Pani lao*.'

He brought me a bucketful of water and then stood astonished in the doorway at the sight of me cooking my own supper.

'*Jao!*' I shouted, and when he did not move, '*Jao!*' I screamed and banged the door in his face.

I had never been a Memsahib in command of a household myself but at that moment I could perfectly understand why all Hindustani grammars composed in the days of the British Raj started their verb chapters with the imperative mood. If you shout at Indian servants and throw your weight about they crumple up at once and you enjoy a sense of power which is very bad for your character. It was really all because I was so angry with B.R. for being so beastly to Durgi who is a very old mule, and it was a shame that the poor innocent *chaukidar* of Arsu had to bear the brunt of my rage.

I added a little water to my *pôtage pahari* and put some more into the minute kettle I carried with me (but hadn't used up till now), warmed it up and stirred in a good spoonful of salt. Then I carried it out to where the mules were grazing on the burnt-up *khud* with the noble intention of dabbing the saline solution on to Durgi's cut. But she would not let me get near her and had I done so she would doubtless have kicked me back to the top of the Bashleo Pass.

When my soup was ready I offered some to B.R. who was sunk

---

* It's come here! and go quickly!
And be careful you pig!

in sulks; he declined without thanks and walked down to the bazaar, no doubt to get a supper more to his liking. I ate as much as I could and it tasted really good. The remainder I poured into the thermos for my breakfast.

The rest-house turned out to be a one-roomed hut, moderately clean but with no thunderbox or lavatory of even the most primitive kind. Since there were no trees anywhere and the moon was only a night past full, answering the call of nature was a very tricky affair. However, I must admit that what the tiny rest-house lacked in size and convenience it more than made up for by the beauty of its situation, perched on a ledge above the village with a lovely view down the valley and a breath-taking one up it. Once again I stood for at least half an hour in the moonlight contemplating the beauty of the Bashleo, and thinking of the good Gujars with their large, beige, blue-eyed demons asleep in the alpine pastures.

On Saturday, June 27th, I was up by 5 a.m. to enjoy my breakfast of tepid *pôtage pahari* out of the thermos. I was annoyed because the *chaukidar* made me pay four rupees for the use of the one-room, lavatoryless rest-house which should certainly be rated as third-class and only cost two rupees. Perhaps he was—justifiably—getting his own back on me for my imperious behaviour of last night.

B.R. was obviously still in a very bad mood and kept grumbling because I had not paid him his usual six rupees, for even though I could not understand what he was saying it was quite clear what he meant. I know I was being very pig-headed, but it was my way of punishing him and I intended not to pay him until we reached Rampur, and then to give him thirty rupees for the past two days and the next three, for I planned to return to Simla by bus. Crossing the Bashleo—though child's play to a mountaineer —had actually taken more out of me than I realised at the time and I had reacted, as I always do when I get overtired, by getting a bad sore throat.

The path from Arsu went uphill to start with, then descended through shady pine woods and I walked most of the way, sliding down the innumerable short cuts on my behind, but eventually we left the lovely shade of the forest and emerged on to the bare brown hills of the sub-Himalaya in the near noonday sun. Here we got our first view of Rampur, the capital of the former Bushahr state, deep down in the Sutlej valley on the further bank of the river and backed by a vast forbidding black hill. We came to the hamlet of Kashiol with a beautiful pagoda-type temple, the lower storey of which was square and built of alternate dry stone and timber courses with two circular upper storeys of wood. How I long to return to Saraj to make a study of these fascinating little-known *pahari* temples, for on this tour I have undoubtedly missed far more than I have seen. The door of the temple at Kashiol was locked and although there was a row of rather disagreeable-looking men sitting on the first-floor veranda of a nearby house, not one of them offered to produce the key: however, they made it quite clear to me that I must remove my shoes on entering the temple courtyard. Before putting them on again I paddled in a nice stream outside the village as it was by now desperately hot and, mounting my mule, I put up B.R.'s huge umbrella for which I was perpetually grateful, and rode Shanti down the path which eventually led to the banks of the great river which was in spate, the water a muddy-brown, foaming and rushing along at a great rate. We could now see very clearly on the opposite bank the little town of Rampur, dominated by a fancy palace with bright red corrugated iron roofs. I found to my dismay that the bridge was a mile downstream and on our way to it we passed through a hamlet with a few shack-shops, at one of which I bought some good eating apples. Then we rode by the mule lines where the poor animals were turned loose on the burning, sandy banks of the river without grazing or shade; close by there were a few ramshackle godowns for the muleteers to cook and sleep in. At last we came to the suspension bridge, which was only wide enough for pack animals, and here we crossed over from Outer Saraj to Rampur Bushahr. There appeared to be no main track leading up to the road, only a maze of rocky footpaths. We had no idea which one to take and the one we chose turned out to be so steep that I cannot think how the mules got up. I panted after them at least a hundred yards in the rear having missed the help of Shanti's tail.

On reaching the main road we were directed to the Circuit House which is at one end of the town while the P.W.D. rest-house is at the other: I reflected how dreadful it would be if I could not get in at the former and had to walk at least another baking mile to the latter. My magic chits had come to an end at Arsu, the last village in which I had stayed under the jurisdiction of Kulu.

Great preparations were going on at the Circuit House: the gates were being repainted, the furniture moved about and everything was spotlessly clean. The *chaukidar* said I must ring up the P.W.D. office for permission to stay the night. Fancy being back in a bungalow with a telephone! So I did as I was told and the permission was refused, the clerk explaining that the War Minister was paying an official visit to the district in two days' time and the Circuit House must remain empty before his arrival so that the servants could keep it clean. Disappointed, I asked the *chaukidar* if I could at least wash there and rest for a couple of hours. He agreed to let me but before I retired to do so a young man came into the sitting-room. He turned out to be an atomic scientist called Shri Sahai. He told me he and his wife were going to have to turn out tomorrow and move to the Forest Commission's rest-house as no one was allowed to stay in a Circuit House at the same time as a Minister. However, he thought it ridiculous that I should not be allowed to stay that night, whereupon he most kindly rang up the P.W.D. office himself and fixed it with the clerk—whom he knew personally and who was dining with him. He invited me to coffee and biscuits with him and his wife, who turned out to be one of the most beautiful young women I have ever seen: and when an Indian woman is beautiful she is more beautiful than any other woman of any other race, for it is not her features only which are perfect, but the rhythmic grace of her every movement.

A Circuit House is, of course, a very grand type of bungalow designed for judges on circuit. I was given a large bedroom with a very high ceiling and a suite of hideous shiny modern furniture, but the great joy was that the nice, clean washroom contained a shower-bath! After standing under it (cold water only which was what I wanted) for nearly ten minutes in a state of complete euphoria, I dried myself and flopped on to my bed where I slept till 4 p.m. under yet another *objet de luxe*—an electric fan.

After my rest I went to call on the Raja and was taken by a servant to the office of his personal assistant. He spoke good

English and told me that H.H. is a young married man of twenty-nine with three children and that the family was at present in Simla, where the Raja, who is an M.P., spends most of his time when he is not attending the *Lok Sabha* in Delhi. The P.A. very kindly offered to show me the palace, which he said was called after his late Highness Maharaja Padam Singh Sahib Bahadur who laid the foundation stone in 1919. It was designed by the then State Engineer, Beer Shand Shukle.

There was an octagonal front hall with red and blue glass windows in geometric patterns, and round the upper part of the walls a three-feet-wide dado of tiles with a design of pink roses in white circles on a green ground. On one side of the hall there was a silver throne with a pair of charming silver lions acting as arms; and above the throne is his late Highness's portrait in oils which the P.A. referred to as 'this snap'. The room beyond it and one or two others on the ground floor were furnished with stiff-looking modern suites and large, tinted, family photographs adorned the walls. I was not taken upstairs.

What I took to be a covered bandstand in the courtyard turned out to be a grandstand, built as recently as 1948 for H.H. and his friends to view displays of folk-dancing. I was extremely proud at being able to decipher *om Ram* inscribed repeatedly round the interior frieze. Tucked away behind the grandstand in a far corner of the courtyard stood the old palace in the Moghul *pahari* style with carved enclosed balconies and cusped wooden arches.

Across the main road from the palace a lesser road leads steeply downhill and then turns left running parallel with the banks of the Sutlej. It is along here that some interesting temples are to be found, but unfortunately I cannot illustrate them with photographs as I had by now run out of film. First there is the Buddhist *gompa*, built at the beginning of this century in the Pagoda Style. Inside there is a vast metal prayer wheel with bands of embossed bronze friezes running round it. On what corresponds to an altar there is a row of highly polished metal Buddha images with twelve small wooden images in front of them, some still bearing traces of faded paint. The walls are covered by paintings of *Bodhisattvas* in familiar postures, which, though they cannot be more than seventy years old, are in the traditional Tibetan style and extremely decorative but damaged by smoke. In the dim light which comes only from the open door, for there were no windows, I noticed on some dusty shelves rows and rows of manuscript scrolls which have doubtless been examined by the Tibetan scholars who knew Rampur Bushahr, such as the Moravian missionary the Rev. A. H. Francke and Mr. H. Lee Shuttleworth, I.C.S.

Further along the lower road through the bazaar, where it runs parallel with the river, I found the Ram temple with superb wood carvings on the ceiling of the pillared hall; then the Narsingh temple with bands of low relief carving in stone in the *pahari* style; and later, the Satya Narain temple which is full of surprises. It is a white marble building of modest proportions built at the beginning of this century and fronted with cusped arches in the Moghul manner leading on to a wide veranda with a looking-glass ceiling. On the square pillars beyond and on the walls to the sides there was an assortment of gods and Rajas brightly painted on panels with European-style backgrounds and looking-glass frames. Also on the veranda there were two life-sized coloured plaster statues of Maharaja Padam Singh and his wife the Maharani wearing the enormous nose-ring which the ladies of *pahari* royal families apparently put on for special occasions. In the sanctuary under a curved Bengal-roofed baldacchino there is a marble statue of Vishnu Narain on a three-storeyed pedestal faced with pink and green tiles, each bearing an embossed rose in its centre. To the right of the main idol stands the most popular *avatar* of Vishnu, the blue God Krishna with his beloved milkmaid Radha, both dressed in real brocade.

The Sahais had most kindly invited me to dinner and we had an excellent curry with a good selection of accompaniments, all prepared by the lovely Shrimati Sahai. The only other guest was the young P.W.D. clerk who had at first refused me permission to stay at the Circuit House. He told us that in a certain village some six miles from Rampur there had been a riot only a few years ago because the authorities had forbidden the villagers to offer up a human sacrifice to their *devi* at their annual *mela*. Subsequently I read in *Antiquities of Indian Tibet** that there is an ancient temple dedicated to Bhima Kali at Sarahan (not the little village of that name where I had stayed below the Bashleo Pass, but the old

* A. H. Francke, Vol. 38 of the *A.S.I.*, New Imperial Series, London, 1914.

summer capital of the Rampur Rajas) where human sacrifices used to be offered every tenth year. The victim was thrown into a deep pit. If a human being was not forthcoming at the appointed time, a terrible voice could be heard calling from the depths of the pit.

On the last night of my month's mule tour I sat up in bed composing a little moral lecture for B.R. about kindness to animals. I planned to ask Shri Sahai to translate it into Hindi the next morning and read it aloud to my muleteer. Meanwhile poor B.R. had had to return to the miserable mule lines on the other side of the river since the *chaukidar* would not hear of Durgi and Shanti staying at his grand Circuit House where there were anyway only 'jeep stables'.

When B.R. turned up after breakfast to get his final orders, I asked Shri Sahai to explain to him that I would take all my baggage with me and tell him that it would be good for him to be able to ride home, as he had been badly shaken by the kick in the chest he had received from Durgi, and that I promised to give him a handsome tip if he reached Simla within five days. Then the young atomic scientist read out my lecture:

'You have looked after me very well on this journey and have been extremely dependable and honest in every way and for all this I am very grateful. I must tell you, however, that it has upset me to see you hit and kick Durgi so frequently. She is an old mule and has done her job extremely well, carrying all my baggage over steep high passes.

'I have kept animals since before you were born: horses, ponies, cows, dogs and cats, and during the past thirty years I have broken in quite a number of horses. I know, and you know too, that it never pays to lose your temper with animals. Durgi kicked you yesterday afternoon because you got angry with her repeatedly and if I had been her I would have kicked you long before.

'Remember that one day we shall all have to answer to God for our treatment of animals and if you are not careful you may find yourself as a mule in your next incarnation. Then you will know what it feels like to be hit and kicked every day. Please try in future not to lose your temper with your mules. They will then serve you all the better.'

Then I gave him his pay for the next five days in a lump sum. He beamed all over his face and seemed to bear me no grudge.

Glossary

Note. The problem of the ever-changing transliteration of oriental scripts into the Roman is always with us. On the whole I have adhered to that familiar to readers of Kipling rather than the more modern forms. I have also deliberately omitted diacritical marks as being comprehensible only to orientalists.

ADHA TODA A common shrub.

AHIMSA The doctrine of the non-taking of life.

ARHAT Buddhist sage.

ASHRAM The home of a religious community; lit. hermitage.

ASHRAMAS The four stages of life according to Hindu philosophy.

AVATAR A divine incarnation.

AYAH A nanny, or a lady's personal servant.

BABU A clerk.

BALU A bear.

BARSELAS Memorial stones, confined to royal families in the Himalayan region.

BATHU Goose-foot, chenopodium.

BEGAR Forced labour.

BHANDAR Temple treasury.

BHANG Wild marijuana.

BHIKKHU A Buddhist teacher, monk.

BIANNA An icy wind.

BODHISATTVA Buddhist Holy man.

BRINJAL Egg plant.

BURFI Fudge-like sweet covered in silver leaf.

CHAI KHANA Shack tea- and snack-shop.

CHAKRA Wheel, in Buddhism, the wheel of the law.

CHAPATTIES Dry wholemeal pancakes eaten in place of bread all over northern India.

CHAPRASSY Peon.

CHARPOY Indian bed in common use.

CHAUKIDAR Caretaker; lit. watchman.

CHAURI BEARERS Wavers of yak's tails at ceremonies.

CHELA Disciple

Glossary

CHHATRI   Umbrella.

CHHOTA HAZARI   Early morning tea; lit. little breakfast.

CHHOTA RASTA   A track; lit. Little road.

DAHI   Curds.

DAK   Mail.

DAK TONGA   Mail pony cart.

DALDA   A modern brand of tinned cooking fat.

DANA   Animal fodder.

DEODAR   Himalayan cedar; *Cedrus deodara*.

DEOTA (Hindi)   ⎫ A local village god, as opposed to Deva, a great
DEVATA (Sanskrit) ⎭ god.

DEVI   Goddess.

DHOJ   A sacred pole planted in front of a hill temple (from Sanskrit *dhvaja*).

DHOOLY   Litter slung on poles, used in hill tracts for carrying people.

DURREE   Cotton rug.

DUSSEHRA   A Hindu religious festival.

DWARAPALA   Figure of a doorkeeper carved at the entrance to Hindu shrines.

GADDI   The throne (lit. cushion on which a Raja sits). Also a nomadic tribe of hill shepherds.

GARBHA GRIHA   The cella of a temple.

GHI   Clarified butter.

GHORAL   A Himalayan deer.

GOMPA   Buddhist temple.

GRIHASTHA   A householder (the second of the four stages of life).

GUR   Unrefined sugar.

GUR (second meaning)   A dedicated man who acts as the mouthpiece of a village god, a shaman.

GURU   Teacher.

HARIJAN   Gandhi's definition of an untouchable, meaning 'child of God'.

JAGIR   A holding of land.

JALEBIS   Sweet sticky fritters.

JANPANIS   Rickshaw men. Teams of four were used in hill tracts.

JHULA   Himalayan rope bridge.

JOGINIS, JOGNIS   Fairies, nymphs, special attendants on the Mother Goddess.

KAIKA   A death and resurrection ceremony peculiar to the hills.

Glossary

KAKUR   Barking deer.

KHANSAMA   Cook.

KHUD   Hillside, precipice. Also sometimes used for a gorge through which a torrent flows.

KILTA   Cone-shaped basket carried on the back, in use all over the hills.

KUTCHERRY   Court.

LAKH   One hundred thousand.

LATHIS   Sticks used by policemen.

LINGA   The phallic emblem of the great God Shiva.

LOK SABHA   Parliament.

LOKAPALA   A guardian deity of northern Buddhism.

LOTA   Brass pot.

LUGRI   Rice wine.

MACHHLI   Fish.

MAHSEER   Coarse fish reaching a great weight which plays like a salmon.

MAIDAN   A flat piece of ground, sometimes a parade ground.

MAKARAS   Stylised crocodiles carved in wood or stone, common in Indian art.

MALI   A gardener.

MANDAPA   A pillared hall, an integral part of Hindu temples in the plains, but less common in the hills.

MANDIR   A temple.

MAUND   About 80 lb. weight.

MELA   A religious festival, fair.

MULLAH   A Muslim minister of religion.

MUSSOCK   An inflated buffalo skin used for crossing rivers in the absence of bridges.

NAG   A serpent, sacred to Hindus and frequently carved on wooden hill temples.

NALA, NULLAH   A confusing word: in the plains it signifies a ditch or canal, in the hills a creek, valley, gorge.

NAMASTE   The current Hindu form of greeting.

NEGI   Village headman.

NEUE PAISE   New cents (replacing the old annas), 100 to one rupee. Usually written *n.p.*

NILGAI   Blue bull, common in the sub-Himalaya.

NIMBU   Fresh lime.

Glossary

PADAMI   The royal lotus sign.

PAGAL   Fool.

PAGARI (pugree)   Turban.

PAHARI   Hill, a hillman or woman.

PAKORAS   Vegetable fritters.

PANCHAYAT   Village council.

PARATAS   Fried chapatties.

PUJA   Worship.

PUJARI   Village priest.

PULIS   String shoes made in the hills.

PURIS   A light dry pancake.

PUTTOO   Tweed dress peculiar to the women of Kulu.

RATH   Lit. a wheel. Chariot, carriage, but also used in the hills for a wheelless litter on which the *devatas* are carried.

RISHI   A sage.

SADHU   A wandering holy man.

SALWAR KAMIZ   The common dress of women in the Punjab, a loose tunic worn over cotton trousers.

SAMADHI   Lit. religious ecstasy. Also used to describe the memorial stone of a holy person.

SANGAM   The sacred confluence of two rivers.

SANGHA BRIDGE   Cantilever bridge of deodar or spruce. Formerly common all over the Himalayan region, now being replaced by metal bridges.

SANGHARAMA   Community, monastery.

SANNYASIN   The fourth and final stage of life: a wandering ascetic.

SATI (Suttee)   A woman who was immolated on her husband's or master's funeral pyre.

SATYAGRAHA   Non-violent non-co-operation.

SHABASH   Bravo!

SHAKTI   The female power of a god, used to denote his wife.

SHAMAYANA   A marquee.

SHIKAR   Hunting, shooting big or little game.

SHIKARI   A hunter.

SHIKHARA   A curvilinear stone temple tower.

SWAMI   Scholar, teacher.

TATHAGATA   A term of endearment for the historic Buddha.

THACH   High altitude grazing ground.

THAIRI   An open-air shrine.

Glossary

THAKUR   Chieftain, approximating to our medieval barons.

THESIL   Sub-district.

THESILDAR   Sub-collector of taxes and magistrate.

TRISHULA   The trident of Shiva and Durga.

ULLU   Owl.

VEDANTA   Doctrine of the Vedas.

WARNA   The throwing up of a live lamb into the air before sacrifice.

YONI   Vulva, worshipped in conjunction with the linga to symbolise the male and female creative power of the great God Shiva.

ZAMINDAR   Landholder, farmer.

Bibliography

Note. The majority of the books given in the Bibliography are now out of print but most of them, including the journals and periodicals, may be found in the India Office Library in London or in the Indian Institute Library in Oxford.

A.S.I. = *Archaeological Survey of India* Reports.
J.P.H.S. = *Journal of the Punjab Historical Society.*

ARCHER, Mildred, *British Drawings in the India Office Library*, 2 vols., London, 1969. (pp. 206-22 list A. F. P. Harcourt's works).
BRUCE, Colonel the Hon. C. G., *Kulu and Lahoul*, London, 1914.
   Mostly about mountaineering, but Chapter 13 'Some History and Folk-lore' is excellent, also the last chapter 'A Lady's Point of View' by the Hon. Mrs. Bruce.
CALVERT, J., F.G.S., *Vazeri Rupi; the Silver Country of the Vazeers in Kulu, its Beauties, Antiquities and Silver Mines*, London, 1873.
   The author was a geologist, but the book is written in a racy style and has numerous coloured lithographs from sketches by the author, including one of the many-towered fort at Bajaura before its gradual disappearance by serving as a quarry for builders.
CHETWODE, Penelope, 'Temple Architecture in Kulu', article in the *Journal of the Royal Society of Arts*, October 1968.
COLLETT, Sir Henry, *Flora Simlensis*, Calcutta, 1921.
   Specifically about flora in the Simla area but also useful for the whole temperate zone of the Western Himalaya.
EMERSON, Sir Herbert, I.C.S., K.C.I.E., *Mandi State Gazetteer*, the 1920 edition was compiled by him and he wrote the chapter on religion and folk-lore which applies to Kulu as well as to the neighbouring State of Mandi.
   'Some Aspects of Himalayan Sacrifice', *J.P.H.S.,* 1921, Vol. VIII, No. 2, p. 185. A fascinating lecture on this subject including a description of the *Bhunda* (rope-sliding ceremony) at Nirmand in Outer Saraj.
FAIRS AND FESTIVALS. *Census of India 1961*, Vol. XIII, Punjab. Part VIIb.

Bibliography

ROERICH, Svetoslav. *Art in the Kulu Valley*, Naggar, 1967.

A rather disappointing book considering that the author must know more about the art of Kulu than anyone else living, illustrated by badly reproduced photographs.

ROSSER, Collin, 'Malana, A Hermit Village in Kulu' (being a chapter in *India's Villages*. Edited M. N. Srinavas), Bombay, 1960.

A social anthropologist's description of this isolated village.

SINGH, Madanjeet, *Himalayan Art,* Unesco Art Books, 1968.

A magnificent publication illustrated by the author's superb colour photographs. The chapter on the Siwalik Ranges is about temples and sculpture in the Kulu valley.

SHUTTLEWORTH, H. Lee, I.C.S., *An Inscribed Mask discovered on the Occasion of the Bhunda Ceremony at Nirmand* [in Outer Saraj], *Acta Orientalia*, 1922, Vol. 1, pp. 224 ff.

'Border Countries of the Punjab Himalaya', *The Geographical Journal*, Vol. LX, No. 4. A lecture read at the Meeting of the Society, May 22nd, 1922.

SIMPSON, William, 'Architecture in the Himalayas', Transactions of the Royal Institute of British Architects. London, 1882–3.

An excellent analysis of temple architecture in the Sutlej valley, Rampur Busharh, but equally applicable to Kulu.

TUCCI and GHERSI (trs. from Italian), *Secrets of Tibet*, London, 1935.

Diary form, the early pages of which describe the Kulu valley.

TYACKE, Mrs., *How I Shot my Bears*, London, 1892.

A fascinating account of big game shooting from a woman's point of view in Kulu, Spiti and Lahul.

TYACKE, Colonel R. H., *A Sportsman's Manual*, Calcutta, 1893. In quest of game in Kulu, Lahoul, Spiti, etc., and a detailed description of sport in more than 130 *nalas*.

An informative and scholarly work on Himalayan fauna.

TYSON, T., *Trout Fishing in Kulu*. Lahore, 1941.

VIENNOT, Odette, *Les Divinités Fluviales Ganga et Yamuna aux Portes des Sanctuaires de l'Inde*. Presses Universitaires de France, 1964.

Treats of the carvings of the river goddesses on the Bajaura temple.

VIGNE, G. T., *Travels in Kashmir, Ladak, etc.,* 2 vols., London, 1844.

He did not actually go to Kulu but there is an interesting account of Mandi.

Bibliography

VOGEL, J. P., *Hill Temples of the Western Himalayas* (Indian Art and Letters, new series, Vol. XX, No. 1).
Indian Serpent Lore. London, 1926.
Deals with the principal *nag* legends of Kulu.
'The Temple of Mahadeva at Bajaura', *A.S.I.*, 1909–10, pp. 18 ff.
History of the Punjab Hill States (in collaboration with J. Hutchison), Vol. II, *Kulu State*, pp. 413–73.

WHISTLER, Hugh, *In the High Himalayas,* London, 1924.
Good chapters on the Rohtang Pass and the Kulu Valley.

YOUNG, G. M., 'Malana and the Akbar-Jamlu Legend', *J.P.H.S.*, 1916, Vol. IV, pp. 98 ff.
A fascinating account of the ceremony which takes place in the early spring of each year at which a minute equestrian statue of the Emperor Akbar is produced, and apparantly worshipped.

YUAN-CHUANG (also transliterated as Huien Tsang), trs. Thomas Watters. London, 1904.
This famous Chinese Buddhist pilgrim was in India between the years A.D. 629–45 and visited Kulu, which he calls Ku-lu-to. See Vol. 1, p. 298.

Index

Index

Index

Index

Index

Manaligarh, 173; Mandankot fort, 168–9, 177; distinguished from Manali, 170; chalet-type temple, 177; stone fragments, 177
Manalsu river, 170; *sangha* bridge, 176
Mandalgar Kothi, 133, 134
Mandanjeet Singh, and Bajaura temple (*Himalayan Art*), 55 and n.
Mandi, Raja of, palace, 98; 101 n., 125, 144, 155
Mandi province, stone temples, 54, 55, 98; *gaddis*, 183; Sikh occupation, 195
Mandi–Kulu boundary, 5
Mandi–Larji gorge road, 44, 51, 130, 131
Mandi–Manali road, 37
Manglaur village, 41–2, 189
Mani-dweep (mythical island), 102
Manikarn, 60, 74, 124; sacred springs, 64, 67–8, 69, 86; the author and, 66–7, 70–1; bus service, 67 n.; modern temple, 68, 69; rest-house, 68, 73; pack animals, 72; public hot springs, 72–3, 124, 178
Markanda (Hindu god), *devata* procession, 15–16
Mashobra village, 5
Master Institute of United Arts, founded by Roerich, 154; and 'Master Building', 156–7; combined with Riverside Museum, 160
Matiana, 13; rest-house, 14–16; flora, 15
Maulana Azad Hospital, New Delhi, 21
Mayapuri, 106
Mazar, 53
Milklu Ram, Ari, 6, 9, 10
Minnikin, Mr., estate manager, 128–34 *passim*, 142
Mongolia, suggested place of Second Coming, 154; Wallace and, 159–60
Mir Izzet Ullah, 53
Moorcroft, William, in Kulu Valley, 51–2; and cavalry horses, 52–3; in Bokhara, 53; and Rohtang, 183, 184; *Travels in the Provinces of Hindustan and the Punjab*, 54, 184 and n., 223
Moravian missionaries, 182, 183, 212
Murlidhar (Krishna the fluteplayer), 120
Muslims, Hindus and in 1947, 147–8

Nagar, 60, 66, 68, 99, 107, 112; transport, 117 and n.; former capital, 117; Raja's castle, 117, 119, 121–2, 143; stone temple, 118; Himalayan architecture, 120–2, 125; temple of Narsingh, 122; temple of Tripura Sundari, 123; British buildings (The Hall, Osborne House), 125–6; tea gardens, 128; Arcadia House, 143,

146; the Roerich's and, 155; route of Manali, 163 ff.
Narkanda, 11, 129, 143; rest-house, 16, 17–18; Tibetan shrine, 17; descent to Luri, 23–4
Naroi, wife of Jamlu, 89
Narsingh (god), 108, 111; at Kulu *Dussehra*, 114; temple at Nagar, 122; at Rampur, 212; stone carvings, 166
Nast, ancient capital of Kulu, 166
National Tourist Board, 7
Nehru, Pandit, death, 8; service of condolence, 37; and Hindu temples, 103 n.; at Manali, 174
Neoli Rani, family temple, 105–7
Nepal, Rana family, 100; Pagoda style architecture, 122, 123
Norway, similarity to Himalayan architecture, 122–3
Nuwani family, foundation, 169

O'Dwyer, Sir Michael, 2
Osborne, General, House at Nagar, 144; and Rennick, 144
Oudh, theft of Ragunathji idol, 121

Padam Singh, Maharaja and Maharani, 211; plaster statues, 212
Pala sculptures, 55
Palampur, 129; mission, 131
Panch Saghat Ram, 68
Papidarm Peaks, 77, 81
Parbatti (goddess), wife of Shiva, 70, 90, 120, 164, 166
Parbatti river, 63, 65, 67, 81, 85, 90, 92, 93; metal bridge, 79; confluence with Béas, 97, 106–7
Parbatti Valley, 57, 60, 94–5, 102, 110; characteristics, 64–5, 74; Horticultural Programme, 65; Project of Atomic Energy, 65; Silver Province (Waziri Rupi), 75, 102, 114
Patala, Kingdom of Sesha, 70
Pathankot, 129
Patlikuhl, 117 n.
Pegler, Westbrook, and '*Guru* Letters', 161–2
Pin-Parbatti Pass, 74
Plach village, 41
Public Works Dept (P.W.D.), 7, 190, 210
Pulchan, 179, 184
Pulga, 74–6, 87; rest-house, 76–7, 78–9, 88, 200; village architecture, 77; Punjabi police force, 77–8; mental deficiency rate, 78
Punjab Hills, 2, 173
Punjab Legislative Assembly, 27

Index

Index